Janet Keller Richard
Bless Jesus !

Unlocking Our Inheritance

Spiritual Keys to Recovering the Treasures of Anabaptism

Janet Keller Richards

UNLOCKING OUR INHERITANCE

To purchase books or to contact the author:
unlockingourinheritance@earthlink.net.

Regarding Anabaptist Reconciliation work, contact:
www.anabaptistreconciliation.org.

Cover photo © 2004 Mark Buckwalter
Cover design by Joe Swartz
and thanks also to Jeremy at TrueLightCommunications

Materials from *Father Forgive Us!*, by Jim Goll, © 2000, and from *Floods Upon the Dry Ground* by Charles P. Schmitt, © 1998, used by permission of Destiny Image Publishers, 167 Walnut Bottom Road, Shippensburg, PA 17257; www.destinyimage.com

Library of Congress Control Number: 2005922189
International Standard Book Number: 1-932864-23-7

Printed by
Masthof Press
219 Mill Road
Morgantown, PA 19543-9516

CONTENTS

ACKNOWLEDGMENTS
AND
DEDICATION

There are so many people who have poured into my life the riches of their own spiritual treasures during the time of writing this book. Five women committed to faithfully pray as I wrote for more than a year. Elaine, Geri, Marian, Marta, and Mary, thank you for depositing a wealth of effectual prayer. May God pour out abundant reward to you! My husband, Rusty, is to be thanked more than any other earthly friend. Thank you for carrying this with me and for every encouragement, every word of blessing, every prayer, and all your listening and advice . . . not to mention enduring long hours, unfinished chores, and distractions as I wrote.

God bless Lloyd and Elaine and Mark and Heather, and the whole "recon prayer team" for such an exciting journey, as we rebuild the ancient ruins together. What a privilege! And I express a grateful heart to John Ruth, Keith Yoder, and Mark Buckwalter for your excellent proofing advice, which I trust you'll see was followed to a great degree! Thank you to Stiftung Schleife and our Reformed sisters and brothers in Christ. Thanks to Light of Hope and Bob Doe, and to Dennis and the "L-dub gang" for grace! Thanks to Karen Neupauer for her talent. Thanks to Masthof Press and Lois Ann Mast for your hard work, and to Joe Swartz for your creative gift. And thanks to my church family and my natural family: Mom and Dad, and all my family siblings and my spiritual siblings, especially at Petra. God bless you all abundantly!

This book is dedicated and consecrated to Jesus.
There is no one else who has loved so purely
and completely and attentively.
You really are love.

INTRODUCTION

This book is meant to be read by looking through the eyes of our *spirit*. According to the Scriptures, we can perceive the things of life from either a spiritual viewpoint, or a natural (carnal) viewpoint:

> . . . we speak . . . *comparing spiritual things with spiritual.* But the **natural man receiveth not the things of the Spirit of God:** for they are *foolishness* unto him: neither can he know them, because they are **spiritually discerned.** (I Corinthians 2:12-14, *KJV*)

> And I, brethren, *could not speak unto you as unto spiritual,* **but as unto carnal,** even as unto babes in Christ. . . .For ye are yet **carnal** . . . (I Corinthians 3:1-3, *KJV*)

As our spirit relates to God's Spirit, we are able to discern spiritual things. The natural part of us will *always* perceive spiritual things as *foolish.* That is why Paul urges us to walk by the Spirit and not by our natural mind, will, and emotions (Romans 8).

The Pharisees missed the time of God's coming to them, mainly because they did not understand this principle (Luke 19:44). They were well versed in the Scriptures and had read the passages which proclaimed the coming of the Messiah. Yet, when Jesus performed miracle after miracle, they could not perceive His glory because they were thinking "naturally" (Matthew 12:24).

Many of those who followed Jesus were tempted to leave Him because of the same misunderstanding. When Jesus taught them to eat His flesh and drink His blood, they grumbled at His "hard saying":

> Therefore many of His disciples, when they heard this, said, "This is a hard saying; who can understand it?" . . . (Jesus) said to them, "Does this offend you? . . . It is the *Spirit who gives life; the flesh profits nothing.* The **words that I speak to you are spirit,** and they are life. (John 6:60-63, *NKJV*)

His words were *spiritual* words explaining the work of the cross, but His disciples could only imagine drinking real blood and eating real flesh, and they became offended.

Our Heritage

In this text my intent is to examine our Anabaptist heritage through the eyes of our spirit. Just as Jesus did not seem like the Messiah to the Pharisees, there are aspects of our own ancestry which will appear much different to our spirits than they will to our carnal souls. As I searched the pages of Anabaptist history, it was always with a desire to understand the *spiritual impact* of our journey as a people group.

With so many different groups of Anabaptists in today's world, we are bound to have differing interpretations of the Bible, just as our forefathers had many different interpretations, yet all served God wholeheartedly. As I share various thoughts and perceptions about the spiritual perspective of our ancestry, you may disagree with some of my words, just as I may disagree with some of your words, were I to read your own thoughts. Yet, we both serve God wholeheartedly.

If you do disagree, I only ask that you don't reject the whole of this book. Rather, place the questionable things on hold and move on, asking the Lord to confirm or clarify them in His time. We are all human, and I may have interpreted some things of history with my own natural soul rather than by the Spirit, though I have prayerfully written each page.

Regarding our historical pathways, I do not claim to be an historian. There are many others who have done the hard work of digging to the foundations of our formation as Anabaptists. I'm grateful for their work, since I've used their discoveries and their source information in my own writing. These fact-finders have shared their treasures with the rest of us in order to help us accurately understand the record of our past.

Finally, I have often marveled about writing this book in the first place. Having grown up in a Methodist church, I began attending a nearby Mennonite church as a young adult who was searching for her place in the family of God. It never occurred to me that the new direction I had taken was leading me towards my ancestral roots as an Anabaptist. With hindsight, I now realize that in order to apprehend His call and purpose for my life, it was important that I understand my past.

My mother, Dorothy (Shirk) Beck Keller, grew up in southeastern Pennsylvania (USA), attending Ephrata Mennonite Church. Earlier in life, her family attended Groffdale Mennonite Church in the same region. My father, David (Ludwig) Keller, grew up as a Dunker Brethren in Mohler's Brethren Church, and later attended Ephrata Church of the Brethren. My father's family lived on the Ephrata Cloister property, and Hans Jacob Keller, my first American ancestor on my father's side, is buried there.

It is with the embracing of my own heritage, that I share the concepts in this book. God has given each one of us a purpose on this earth. He has made us who we are for a reason and we are part of His divine Kingdom plan. But before we can fully understand our purpose in the *present* and *future*, we must first understand the *historical foundations* that made us who we are today, and how they have spiritually impacted our lives.

- Janet Keller Richards

A FEW THINGS TO KNOW
BEFORE YOU GET STARTED

You may not be an Anabaptist, but you have picked up this book because you *are* interested in understanding how heritage can significantly impact a person's spiritual life. If that is the case, please come along on the journey. For those who are reading this as Anabaptists, you were either *born* into an Anabaptist heritage, or you have joined yourself with Anabaptism because your personal convictions of faith agree with its tenets. I also welcome you to join the search for spiritual treasures. Then there are those who have not given much thought at all to your heritage, but you are spiritually thirsty and eager to learn. Whatever your reason for picking up this book, you are invited to walk with me through time. Because my own heritage is Anabaptist, I will often refer to "our" heritage as I write, but everyone from every background can consider what is written for their encouragement and spiritual growth.

Before we begin our journey together, please allow me to clarify several things before you begin reading, so that everything may be received and understood in its proper context.

1. Chapter sequence is important and intentional. Each chapter builds on ideas which have been established previously. In order to gain the most from this book, it is best to read it in the order it has been written. You will find some repetition of thoughts or Scriptures as the book progresses, but only for the purpose of adding another "layer" to an idea which has already been introduced.

2. Though I have addressed present-day Anabaptism as a whole, I realize our cultural ethnicity and our spiritual influences

differ greatly, since Anabaptists are spread all over the globe. Even in my own geographical region of southeastern Pennsylvania (USA), Anabaptists are so diversified that what is written will apply in varying degrees from group to group. It will also vary for each individual, since no one family line of heritage is exactly like all the others. I trust God will give what is needed and reveal His heart concerning each chapter as it applies to particular groups, denominations, and individuals.

3. Our history as a people group is intertwined with the history of other denominations within the body of Christ, particularly the Swiss Reformed Church and the Catholic Church, as well as the Lutherans, Calvinists, and others. Though I have written about ancient attitudes and actions of various groups against our Anabaptist ancestors, it is always with the understanding that we have all "sinned and come short of the glory of God" and we are all being transformed into God's image (Romans 3:23 and Romans 8:29). It is *never* with the intent of attacking or defaming any of these groups in any way. In Christ, the dividing walls of hostility have been brought down (Ephesians 2:14).

   I have used capital letters to denote the historical State Church systems (Catholic and Reformed) which existed in Europe during our ancestors' time, in order to differentiate between these specific religious groups and the greater *church* of the Bible which is comprised of all Christians from every generation, nation, and Christian tradition.

4. One of the goals of this book is to delineate both strengths and weaknesses within Anabaptism. Included at the end of each chapter are prayers which are intended for your personal growth in light of what is written. They are a means, not an end: a starting place of "prayer and supplication" that will help us walk into our spiritual purposes (Philippians 4:6). They are for strengthening our spirits and building faith, as well for bringing cleansing and restoration. These chapters and prayers are not meant to counsel those who may need more in-depth ministry.

Though some Anabaptist groups are accustomed to silent prayer, just as Daniel, Ezra, Nehemiah, David, and others cried *aloud* in their times with God, I strongly recommend praying these prayers out loud. The Scriptures declare the tongue has the power of life and death, and that applies also to prayer (Proverbs 18:21). Just as a bit in the mouth of a horse makes it obey, our tongues can turn the course of our lives if used to **speak** life (James 2:2-12). So for our own personal edification, I believe it is important to speak these words as you pray.

5. Later in this book, we'll discuss why some groups of Anabaptists only read the King James Version of the Bible. I have chosen to use different translations, depending on which version I understood as best interpreting the Greek or Hebrew meaning of a certain verse or passage. Unless noted, all Scripture quotations are from the *New International Version* (*NIV*) of the Bible, ©1973, 1978, 1984, by International Bible Society. All rights reserved. Used by permission of Hodder Head-line Plc.

Scripture quotations marked with the other abbreviations are from these versions:

KJV = King James Version
NKJV = New King James Version, © Thomas Nelson, Inc., 1982.
MKJV = Modern King James Version, © 1962, 1990; third ed.: 1993,
   by Jay P. Green, Sr.
NASB = Scriptures taken from the *New American Standard Bible,*
   © The Lockman Foundation, 1960, 1962, 1963, 1968, 1971,
   1972, 1973, 1975, 1977, 1988.
NRSV = New Revised Standard Version, ©1989 by the Division of
   Christian Education of the National Council of the Churches
   of Christ in the United States of America.
RSV = Revised Standard Version, © Division of Christian Education of
   the National Council of the Churches of Christ in the United
   States of America, 1946, 1952, 1959, 1973.
WEY = Weymouth New Testament, Grand Rapids, Mich.: Kregel Publi-
   cations.
BBE = Bible in Basic English, Cambridge Press in England, 1965.

All emphasis within Scripture is my own as the author. Parentheses within quotations are mine unless otherwise noted. Please note that capitalization and punctuation may vary depending on a particular version. Use of Scripture is granted by permission.

Other study helps which I used regularly throughout the book include:

> ~ *Word Study Greek-English New Testament* edited by Paul R. McReynolds (Wheaton, Ill.: Tyndale House Publishers), 1998.
> ~ *The Exhaustive Concordance of the Bible* compiled by James Strong, STD, LLD. (New York/Nashville: Abingdon-Cokesbury Press), 1890.
> ~ *Online Bible*, Version 2.5.2, Online Bible Software, 1995. Ken Hamel, Box 168, Oakhurst, NJ 07755.

6. Regarding the use of certain nouns and pronouns, I have chosen not to capitalize the name of satan, even though it means breaking grammatical rules. When referring to God, words or pronouns like His, He, the One, Savior, etc., will be capitalized in honor of His name.

7. Though this book is designed for individual reading, it can also be used as a group study resource, since each chapter subject stands well on its own merit. It may also be beneficial to consider these topics as a basis for group prayer.

Part One

Nuggets of Spiritual Gold

By historical accounts, the United States gold rush of 1849 started when someone saw gold nuggets lying out on the open ground. Their discovery eventually led to thousands of people streaming to California with dreams of striking it rich. Within Anabaptist history, there are also nuggets lying around which are spiritually as precious as gold. Some are even out in the open, visible to us as we turn to look at the strengths of Anbaptism. By allowing God to shine His light on the past, these nuggets will sparkle and catch our eye. Then all we need to do is pick them up and put them in our hearts; and our lives will be richer by their treasure.

~ 1 ~

A GOD-GIVEN HERITAGE

We all have a heritage if we're alive and I assume if you're reading this, you are alive. In some Anabaptist circles where I live, having an *Anabaptist heritage* means that within the first five minutes of meeting someone, you will have taken time to find out who their parents are and where they grew up and whether you share any common relatives. If you are a "dyed in the wool" Anabaptist, you might even have a book which traces your family's roots back to early ancestors in Europe. For many, Anabaptist *heritage* gives us a place of social connection.

Anabaptists are descended from men and women who were martyred for their faith. Thousands of their forefathers endured heinous torture and imprisonment, singing joyfully as they were led to their executions. They spoke fervently of their Savior's love while being burned to death at the stake.

This is the faith-filled heritage God has intentionally written into your life. He knew you would be born into your family, your country, and your generation. He chose your DNA, or genetic fiber, for His purposes. Paul writes in Acts:

> From one man he made every nation of men, that they should inhabit the whole earth; and *he determined the times* set for them and the *exact places* where they should live. (Acts 17:26)

The Scriptures tell us ". . . the gifts and the calling of God are irrevocable" for the Jews (Romans 11:26-29, *NASB*). In the same way, the *gifts* and the *calling* of the Anabaptists are meant to be received as part of God's purposeful blessings for us, and for the whole body of Christ. In the rest of this book we will explore some of these gifts, and the call which has been placed into our lives through heritage. We will also look at our past to discern where these blessings may have been laid aside in order to restore them for this present generation.

Looking Back Into History

It may be difficult for some to understand the connection between historical events and our present day lives. After all, what difference does it *really* make that ten or fifteen generations ago, those in our heritage were severely persecuted? How does it (or does it?) affect me? How does it affect my church fellowship or my denomination?

The prophets Isaiah and Jeremiah answer these questions, at least in part. Jeremiah promises that our souls will come to the place of *rest* if we walk in the old (ancient) paths where the good way of faith exists. And Isaiah, in calling his people to God, urges them to look back at their own spiritual ancestors:

> Thus says the Lord: 'Stand in the ways and see, And *ask for the old paths, where the good way is*, And walk in it; *Then you will find rest* for your souls. . . .' (Jeremiah 6:16, *NKJV*)

> Listen to me, you who *pursue righteousness* and who *seek the Lord*: *Look to the rock from which you were cut* and to *the quarry from which you were hewn*; look to Abraham, your father, and to Sarah, who gave you birth. (Isaiah 51:1-2)

We know Abraham and Sarah did not actually give birth to the people Isaiah was addressing. He was speaking figuratively about their *spiritual* ancestral mother and father, instructing the Israelites to reflect all the way back to the place where their faith as a nation had begun. Similarly, it would be good for us as modern day Anabaptists who are *pursuing righteousness* and *seeking the Lord*, to look back to the "quarry from which we were hewn" in order to understand and examine whether we are following the Lord with the same passionate spirit of our early ancestors.

As we look at our Anabaptist lives today and compare them with those who went before us, do we see any discrepancies? Our early forefathers shared their faith with a strong and holy zeal: are we filled with their same boldness? Are we *compelled* in our spirits as they were, to obey the great commission of Jesus to "Go into all the world and preach the gospel to every creature," or does the idea of witnessing seem frightening or uninteresting (Mark 16:15)? Many of our ancestors were filled with joy even though all their worldly goods were confiscated: are we filled with joy and free from attachment to "things," or do we worry about having enough money, or preparing for a comfortable retirement? They were marked with great peace and a deep love for their Savior, even in light of martyrdom: do we have peace and a deep, heartfelt love for God, regardless of our circumstances? The *Schleitheim Confession of Faith*, an early statement of Anabaptist beliefs, called the religious works of the State Churches an . . .

> . . . abomination . . . to Christ Jesus, who has freed us from the servitude of the flesh

Are we experiencing our ancestors' same freedom from religious works in our own worship services? [1]

If you are like myself and most Anabaptists alive today, an honest response to these questions will reveal that some of the "fruit" which has grown on the tree of Anabaptism looks very different from the fruit of the young sapling which God planted in the 1500s. Things have changed, both positively and negatively since the time of our ancestors.

Anabaptists have a good heritage. In the following chapters, we will unearth it from its resting place, brush it off, and examine it carefully. We'll consider its blessings and we'll look at its weaknesses. We'll prayerfully seek God all along the way and apply the wisdom of the Scriptures, that we may find the "good way" in the ancient paths.

Thank You, heavenly Father, that You have given me a rich heritage. Thank You that I am from Anabaptist descent.

Help me to understand and to receive as my own, all the truths You revealed to my ancestors. As the Bible says, when I read the pages of this book, "divide between my soul and my spirit by the Word of God: discern the thoughts and attitudes of my heart.[1] *"Enlighten the eyes of my understanding, that I may know the hope of my* calling *and the riches of the glory of Your inheritance in the saints."*[2] *"Guide me into all truth."*[3]

Thank You that You have gifts and a spiritual call for me through my heritage. Show me those gifts, reveal to me the call. Help me to receive everything You have for me. And hide me under the shadow of your wings.[4] *Thank You,*

In Jesus' Name, Amen.

---

[1] Hebrews 4:12; [2] Ephesians 1:18; [3] John 16:13; [4] Psalm 17:8.

GRACE IN THE FIRE

A young Italian student named Algerius became a true Christian and was baptized.[1] He was soon arrested for his "heretical" faith and spent several years in a prison of testing, trial, and suffering. When he could not be dissuaded by nobility or by the State Church to renounce his beliefs, he was condemned to death.

The year was 1557 and the place was Rome, Italy. The method of execution was unusually cruel. Stripped bare to his waist, his executioners poured boiling oil over his head and body so that when Algerius rubbed his face with his hand, he pulled off his skin and his hair. He was then burned to ashes, dying as a martyr for Christ.

While Algerius was in prison in Padua, he wrote these words to encourage his fellow believers:

> . . . here (in prison) I have whom I may take for companions, comforters and examples, since I see some stoned; others cut in twain; some roasted! others fried in pans, ovens, and chaldrons of oil; some whose eyes are put out; others whose tongue is cut out; these with their skin pulled over their head; others with hands and feet cut off; some that are cast into fiery furnaces; others given as food to wild beasts; yea, it would require too much time were I to relate it all.
>
> . . . And for all these there is but *one remedy, one medicine, which can **cure** all their infirmities*; and this remedy gives to me also **strength, and life, and cheerfulness** to suffer all these fears and afflictions, which are but momentary, and not worth speaking of; this is *the hope which I have placed in heaven.*[2]

In another part of his letter, he shares about his great inner peace and joy, in spite of his circumstances:

> In a dark hole I have found *pleasure;* in a place of
> bitterness and death, *rest and hope of salvation*; in the abyss
> or depths of hell, *joy*; where others weep, *I have laughed*;
> where others fear, I have *found strength*; who will believe
> this? In a state of misery I have had very *great delight;*
> in a lonely corner I have had *most glorious company*, and
> in the severest bond, *great rest*. All these things, my fellow
> brethren in Jesus Christ, the gracious hand of God has given
> me. . . .
>
> He comforts me; He fills me with joy; He drives from
> me bitterness and renews within me strength and sweetness;
> He makes me well; He sustains me; He helps me up; He
> strengthens me. *Oh, how good is the Lord*, who does not
> suffer His servants to be tempted above that they are able!
> Oh, how *easy, pleasant and sweet* is His yoke! . . . He gives
> us cheerful mind and peaceful heart. [3]

Like many of our forefathers, Algerius had found the
secret of life, though faced with excruciating pain and a gruesome death; he had found the *love of God*. He endured all for his
heavenly Bridegroom, as our ancestors lovingly called God in
final letters written from their prison cells.

It was said of Anneken Van Den Hove, who was buried
alive at Brussels, Belgium, in 1597, that . . .

> . . . she *so loved her dear leader, Christ Jesus*, that she
> followed Him not only to the marriage at Cana, but also, so
> to speak even to the *gallows-hill** . . . she will meet her
> *heavenly Bridegroom*, be joyfully welcomed and received
> in the heavenly halls of immortal glory. . .[4]

Hans Langmantel, a wealthy German nobleman who was
beheaded by the sword in 1529, envisioned meeting the Bridegroom on the other side of death:

> Grant, Lord, that . . . when they shall led us to death, we . . .
> may go to meet Thee . . . in the true, adorned wedding gar-
> ment, at the marriage feast, prepared for Thy Son,
> *when He shall receive His bride with everlasting joy and
> delight.*[5]

Christiaen Rijcen, incarcerated in Flanders, Holland, was tortured and then burned to ashes on April 7, 1588. From prison he writes to encourage his wife to love God as a bride loves her husband:

> O my dearest love, trust with all your heart in the Lord, and do not forsake your friend, *that loves your soul,* since you have found Him, *as the bride* in (*Song of Solomon*) (3:4);* but cleave faithfully to Him, and *take Him for your Husband,* and for a Father for my children . . . be also faithful to your *Husband Christ. . . .*[6]

Our ancestors did not suffer and die for the sake of doctrine or theology. They did not even suffer and die for the sake of the "true church" which was made up of believers gathering in worship. They died because they loved. They gave themselves for Jesus who loved them as a "fragrant offering and sacrifice to God" (Ephesians 5:2).

They were sent as galley slaves to row in the ships of Rome's armies. They were starved to death in prisons. They were stretched on racks until blood ran down their feet. They were hung upside down and they were buried alive. They were drowned. They were scourged and branded with hot irons and banished from their homelands. They were strangled, hanged, and cut in pieces. Their children were taken away and given to strangers and all their earthly possessions were sold and given to the State Church and to those who betrayed them.

But in all these things, they were more than conquerors through Him who *loved them* (Romans 8:37). They endured all sorts of suffering and ridicule because they had discovered *relationship* with their heavenly Father and Brother. For them, the words of John were true:

> There is *no fear in love.* But **perfect love** drives out fear . . . We love because **he first loved us.** (I John 4:18, 19 *NIV/(KJV)*)

The fears of our early ancestors were washed away by the intense and perfect love they had found. God loving them—God as *Perfect Love*—gave them the willingness to die for a faith that had become very real. George Blaurock and Hans Van Der Reve were burned alive near the town of Clausen, Switzerland, in 1529. While they were imprisoned, they wrote of the Father they had come to know:

> Lord God, I will praise Thee now and until my end; because Thou hast given me faith, by which I have learned to *know Thee*. . . . For this I will now magnify and praise Thy glorious name forever, because Thou dost always *show Thyself a merciful dear Father*. Cast me not off but receive me *as Thy child* . . . that I may be *Thy child and heir*. . . . Thy *Holy Spirit protect and teach me*, that in all my sufferings I may ever receive Thy consolation, so that valiantly fighting, in this conflict, I may gain the victory.[7]

The Divine presence enabled many of our ancestors to love even their torturers as Jesus had forgiven His enemies. A memorial left by George Blaurock and Hans Van Der Reve included this prayer for those who hated them:

> I sincerely pray Thee for all our enemies, O Lord, however many there may be; *do not lay their sins to their charge;* Lord, I entreat this according to Thy will. (Acts 7:60)[8]

Leopold Schneider, beheaded at Augsburg in 1528, also forgave:

> He that would here bring his gift to the altar, and remembers that his brother has aught against him, must leave his gift at the altar, and first go and be reconciled to his brother, and then come and offer his gifts (Matthew 5:23, 24). Therefore, I beseech Thee, O God, graciously to *forgive those who put me to death*.[9]

Many others walked in the same spirit of these men, blessing their persecutors (Romans 12:14). Some who were about to die actually comforted their executors, who were troubled about having to put to death "good people." Without hatred or judgment, these Anabaptist hearts stayed free of bitterness and remained in the grace and joy of the Lord.

The Joy of God

God's presence brings joy, and joy brings strength, just as Nehemiah 8:10 says, ". . . the joy of the Lord is your strength." It was because they walked with God that the testimonies of our forefathers are full of joy.

Hendrick Sumer and Jacob Mandel were drowned in Baden, Switzerland, in 1582. When they heard about their death sentence, they were filled with joy, and,

> . . . rejoiced from the heart, and were *glad and of good cheer*; they also said that it was a *greater joy for them than if they were to go to a marriage*; yea, they were of *very good cheer*, that God had counted them worthy, that they should glorify His name through such a righteous death. . . .[10]

In other places of persecution in 1529, Anabaptists sang like Paul and Silas in their prison cells:

> . . . they filled all the prisons with them, intending to deter them by fear; but they *sang and rejoiced in prison,* so that their enemies who had cast them into prison were more troubled and afraid than the prisoners. The knew not what to do with them. . . .[11]

About 350 Anabaptists were put to death near Alzey, Germany, in 1529. They died in rejoicing, as each one . . .

> . . . *went joyfully to meet death*; while others were being drowned, and executed, the rest who were yet alive and waited for death *sang until the executioner took them.*[12]

Arent and Ursel Van Essen, of Maestricht, Holland, died in 1570. They were severely tortured, Arent seven separate times, and Ursel twice on the rack and once hung up, her bare

skin scourged with rods. When they found they were to be
executed, they praised God, and . . .

> . . . *greatly rejoiced*, because they were to be counted worthy
> to die for the name of Christ; and were *full of joy that day*
> *and night, thanking and praising God,* and thus waited for
> the day of their redemption..[13]

They died in full faith, burned to ashes in prepared huts
of straw and wood that were set ablaze by the executioner's
storch.

Maeyken Wens died on October 6, 1573, at Antwerp,
Belgium. After her sentencing, she rejoiced in a letter to her
minister:

> And now I can also not write much, because I have been sen-
> tenced; nevertheless I was so *full of joy,* that I *should not be*
> *able to express it with the mouth, the Lord be forever praised*
> *for the great grace He has shown me,* who has feared so much.
> Oh, what a strong God we have, compared with what we see
> the wicked have. Oh, let us have good courage...[14]

Pieter Saymer was ready to die for Christ in July 1588 in
Frieburg, Bavaria. He was willing to give his life *twice*, if it were
possible, for the sake of the gospel:

> . . . his end was announced to him . . . which caused his *heart*
> *to leap for joy,* and he *greatly thanked and praised God,*
> saying then: "I have one head, and if I had two, or still more,
> I would rather suffer them all to be cut off than to renounce
> my faith.
>   There was much people present, and some wept over
> him when he was led out; but he said: "You need not weep
> over me, for *I am of good cheer in God;"* and he *sang for*
> *joy,* which the priests would not tolerate . . . while he was
> kneeling in prayer, the executioner struck off his head,
> which when it fell down to the ground, rolled about won-
> derfully, and finally lay still with the face turned toward
> the executioner, at which the people greatly
> marveled.[15]

Even as they wasted away in prisons, the early Anabaptists lived and died with joy. Ulrich Schneider was seized and imprisoned in 1635. Taken to the Othenbach dungeon in Zurich, Switzerland, he was stripped in his bonds and fed only bread and water. He remained there in much suffering until he committed his spirit to God and died in 1639. While he was in prison, his children were driven out and put among strangers and his property sold, the monies kept by the authorities. Yet even in their poverty, these

> . . . cast out and forsaken ones *joyfully* bore the spoiling of their goods.[16]

Grace in the Fire

We have a heritage passed down to us through the years from men and women, youth, and even children, who boldly and joyfully gave up everything for love. They did not give in to fears or to doubts, but in pouring out their petitions and prayers, received from Christ the grace they needed to bear their own personal crosses with victory (Philippians 4:6,7).

We have the same privilege. In this time and age we are seeing wickedness increase. The "birth pains" before Jesus' return for His bride, the church, are evident all around us. Yet, we do not need to fear. We can have the same holy and heart-filled assurance and confidence of those who have gone before us.

It is as we *know* God's *perfect love* which so comforted their hearts, that our own fears are cast out.

> And hope maketh *not ashamed*; because **the love of God is** *shed abroad in our hearts* **by the Holy Ghost** which is given unto us. (Romans 5:5, *KJV*)

Through our Father resident within us by His Spirit, we are heirs to a heavenly grace that will face any fire without shame, whether it is the real fire of being burned at the stake like our ancestors or the fire of ridicule, rejection and suffering for the sake of Christ.

His love is more than enough, as it was more than enough for our forefathers. This is part of our inheritance in Christ. When we know God and His perfect love is in us, nothing will ever be able to take Him away from our hearts.

> *. . . Who shall separate us from **the love of Christ?*** Shall tribulation, or distress, or persecution, or famine, or nakedness, or peril, or sword? As it is written, For thy sake we are killed all the day long; we are accounted as sheep for the slaughter. Nay, in all these things we are *more than conquerors through him that **loved** us.* For I am persuaded, that neither death, nor life, nor angels, nor principalities, nor powers, nor things present, nor things to come, Nor height, nor depth, nor any other creature, *shall be able to separate us from the **love of God**, which is in Christ Jesus our Lord.* (Romans 8:31-39, *KJV*)

A reminder to pray the following prayer aloud, that your heart may "hear," and you may be built up by your tongue's confession. Also, allow yourself sufficient time to pray thoughtfully, when your soul is quieted from schedule and other distracting influences.

Father, help me to pray. As I have read about the faith of my ancestors and of their great love for You, I confess my own personal need. I need to know You much more deeply.

Let Your love become the foundation of my life. I want to know how wide and deep, and high and long is Your love for me.[1] If I know Your love, everything else in my life will be at peace. More than anything else, fill me with Your perfect love, and wash away all my fears.

Father, I also need more joy in my life: please give me joy like my early ancestors. As they knew You, I want to know You and to be so full of joy that I am strong and bold.[2] Let the joy of the Lord be my strength and let joy also strengthen my family and my church congregation. Come and fill us with Your joyful presence.

Thank you that my ancestors loved their persecutors. Please give me that kind of love and forgiveness towards those who reject me and persecute me. If there is any place in my heart where I have not loved those who have spoken a word against me, enable me to forgive. If there is one who has acted against me or rejected me, whom I have not loved, help me to forgive them. I can't love them by my own strength, so I ask You to give me Your love for them.

God, You are love.[3] Thank You for giving Yourself to me.[4] I give myself to You and ask You to deliver me from all my fears and to protect me from the evil one.[5]

In Christ's name, Amen.

---

[1] Ephesians 3:16-19; [2] II Corinthians 3:12; [3] I John 4:16; [4] John 14:16-18; [5] Psalm 34:4 and John 17:15.

~ 3 ~

FREEDOM FROM RELIGION

Imagine that only one church denomination is permitted in all of society and by law, you must attend its services. You are also forced to tithe and to obey its doctrine. You have no choice in the matter even if you disagree with its teachings, because rebellion against this church will mean physical imprisonment or execution and, according to its leaders, spiritual damnation. Many of the leaders of this church are corrupt and much of its doctrine is full of error and all of the people in society suffer the consequences.

For more than a thousand years this was the church which ruled over much of the European continent. Influencing entire kingdoms by its connections with political rulers and town councils, this church was firmly entrenched in power as our first ancestors were born. They grew up attending its services and being taught according to its doctrine.

That is why we must understand this church if we are going to understand our own heritage. Why did its leaders consider our forefathers such heretics? Why did our ancestors eventually insist on a complete separation from this one Church? As we answer these questions, we'll also begin to grasp why our forefathers passionately pursued *freedom from religion*.

The "State" of the State Catholic Church

It was Constantine, a ruler in the early fourth century who first declared that everyone in his empire had to become Christian. Pagans, Jews, Moors (Muslims)—absolutely everyone—had to "convert" or be killed. From his statewide church model, the *State Catholic Church* arose to become the only lawful church in existence in much of Europe. Consequently, Europeans living during its reign did not *join* the Church; in a sense they were *born into* Church.

Practices and lifestyles of Church leaders were often an abomination to God, yet they led mass, heard confessions, and gave communion.[1] But because of the Church's power and control, their wickedness went unchallenged. Pope Gregory VII (1066 AD) made these declarations about himself and about all popes who would rule after him as head of the State Catholic Church:

> To the Pope belongs the right of making new laws. All the princes of the earth shall kiss his feet. He has the right of deposing emperors. The sentence of the Pope can be revoked by none. He can be judged by none. None may dare to pronounce sentence upon anyone who appeals to the Pope. He never has erred, nor can he ever err. He can loose subjects from the oath of fealty (oath of loyalty). The Pope is holy. He can do no wrong.[2]

Popes, bishops, cardinals, and other leaders "bought" their way to influence and gave political favors to strengthen their own power. One archbishop committed murder to gain political allies, but the pope pardoned him.[3] Another pope poisoned men, lived unlawfully with a woman and their children, and at will took away the crown of a king and gave it to someone else.[4]

Influence was also used to make them rich. Cardinal positions were sold.[5] Commoners were told they could lessen the penalty of their sins by paying money to the Church. These payments were called "indulgences" and were sold by the thousands. Fake "holy" relics with claims of healing virtue and blessing were also sold, all to feed the extravagant lifestyles of the Church rulers.[6]

In *The Story Of Liberty*, Charles Coffin writes of Martin Luther's reaction as he visits the "holy city" of Rome, while still serving as a priest in the Catholic State Church:

The longer (Martin Luther) stays in Rome, the more he is dissatisfied with what he sees. He discovers that the Pope, the cardinals, the bishops, and priests are, for the most part, very far from being the pure men he had supposed them to be. The Pope is a military chieftain. The cardinals are living sensual lives. The money which is contributed by the good people of every land for the Church is squandered in riotous living or for the support of armies. It is no longer holy Rome; the city instead is a sink of iniquity. Crime goes unpunished. Men are robbed and murdered at noonday. The (positions) of the Church are bought and sold, just as men buy and sell houses or cattle. The nunneries and monasteries, instead of being retreats for prayers, meditation, and holy living, are vile places. Cardinals, bishops, priests, monks, and nuns, all live upon the treasure contributed by the people, or taken from them by tithes, or obtained by the sale of indulgences and pardons. (Martin Luther) turns his steps homeward, sick at heart with what he has seen.[7]

Grand processions of pomp and ritual were held in major centers of religion with pope, priests and cardinals parading in their luxurious velvet and jeweled gowns, hats, slippers and robes. There were richly decorated, massive marble cathedrals and sumptuous feasts, with every kind of delicacy, held for those who served in the "holy" city.[8]

Like the Pharisees of Jesus' day, many leaders within the State Catholic Church tied up heavy loads of duty to weigh down the poor, while neglecting to carry any of the weight on their own shoulders (Matthew 23:4). Jesus perfectly describes the true condition of many of these leaders in one simple condemnation of the religion of the Pharisees:

> Woe to you, scribes and Pharisees, hypocrites! For you cleanse the *outside* of the cup and dish, but *inside* they are full of *extortion* and *self-indulgence.* (Matthew 23:25)

Reforming the Church

By the early 1500s, things were beginning to stir toward change, partly because of one simple *machine.* The printing press had just been invented, which allowed many more Bibles to be made. More Bibles meant more people reading the Scriptures. More people reading the Scriptures caused a greater awareness of the deep corruption and error within the State Catholic Church.

A growing number of people desired reforms that would bring an end to its apostasy. They had received a revelation of grace and of faith, and their hearts were grieved by the deplorable religion of the State Catholic Church. Martin Luther, Ulrich Zwingli, John Calvin, and other leaders like them were moved to action, and birthed a new "Reformation" theology based on faith and on a more complete understanding of the Word of God.

Although the State Catholic Church had maintained power for centuries, ruling nobles and town councils lined up with this new Reformer theology and suddenly changed the allegiance of entire regions. Whole towns and political domains were "Reforming" as they turned away from the State Catholic Church.

Even as they came under attack by the State Catholic Church for abdicating, the Reformers made some progress towards change. Yet they decided to keep the one-Church State system, which meant everyone in society was still required to attend their church and to obey its rules. Like the State Catholic Church, religious leadership of the people still remained under the umbrella of the government's responsibility.[9] In *The Anabaptist View Of The Church*, Franklin Hamlin Littell writes,

> . . . the Roman Catholics and Reformers were still thinking in terms of the church pattern of the Middle Ages: *religion* was a certain phase of civilization, controlled and bounded by the *agreement of princes.*[10]

Using the Scriptures to back up their decision for a one-Church society, the Reformers taught the biblical parable of the *wheat and tares*, applying it to the Church: that the "tares" (the wicked of society) and the "wheat" (those who actually lived their Christian faith) existed together *within the Church* and would only be separated out at the end of the ages, when Jesus returned (Matthew 13:24).[11]

The "True Church"

Certain men and women who agreed with the Reformers concerning faith, believed a more radical change was necessary. They believed the church needed to *look* and *live* like the New Testament model.[12] They were our ancestors, the *Anabaptists*. When they proclaimed that the biblical image of the church *only included true believers* and excluded the unbelieving people in society, both State Churches set about to silence them. They hated this teaching, as did the ruling kings, queens, and nobles, since in their minds the Anabaptists' "disobedience" to the State Churches was also disobedience to the government. To State Church leaders, the Anabaptist version of a church without governmental controls could only lead to anarchy and social chaos.[13]

Yet the early Anabaptists pressed ahead, convinced in their spirits that the body of Christ needed to be pure and undefiled. As they grew, they made incredible strides away from the *religion* of the State Churches. Their worship services were without pomp and ritual. Their leaders wore no special robes. Meeting places were no longer great marble structures. Instead, Anabaptists met together in the forest or field or in private homes, often around a common meal of brotherhood. Their worship was simple praise and prayer and their study of God's Word was personal, without needing a priest to mediate. Believer's baptisms were done with a bucket or ladle and without the superstitious blowing, exorcism, anointing, crossing, or applying saliva which accompanied infant baptism in the State Churches. Communion was administered by distributing ordinary bread and wine to all the participants, rather than by "holy" wafers given only by the priest, and without the cup.[14]

God was restoring His people and cleansing His church, as they returned to *Christ* as the center of their worship. He was bringing correction to centuries of "error concerning the Lord":

> See, a *king will reign in righteousness and rulers will rule with justice.* Each man will be like a *shelter* from the wind and a *refuge* from the storm, like *streams of water* in the desert and the *shadow* of a great rock *in a thirsty land.*
> *No longer will the fool be called noble nor the scoundrel be highly respected (as noble, rich and liberal).* For the fool speaks folly, his mind is busy with evil: He *practices ungodliness* and *spreads error concerning the Lord*; the *hungry he leaves empty* and from the *thirsty he withholds water.* The scoundrel's methods are wicked, he makes up evil schemes to *destroy the poor with lies,* even when the plea of the needy is just. *But the noble man makes noble plans, and by noble deeds he stands.* (Isaiah 32:2-9)

As the good news spread through the zeal of our Anabaptist forefathers, the people of the church once again became a "shelter" and "refuge" for each other. These new believers were "noble" men and women who made "noble plans" and stood by "noble deeds." Rather than "destroying the poor with lies," the *true church* helped the poor, and shared possessions with the needy, as we shall discover in a later chapter.

In this newfound church, leaders actually *lived* their faith instead of "practicing ungodliness." And rather than "spreading error", they endeavored to teach according to scriptural truths as God gave them understanding. The essence of verse five came true within their fellowships: no longer was the "fool called noble" or the "scoundrel highly respected," but leaders *served* their flocks, and believers loved one another. This was the *radical faith* of our forefathers, who turned away from pursuing *religion* and determined in their hearts to follow God.

We know that not everyone within the State Catholic Church during the Middle Ages walked corruptly: there *were* godly men and women of this Church who truly wanted to know God. We also know many of the Reformers desired to walk uprightly and to love God. Yet it was the early Anabaptists who saw a revelation of freedom from the religious practices of the State Churches. They saw the "new thing" God was doing:

> Forget the former things; do not dwell on the past. See, *I am doing a **new thing**!* Now it springs up; do you not perceive it? I am *making a **way in the desert*** and streams in the wasteland. (Isaiah 43:18-19)

Today, partly through their influence, the "new thing" of their day has become the standard church model for Christianity. Now, a true ***believer's church*** is normal: in fact, it has become so much the norm, it's now an "old treasure" in body of Christ, just as Jesus taught:

> . . . every teacher of the law who has been instructed about the kingdom of heaven is like the owner of a house who brings out of his storeroom ***new treasures as well as old***. (Matthew 13:52)

Though it took hundreds of years and much bloodshed, the truth of a church comprised only of *the brethren* took hold in Europe and later in North America and other parts of the world. The Anabaptists— along with other people groups like the Huguenots of France, the Waldensians, and the early "Donatists"—played an important role in the eventual widespread practice of this more accurate version of a believing New Testament Church.[15]

Their great revelations are part of our gifts and call. *We* are to be those who perceive the "new thing" and the "new treasures" of our day and age. We are to be a people who see the revelations of the Scriptures and walk in them. We are to live like the New Testament Church, as our forefathers endeavored to live. And *we* are to be a church who walks in the glorious gift of ***freedom from religion*** as we serve our God with the same passion of our ancestors.

Father, thank You again for a good heritage. Thank You for the depth of spiritual insight You gave to my forefathers. Though I may not feel so bold or so wise, I humbly ask for spiritual insight as well. According to Your promise, I call to You and ask You to show me "great and mighty things" which I have not yet known.[1] You gave my ancestors great understanding from Your Word through the Holy Ghost. I also ask to understand Your Word by Your Presence in my life. I want to know all that You have freely given me.[2]

Lord, my early ancestors were able to see the difference between true faith and religion. Show me true faith and give me "ears to hear" the difference between the two.[3] I want to live by faith and not religiously. Open my eyes, that I may see.[4]

Father, just as my forefathers imitated the New Testament church, show me the "old treasures" within the church of Acts. Teach me about the early church and their ways and speak to me about my own life through their example.

Thank You that You have promised to finish what You've started in my life.[5] Thank You that You love me.[6] Thank You for hearing me and answering my prayer.[7] Thank You for being my Shepherd.[8]

I ask these things in Jesus' Name, Amen.

---

[1] Jeremiah 33:3; [2] I Corinthians 2:12; [3] Mark 4:22-24; [4] Matthew 13:16; [5] Philippians 1:6; [6] Isaiah 43:4; [7] Mark 11:24; [8] Psalm 23:1.

~ 4 ~

SALVATION BY GRACE
THROUGH FAITH

The greatest spiritual gift given to the early Anabaptists
was the gift of *salvation by grace* through faith. Most of us are
familiar with this biblical concept, but only a few years prior to
Anabaptism's beginnings, the word *salvation* held an entirely
different meaning in the State Catholic Church.

For hundreds of years, God's grace had been mostly forgotten. Salvation was deemed as something to be *earned,* rather than
received through faith. A person was mainly saved from hell by the
"holy" sacraments: communion, infant baptism, marriage, sacred
orders, holy matrimony, penance (for sins), and extreme unction.
Acts of obligation and ritual were thought to have *more* redemptive
power than a person's trust in Christ's sacrifice.[1] And since the Bible
was only available to the leaders of the State Catholic Church, the
"sheep" of their fold could only assume their teachings were true.

True Salvation

It was out of this "aimless conduct received by *tradition*
. . ." that our early forefathers were given the revelation of *grace*
(1 Peter 1:18). It came to them mainly through the writings and
teachings of the Reformers who saw truth's light and received
God's *free gift.* As our early Anabaptist forefathers read their
essays and heard their preaching, their spirits lit up and they
also accepted salvation, free of religious works, and free of
obligation to any Church system.

What an incredible gift! Salvation by grace through faith completely overtook the hearts of our early Anabaptist forefathers. It was so real to them, they considered ". . . everything a loss compared to the surpassing greatness of knowing Christ Jesus . . ." (Philippians 3:8). And though they would soon be surrendering their lives for what they believed, but they didn't fear because they had already crossed a line into eternal life. Their spirits had forever been sealed in a heavenly covenant.

This Gift of Our Heritage

This gift is part of the heritage to which we lay claim. Our forefathers came out of a religion based on doing good works, to discover that the Bible taught a much different gospel. They saw a great chasm between the State Church's practice of striving to be righteous by doing deeds, and the Scriptures' true righteousness which is offered freely. In the *Dordrecht Confession* (1632), a statement of faith written by our ancestors, article six affirms their belief in salvation by faith, rather than by works:

> . . . For neither *Baptism, Sacrament*, nor *Church-Fellowship*, nor any other *external ceremony*, can without faith, the new birth, and a change or renewal of life, . . . *qualify us* that we may please God. . . . But on the contrary, we must go to God "with a sincere heart in full assurance of faith," and *believe in Jesus* . . . through which faith we obtain the *pardon of our sins*, become sanctified, justified, and children of God . . . as we are *born again of God* from above, *through His incorruptible seed* from above.[2]

Our ancestors read the same verses that you and I read today, calling us new creations in Christ:

> Therefore, if anyone is in Christ, he is a *new creation;* old things have passed away; behold, all things have become new. Now all things are of God, who has **reconciled us** *to Himself through Jesus Christ,* and has given us the ministry of reconciliation, that is, that God was in Christ reconciling the world to Himself, *not imputing their trespasses to*

them...For He **made Him** who knew no sin **to be sin** for us,
that **we might become the righteousness of God** in Him.
(II Corinthians 5:18-21)

This is our gift. The literal translation of the word *recon-ciliation* in this passage means to make a mutual exchange. Jesus made a **mutual exchange** on the cross, taking onto *Himself* all *our sin*, and putting *in us* His *righteousness*. Think for a moment about Jesus' righteousness. He is completely spotless. He has not one tiny blemish of sin, or one speck of anything unholy. He is the purest pure. He is perfect and seated in the Holy of holies, heaven's royal court. That is the righteousness He gave to our Anabaptist ancestors. That is the same gift He gives to you and me today. He wiped out our sinful record by making us the very *righteousness of God.*

Our Spiritual Position in Christ is a Gift

Yes, there is a practical outworking of this righteousness which will continue for the rest of our lives. But the writer of Hebrews promises, "For by one offering He has *perfected forever* those who are *being* sanctified" (Hebrews 10:14). As we are learning and growing in our faith, God, who exists outside of time and space, has provided the blood of Jesus to cover our entire life.

We also understand that James calls us to add to our faith *deeds*, showing evidence of our faith by the way we live our life (James 2:18). But the foundation of all of the good "works" we do is based on knowing that Christ has made us "right" before God, through His shed blood and broken body. We receive *His* righteousness and then follow Him in an obedient lifestyle, out of our love for the One who demonstrated His unending love by *changing places with us* (Romans 5:8).

The gift is absolutely *free* and there is nothing we have to do in order to be assured of God's complete and total approval, and of eternal life with Him. It is *guaranteed* through the Holy Spirit. He says in Ephesians 1:13 and 14:

> In Him you also trusted, after you heard the word of truth, the gospel of your salvation; in whom also, having believed, you were *sealed* with the *Holy Spirit* of promise, who is the *guarantee of our inheritance* until the redemption of the purchased possession. . . . (*NKJV*)

Because we have been made spiritually *right* and *perfect* in God's eyes, we are now able to come before Him anytime we wish, and boldly, because He does not remember our sins:

> For by one offering He *has perfected forever* those who are *being* sanctified. But the *Holy Spirit also witnesses to us.* . . . This is the covenant that I will make with them after those days, says the Lord: I will put My laws into their hearts, and in their minds I will write them," then He adds, "Their *sins and their lawless deeds I will remember no more.*" Now where there is remission of these, there is *no longer an offering for sin.*
>
> Therefore, brethren, having *boldness to enter* the Holiest by the blood of Jesus . . . through the veil, that is, His flesh, and having a High Priest over the house of God, let us *draw near with a true heart in full assurance of faith*, having our hearts sprinkled from an evil conscience and our bodies washed with pure water. Let us hold fast the confession of our hope without wavering, for He who promised is faithful (Hebrews 10:14-23).

The mysteries of the cross baffled the angels and hold endless treasures for us to discover (I Peter 1:10-12). Not only have we been made righteous, but we have bseen *forgiven* and *healed* (Isaiah 53:4-5). He was rejected on the cross, that we may be fully *accepted* by the Father in heaven (Ephesians 1:5,6). He was punished, that we may have *peace* (Isaiah 53:5). Jesus was cursed, that we might be *blessed* (Galatians 3:13-14).

Wherever we are along the highway of holiness which leads to eternity, we can always grow in our understanding of *all* that Jesus has provided for us (Isaiah 35:8). If you are interested in learning more about the depths of the "exchange" which occurred when Jesus died, I recommend reading chapter 17, "Divine Exchange," in Derek Prince's book *Blessing or Curse— You Can Choose* (listed in the "Recommended Reading" section).

For All Who Choose

We are not automatically placed into this glorious salvation, just as attending the State Church during our ancestors' time did not make anyone a true believer. Each and every person on earth must choose to receive this free gift for themselves. For this reason, I have written two prayers at the end of this chapter: the first prayer is for those who would like to receive salvation, or who have questioned whether their relationship with God is forever sealed by Jesus' blood. The second prayer is for all who want to receive a deeper revelation of this great gift.

If you do pray the first prayer, I encourage you to tell someone in whom you have seen or sensed the light of Jesus. Romans 10:9-10 tells us that with the *heart we believe unto righteousness*, and with the *mouth we confess and are saved*. If you want information on how to grow in your faith as a new believer, see the "Recommended Reading" section.

Remember to pray these prayers aloud, to build your faith and establish your heart as your ears hear the proclamations that your mouth is speaking.

Jesus, thank You for showing me that You love me by coming to earth and dying in my place. I agree with You that I am a sinner. Please forgive me for all that I have done which was in rebellion to Your will. Through the blood You shed in my place, please take my sins and exchange them now for Your righteousness. Cleanse me from all my unrighteousness and make me like You. I choose to receive Your gift of righteousness. Please fill me with Your Spirit and come live in me for the rest of my life. (Acts 2:38-39). Teach me everything I need to know about being made the righteousness of God in Christ and fill me with Your love. Thank you.

In Your Name, Amen

You may or may not feel anything if you have prayed the above prayer sincerely. Whatever you do or do not feel, be assured God has heard your prayer and has answered by making you *right* in His sight! (I John 5:14-15).

A prayer for all Anabaptists:

Righteous God, thank You that my forefathers knew Your salvation. And thank You for giving me the same great gift, and for making me righteous like You. Open to me more and more, the deep realities of my salvation. Show me greater things about the exchange You made for me on the cross. I want to grasp all that Your death has accomplished for me, and I want to know Your resurrection life (Philippians 3:10).

Where I have depended on my own strength or on my own "works" to make me right before You, I ask Your forgiveness. Through Your shed blood, cleanse me from anything which causes me to want to live by my own righteousness. I choose Your righteousness as the only righteousness that I need to stand in Your presence or in the presence of men. If there are any dead works or religious works in me, please show me where they exist in my life and give me the strength to admit them to You.

Thank You that as You point out these areas in my life which need to be changed, You will give me the power and the understanding I need in order to turn from them and walk on the paths of true *and godly righteousness (Psalm 23:3). I ask all of these things through Jesus, trusting You to be my Shield and my Defender.*

Amen.

Other Scriptures on our righteousness and the gift of eternal life:

Ephesians 2:8: "For by grace you *have been* saved *through faith,* and that not of yourselves; it is the *gift of God. . . ." (NASB)*

Romans 6:23: "For the wages of sin is death, but the *gift of God is eternal life* in Christ Jesus our Lord."

Romans 5:17: "For if by (Adam's) offense death reigned through the one, much more those who receive abundance of grace and of the *gift of righteousness* will reign in life through the One, Jesus Christ." *(NKJV)*

Isaiah 61:10: "I will greatly rejoice in the Lord, My soul shall be joyful in my God; For He has clothed me with the *garments of salvation,* He has covered me with the *robe of righteousness,* as a bridegroom decks himself with ornaments, and as a bride adorns herself with her jewels."

Romans 3:21-24: "But now the righteousness of God *apart from the law* is revealed, being witnessed by the Law and the Prophets, even the righteousness of God, *through faith in Jesus Christ, to all and on all who believe.* For there is no difference; for all have sinned and fall short of the glory of God, *being justified freely by His grace* through the redemption that is in Christ Jesus. . . ." *(NKJV)*

Hebrews 9:12-15: "Not with the blood of goats and calves, but with His own blood He entered the Most Holy Place once for all, *having obtained eternal redemption.* For if the blood of bulls and goats and the ashes of a heifer, sprinkling the unclean, sanctifies for the purifying of the flesh, *how much more shall the blood of Christ,* who through the eternal Spirit offered Himself without spot to God, *cleanse your conscience* from dead works to serve the living God? And for this reason He is the Mediator of the new covenant, by means of death, for the *redemption of the transgressions* under the first covenant, that *those who are called may receive the promise of the eternal inheritance." (NKJV)*

~ 5 ~

EVANGELISTIC ZEAL

Time and time again, Anabaptists' tongues were screwed shut, singed with a hot iron or impaled with a stick so they could not speak out and testify of their faith. Some had their tongues cut out completely. Others were gagged by rags which were stuffed into their mouths. Witnessing was such an expected part of an Anabaptist's life that even in dying, their persecutors knew they would share their message unless it was silenced by force.

When they were allowed to speak, they did so with fervor. Anabaptist forefathers Hendrick Sumner and Jacob Mandel died in 1582 in Baden, Switzerland. As they were led to the place of their execution,

> . . . they spoke boldly to the people, and exhorted the great multitude that had gathered, that they should repent and turn from their sinful life to God, and then both joined their voices in raising a joyful, sweet, and heartfelt song of praise to the Lord. . . . Thus they sang till close to the water's edge, where they were to be drowned.[1]

Andries Pirchner was beheaded in 1584 in Schlanders, Italy. While in prison, he was tortured three times on the rack to betray the names of those with whom he had fellowshipped. His response to his persecutors expressed his great desire to see others come to meet the One who had saved His soul:

> He said he would rather die than betray, as Judas had done . . . but in regard to his faith, that he "would *willingly and gladly declare and not keep silence* about what he had done or not done; he had made God in heaven a promise in Christian baptism, to which he would adhere. . . . Moreover,

> he would . . . patiently suffer death, and also *request nothing
> else, than that by his blood and suffering he might induce
> some poor souls to repentance and to the confession of the
> truth."* [2]

Melchior Platser was beheaded in Rankweil in Feldkirch in 1583. As he was being led to the place of his execution he called out to the crowds:

> Brother Melchoir began to speak to the people with *great
> zeal,* and *exhorted them* to think of their ungodly life in which
> they were sunk, and that they should no longer thus perversely
> boast themselves Christians. . . . (Later), he again warned
> the people that they should beware of the false prophets who
> thus uphold, comfort and strengthen them in unrighteousness,
> and promise them liberty and life, in order that they should
> the less desist from wickedness. . . . He spoke so earnestly
> and much to the people, that the sweat rolled from his face.
> The executioner dried off his face and said: 'Speak freely,
> I shall not hurry you'. . . ."[3]

Thomas Han was tortured severely and accused of "seducing many" to the "sect" of the Anabaptists. He said to his accusers:

> (Adult believer's baptism) is the true, Christian baptism,
> and not *ana*baptism; and *if I could convert the whole world,*
> I would gladly die three times if it were possible.[4]

In Bern, Switzerland, in 1672, forty Anabaptist prisoners were released through the political intercession of a man of influence, upon the promise that they would leave Switzerland and never return. When one of these men was asked by a Netherlands brother why they had not avoided more severe persecution by leaving Bern at an earlier time, they responded that their primary reason for staying was the *spiritual harvest* which had been occurring:

> . . . the churches (in Bern) '*greatly waxed and increased,* so
> that, though under the cross, they nevertheless flourished as

a rose among thorns, and that *further increase could daily be expected*, because many persons manifested themselves, who saw the light shine out of darkness and began to love the same and seek after it; that the ministers *considering this in their heart, found themselves loath to leave the country, fearing that . . . this promising harvest might be lost, . . .* and hence, they chose rather to suffer a little than to leave, *in order that they might yet rescue some souls from perdition, and bring them to Christ.*[5]

They had chosen to remain for the sake of the gospel rather than leave to escape heavy suffering. In their zeal, they sacrificed their own comfort and ease. This, and their concern for unbelieving spouses who would be left behind, caused them to stay in Bern under the weight of persecution.

We Are Called

In the face of torture and death, the voices of our forefathers heartily proclaimed the gospel, spreading far and wide to preach the good news. Evangelism was carried out as a core activity of their new faith, considered a part of *loving God* and of *showing love* to those in the world who needed God's love.[6] These new Anabaptists believed that every single Christian was called to fulfill the command of Christ to witness. The Great Commission of Jesus is quoted in historical court records more than any other Scripture, as Anabaptists explained to authorities the reason for their actions:[7]

> (Jesus) said to them, "Go into all the world and preach the good news to all creation. Whoever believes and is baptized will be saved, but whoever does not believe will be condemned. (Mark 16:15)

Missionary outreach to the lost was a central theme of Anabaptism from the very start. In Switzerland, the original Zurich group of Anabaptists which included Felix Manz, George Blaurock, and Conrad Grebel, scattered over a larger region to preach and teach and to baptize those who believed.[8] George Blaurock preached so effectively that he held a mass baptism in Zolliken where the first Anabaptist church developed. His short but effective ministry continued in the region of the Tyrol before his imprisonment and subsequent execution.[9]

The well-known "Martyr's Synod" which met in Augsburg on August 20, 1527, discussed strategy for evangelical outreach. Called a martyr's synod because most of those present later died for their faith, these men mapped out a plan for preaching the gospel to South Germany, Switzerland, and Moravia.[10]

Balthasar Hubmaier, another early ancestor, baptized about three hundred—most of the people in the village of Waldshut—using a milk bucket and water from the town square.[11]

Hans Hut is recorded to have won as many as a thousand converts within his short time of ministry, and Leenaert Bouwens baptized more than *ten thousand* new believers within a little more than thirty years.[12]

The Hutterites of Moravia, named after their primary founder, Jacob Hutter, sent out missionaries to trek all over European soil, preaching the gospel, baptizing, and bringing new believers into the fellowship of community. Thousands upon thousands were impacted by their witness. At the height of their one hundred years of intentional and planned missionary activity, they held many baptisms at their communities in Moravia—as many as seventy-two in a single day.[13]

As the Anabaptist movement grew, the witness of our early forefathers became so powerful that it affected nations, converted entire towns and spread quickly, even while persecution mounted. As Peter Hoover writes in *The Secret Of The Strength*:

> Within thirty years of the first baptisms . . . the movement drew incredible thousands—perhaps more than a hundred thousand converts to Christ, and this in the face of the bitterest persecution.
> Congregations of Anabaptists sprang up almost overnight. . . . Ten years later (after the beginning of Anabaptism), the movement had reached the far corners of the German world . . .

> whole towns were reported to have "gone Anabaptist." In
> Moravia, Anabaptist communities eventually numbered 60,000
> members. In the Netherlands, Belgium . . . Holstein, and along
> the Baltic Sea to East Prussia, the movement raced like fire.[14]

There are many reasons our ancestors raised their voices in proclaiming the good news of Jesus, the foremost being their deep love for God. Like the original spiritual birthing of the apostles, they had met His Holy Spirit and the result was that they witnessed in their own "Jerusalem, and in all Judea and Samaria, and to the ends of the earth." (Acts 1:8). They simply could not be silent because the Lord of the universe had come to dwell within and they wanted to tell others.

Their witness was also fueled by a belief that the end of the world was near.[15] As they looked at the tumultuous days in which they lived, many felt Jesus' return was imminent and that He would soon establish His church and His rule on earth.[16] They saw in their Anabaptist communities a church of faithful believers who were preparing for the Lord's return and for the glorious reign of God on earth.[17]

Only God, who can see all of time from His eternal perspective, knows the historical ramifications of our ancestors' witness. Personally, I believe their testimonies in word and in deed, like the blood of Abel, "still speak" in the heavenly realm (Hebrews 11:4).

Ask the Lord of the Harvest

As Anabaptists today, some of us really desire to share our faith and are becoming more and more effective. Others want to tell people about Jesus, but feel inadequate or awkward as we attempt to speak out. For the rest of us, evangelism has simply not been a great desire in our hearts. I confess, I am among the latter group. In a later chapter, we will look at some causes and effects for the disparity that exists between the overall witness of present-day Anabaptists and that of our early forefathers.

As I have seen the great gift of evangelism within my heritage, I have begun asking God to give me a heart for those who are lost. I want to share His love, but with His passion and not out of a sense of religious duty. I choose to obey, yet sense I need the zeal and the fire and the deep conviction my ancestors possessed, in order to walk effectively. Like the disciples, I desire His power, signs, and wonders to accompany "those who believe," that all who need Jesus so desperately in these times will be able to see His glory (Mark 16:17).

Two times, Jesus instructed His disciples to *ask* the Lord of the harvest to send out laborers because the harvest was *plentiful* (Luke 10:2; Matthew 9:38). Paul writes that if there is no one to go and tell those in the world about Jesus, they will not come to faith:

> . . . Everyone who calls on the name of the Lord shall be saved. . . . And how are they to believe in one *of whom they have never heard?* And how are they to hear *without someone to proclaim him?* . . . So faith comes from what is heard, and what is heard comes through the word of Christ. (Romans 10:13-17 *NRSV*)

Several translations use the word "preacher" for the one who is sent out. Yet, the true translation of the Greek is more accurately translated as "one who proclaims," just as our ancestors believed correctly that *every member* of the fellowship is called to share the good news. In their understanding, the Great Commission of Christ was "binding" upon every single member of the church.[18]

"Unless the Lord builds the house, its builders labor in vain" (Psalm 127:1). Our witness is effective through God *in us*. He is our zeal and He is the One who gives us all that we need. No matter how passionate or dispassionate we are about witnessing, we may ask God to raise us up once again with true evangelistic fire, that the world will know His love. As we ask, He will answer and restore what has been lost through the generations. He will answer, because we are asking according to His desires and His will. *He* will do it, because He is faithful to conform us to the image of His Son, who spread the news of the Kingdom of heaven wherever He went (Romans 8:29 and Matthew 4:17).

God, here I am. Hear my prayer. Give me Your heart for those who are perishing. You love them as much as You love me.[1] Lord of the harvest, I am willing to be a harvester. I want to see the lost the way You see them: give me Your spiritual eyes and Your understanding.

Thank You for the witness of my ancestors. Thank You for their boldness, and their passion to fulfill Your Great Commission. Lord, I need the desire and the zeal of Thomas Han, our early ancestor who wanted to convert the whole world. I need a love that is unquenchable and that cannot be silenced. I need a love that will enable me to sacrifice in order to reach those who are lost. Give me Your love to share with others.

You love the whole world so much, you died for whoever would turn to You.[2] In obedience to Your command, I ask You, raise up in me and in all Anabaptists, a holy and powerful witness and send us out as laborers in the fields.[3]

Change us, God. Fill us with Yourself, give us Your gifts and "clothe us with power" to be Your witnesses in our own towns—our "Jerusalems"—and even to all nations.[4] Give us signs to accompany us, that Your Name will be exalted wherever You send us.[5]

Thank You for Your promise to equip me with everything I need to do Your will, and to work in me what pleases You.[6] I entrust myself to You in all these things. Thank You that I am saved, through Your blood.

In Your Name, Lord Jesus, I ask all these things. Amen.

---

[1] II Peter 3:9; [2] John 3:16; [3] Luke 10:2; [4] Luke 24:47-49; [5] Mark 16:15-18; [6] Hebrews 13:21.

A CHANGE OF MIND

When I was a young adult and single, I had determined in my heart that I wanted to marry a farmer. In the agrarian region where I grew up in Lancaster County, Pennsylvania (USA), to be a farmer's wife was a privilege. Naturally then, most of the young men I associated with lived on a farm. Now, if *God* had planned for me to become a farm wife, it would have been "well with my soul" as the hymn goes, and I would have happily perfected my homemaking abilities around Spring planting and harvest times. But my dream would never come to pass.

At the age of twenty-three, I took a walk in the fields near our home. I had just ended a dating relationship with a young man and I was afraid, discouraged, and to be honest, a little miffed at God. I did not want to be single, but dating simply was not working. As I poured out my fears to God, I came to a point of surrender, promising Him I would not pursue or become involved in one more relationship unless He made it pristinely clear that "this man was the one" for marriage, even if the commitment I was making meant I would remain single for the rest of my life. I had given up.

About one month later, I met the man who would eventually become my husband. He was not a farmer. Instead, God had chosen someone very unlike my image of a lifetime partner. But *His* choice was right, enabling by our marriage a Divine awakening of who I really was, through my husband's encouragement and wisdom.

I'm fully convinced that if I had not laid down my own ideas for marriage, I would not have been able to see or perceive the person whom God had chosen for me, since my heart and mind had been so focused on my own plans. I am so glad God enabled me to repent of my own ways that day as I surrendered to Him. As hindsight always has "20/20" vision, I now understand I would have made a very poor farmwife, because I'd much rather be writing or doing other things than washing dairy cows at milking time or throwing hay bales into the loft. Many blessed women are called to be farm wives and it is a high calling, but I am grateful that by God's grace I changed my mind to agree with God's way for my life.

Changing Our Minds

That's what repentance means. One Greek translation of the word *repentance* is *a change of mind*. Paul writes to Timothy to patiently teach:

> . . . in humility correcting those who are *in opposition*, if God perhaps will **grant them repentance**, so that they may **know the truth**, and that they may *come to their senses*. . . . (II Timothy 2:25-26)

Applying this Scripture to our own lives, God desires that wherever we are consciously or unconsciously opposing His ways, we receive His truth through changing our minds. In a moment, we'll look at the gift of repentance, or changing their minds, which was given to our forefathers. But, right now we need to examine some current day perceptions about repentance so we may understand its blessings.

Repentance is a gift. It is a *blessing* from God. Amazing to our hearts as that may seem, one of the translations of the word *grant* in the scripture from Timothy is to *bestow a gift*. That gift is given to us because God is treating us kindly, wanting us to change our minds for our sakes, just as changing my mind from my own way of thinking enabled me to suddenly be able to see the husband whom God had chosen. Romans 2:4 says, ". . . *God's **kindness** leads (us) towards repentance."*

To many of us, repentance is not seen as a positive gift but as a negative obligation. We'd rather keep our error or sin tucked away inside because we are afraid of how others will respond if they know about our struggles. Our approach to God is with the same attitude, assuming He is upset at us when tell Him about our failures. Those coming from more conservative Anabaptist backgrounds may also associate repentance with "sinners" who stand in front of the church to confess their disobedience or sit on the front pew as a disciplinary measure.

God never condemns His children when they come to Him in repentance. Because of the exchange on the cross (chapter four), He promises He will never be angry at us again:

> To me this is like the days of Noah, when I swore that the waters of Noah would never again cover the earth. So now I have **sworn not to be angry with you, never to rebuke you again**. Though the mountains be shaken and the hills be removed, yet **my unfailing love** for you **will not be shaken** nor my **covenant of peace** be removed," says the Lord, who **has compassion** on you. (Isaiah 54:9-10)

Through our righteousness in Christ, God as *sworn* not to be angry with us! Now, His unfailing love and His compassion are the sure foundation of our faith. These are more firm than the even the mountains of earth.

God's purpose for calling us to come to Him in repentance is to help us see and understand truth so we may find healing and walk in His blessing. Repentance is for *our benefit*, so we may know God more intimately. As we are able to see things God's way rather than our own way, we will find closeness to God.

Think how full of victory our lives would be if we always saw our circumstances from Jesus' perspective. We would walk in perfect rest and in great joy: we would always know love and we would always have full trust: we would always overcome every obstacle. Repentance is a call to allow God to bring our thinking into line with His thinking, so we will experience more and more overcoming victory in our lives.

God repeatedly implores His people in both the Old Testament and the New Testament to repent for the purpose of *finding His blessing*:

> Job 36: 7-11: He does not take his eyes off the righteous; he enthrones them with kings and exalts them for ever. But if men are bound in chains, *held fast by cords of affliction, he tells them what they have done—that they have sinned arrogantly.* He makes them listen to correction and *commands them to repent of their evil.* If they obey and serve him, *they will spend the rest of their days in prosperity and their years in contentment.*

> Isaiah 59:20: *"The Redeemer will come* to Zion, to those in Jacob who repent of their sins," declares the Lord.

> Proverbs 28:13: He who covers his sins will not prosper, But whoever confesses and forsakes them *will have mercy (NKJV).*

> Ezekiel 18:30-32: ". . . Repent! Turn away from all your offences; *then sin will not be your downfall.* Rid yourselves of all the offences you have committed, and *get a new heart and a new spirit.* Why will you die, O house of Israel? For I t*ake no pleasure in the death of anyone,"* declares the Sovereign Lord. *"Repent and live!"*

> Acts 3:19: *Repent,* then, and *turn to God,* so that your sins may be wiped out, *that times of refreshing may come* from the Lord . . .

> James 5:16: Therefore confess your sins to each other and pray for each other *so that you may be healed.*

> Isaiah 30:15: This is what the Sovereign Lord, the Holy One of Israel, says: "In *repentance and rest is your salvation,* in quietness and trust is your strength . . ."

When sin or error exists in our lives, we will automatically walk in a way other than God's way, unable to see God clearly in that area of our lives. That is why Paul instructs us to

". . . be transformed by the renewing of your minds, *so that* you may discern what is *the will of God* . . ." (Romans 12:2). As we renew or "renovate" our minds and bring them into agreement with God's mind, we will then be able to understand His good desires for us. What a blessing to have a Heavenly Father who cares about us so much that he leads us to repent!

Anabaptist Repentance

Without repentance, our early ancestors would not have birthed a new, *true church*. The church of the Dark Ages was full of doctrinal error and as the fledgling Anabaptist movement grew, a deep sifting and sorting of truth from untruth was required. As a result, they experienced much *changing of their minds* as they examined what they had been taught within the State Church systems.

One primary example of their repentance was the doctrine of baptism. In the State Church systems, baptism was done in infancy because they believed it assured the salvation of any babies who died, since the rate of infant mortality was so high. As the early Anabaptists read the Bible, their eyes were opened to understand that baptism is actually a sign for those who have received Christ as their Savior (Acts 2:38). From this discovery of truth, our ancestors were baptized in accordance with the change of mind they had received from God.

Our forefathers also repented from many other State Church teachings. They discarded forced tithing and mandatory church attendance and made them both *voluntary*. They rejected the pope or any other man as the head of the church, giving that honor only to Christ, the perfect Head. They denounced indulgences and relics of the State Church as false and fake. They taught Matthew 18 as an appropriate practice of church discipline, rather than the State Church's use of force in dealing with those who erred. And they rejected priests or other men as mediators between God and man, believing instead that every person had direct access to God's presence.

Strongholds of the Mind

Some of the doctrinal errors they uncovered had been a part of the belief system of the State Catholic Church for more than a thousand years. In the Bible, this type of established mindset is called a *stronghold*. The Greek translation of a stronghold is *a castle or a fortress*: in other words, it is a way of thinking which has been firmly established and fortified in the minds of men.[1] In II Corinthians, Paul talks about pulling down these mental strongholds:

> For though we live in the world, we do not wage war as the world does. The weapons we fight with are not the weapons of the world. On the contrary, they have divine power to **demolish strongholds**. We **demolish arguments** and every **pretension** that sets itself up against the *knowledge of God*, and we **take captive every thought** to make it obedient to Christ. (II Corinthians 10:3-5)

Strongholds, arguments, pretensions, and thoughts all have to do with the way the Corinthians were *thinking*. Paul called them to *demolish* every mindset that was against the knowledge of God, because there were false teachers who had been trying to sway them from the pure gospel of Jesus Christ.

Just as the actual building of a castle stronghold takes years to complete, mental strongholds usually develop over a period of time because of the repetition of sinful practices or beliefs. Like their description they are *strong*, having the power to affect entire nations and people groups, as well as individuals.

Repentance, a change of mind, enables those strongholds of thinking to be brought down. For example, when our Anabaptist forefathers taught salvation by grace through faith, many people began to think differently than they had been taught their whole lives. (Matthew 11:12). They started to see that religious sacraments and religious duty were not the way to heaven, and a stronghold began to be dismantled. Thousands of people then experienced the freedom of knowing Christ in true salvation.

Like our ancestors, God calls us to tear down every habitual way of thinking which sets itself against knowing God. As the Corinthian passage says, we use weapons to do so, but not physical weapons. Our weapons are not carnal (of our flesh), but they are spiritual in nature and mighty in God. *One of those weapons is repentance.* As God gives us gifts of repentance to change our mind, we start bringing down the mental strongholds of our lives, of our families and churches, and of our denominations, and we begin walking in obedience to Christ.

Strongholds of thought still exist today, both in society and in the church, but many of these "castles" in the church are slowly being dismantled. For example, forty years ago Christians typically believed only one translation of the Bible was acceptable, but today most think differently. Then, the King James Version which was first completed in the early 1600s, was thought to be the only "true" version. But in recent years many other accurate translations have been completed, aided by the 1947 discovery of the ancient Dead Sea Scrolls which were found in a cave in the Middle East. These other translations are now widely acceptable in most of Christendom. For many people, the King James Version is still their favorite version. But, if it is their only *acceptable* translation, they may still be living under the influence of a stronghold of the mind such as legalism, which we will study in a later chapter.

Thinking Differently

Both John the Baptist and Jesus began their ministries by preaching, "Repent, for the Kingdom of heaven is near" (Matthew 3:2 and 4:17). Their message to the Jews who had been practicing Judaism for thousands of years was, "Change your mind: think differently, because now there is a new and better way nearby, called the Kingdom of heaven." Our ancestors also found that new and better way, apart from the religion of the

State Church systems. Thinking differently led them to a discovery of the Kingdom of heaven in their midst. Repentance was part of their spiritual victory because it set them free to worship God in spirit and in truth (John 4:24).

To identify strongholds in our own minds or in our families and churches, we begin by asking God to reveal any error in the way we think about our faith. He will be faithful to show us where we need to think differently, promising to direct our paths and to give us understanding (Proverbs 2:6 and 3:6). And as we change our minds, the truth will make us free, just as it freed our ancestors to follow God with all their hearts, souls, minds, and strength!

Heavenly Father, thank You for helping my forefathers think in a whole new way. You led them to change their minds, and You set them free by Your truth.

I also want to be free. Help me to change my mind to agree with Your truth. Show me if there are any errors in the way I think about You, or about my faith. If there are any strongholds of thinking in my life, or in the life of my family or my church congregation, show us what they are and help us as individuals and as a corporate church to make all our thoughts obey You.[1] Give us Your strength to "demolish these strongholds" as You reveal them. Help us change our minds, Lord, for You are our Helper[2] and we cannot change ourselves, but with You, all things are possible.[3] Give us Your courage and Your power.[4]

Thank You that You help me to want *to obey You, and to do what pleases You.[5] I know You love me. Help me love You with my* mind, *as well as with my heart, soul and strength.[6] I accept You alone as my stronghold—my castle, my fortress (II Samuel 22:3; Psalm 18:2)—and I "pull down" every religious stronghold and every other stronghold which is not of You, through the blood of Jesus shed for me. I cut and reject every tie to those strongholds in Jesus' Name. Lord Jesus, renew and heal my mind and be my stronghold for the rest of my life.*

I ask all these things in Your name, Amen.

---

[1] II Corinthians 10:5; [2] Hebrews 13:6; [3] Matthew 19:26; [4] Acts 4:29-31; [5] Philippians 2:13; [6] Mark 12:30 and Matthew 22:37.

~ 7 ~

TWO BAPTISMS

The name "Anabaptist" means "re-baptizer" and was used long before our ancestors' times as a derisive insult against anyone who baptized adults. Adult baptism had been forbidden by imperial law for almost a thousand years and was punishable by execution, since the State Church believed in and practiced infant baptism.[1] As a result, the life of every Anabaptist was automatically put in danger by their obedience to this symbolic act of faith.

Of course, Anabaptists did not believe in infant baptism. But our early forefathers did believe in *two baptisms*, so in a sense the authorities were right; they *were* "re-baptizers." The first baptism they believed in was accomplished by God's hand. The second was done with water by the hand of men. One was an *internal* baptism and the other was *external*. Listen to their words, as written in the *Ausbund Confession of Faith*:

> I believe and confess that there is a Christian baptism that must take place *inwardly* and *outwardly*: **inwardly with the Holy Ghost and with fire:** but **outwardly with water** in the name of the Father, the Son, and the Holy Ghost (Matthew 28; John 1; I John 5; Mark 16). The inward baptism is . . . as John the Baptist said, 'I baptize you *with water* . . . but He who cometh after me . . . is stronger than I. He will *baptize you with the Holy Ghost and with fire.'*
>
> Christ confirmed these words when He commanded His disciples (Luke 24 and Acts 1) not to depart from Jerusalem, but to *wait for the promise* of the Father. . . . For John baptized you **with water**, but ye shall be **baptized with the Holy Ghost** not many days hence.'[2]

Letters written from prison cells by our early ancestors are full of the overcoming faith which accompanies the Spirit's "fire" within. The Holy Ghost was the fuel, the oil, the source of the flame which lit up their souls as He lived *in* them, according to the promise of Jesus:

> And I will pray the Father, and he shall give you another Comforter, that he may **abide with you for ever;** Even the **Spirit of truth**; . . . for he dwelleth with you, and shall be **in you.** *I will not leave you comfortless: I will come to you.* (John 14:16-18 *KJV*)

Hans Bret, a young Anabaptist believer, was twenty-one years old when he was apprehended by authorities and taken to prison in Antwerp, Belgium. After about eight months he was burned at the stake, but not until they screwed his tongue and singed the end of it with a hot iron so he would be unable to witness. Even so, the presence of the Comforter was evident in him as he cheerfully motioned to the brethren while he walked to his execution site.

In a letter written to his mother from his prison cell prior to his death, Hans writes joyfully of God's presence with Him through the Spirit:

> . . . I thank the Lord and praise Him for His unspeakable grace, that He gives me *strength by His Holy Spirit*, so that my mind is unchanged, the Lord be thanked. And I trust in the Lord that *He will give me strength by His Holy Spirit*, even as He through grace has hitherto done to this hour . . . for which the Lord be praised forever.[3]

In a prison letter written by seven believers in Gmuend, Swabia, Germany, in 1529, we also sense the strength of God's Spirit as they pray to "cheerfully and valiantly" lay down their lives:

> . . . Send *Thy Holy Spirit,* even as Thou, O Christ, has until now not withdrawn, but *graciously imparted Him to me.*
> . . . *fill us with Thy Holy Spirit*, which we entreat of Thee

from the bottom of our hearts; so that we may continue steadfast unto the end, and *cheerfully and valiantly* enter upon the suffering which now awaits us, and that we may fear no agony or pain.[4]

These seven died boldly and with grace, beheaded by the sword. In a letter written by Hans Langmantel (beheaded in 1529), he asks for the Spirit's power, love, and joy:

O God, our heavenly Father, come with the *power of Thy Holy Spirit,* that Thou mayest *rejoice* our mind, heart and soul; give . . . us a manful (excellent) heart. . . . Let us *enjoy* the faithfulness which Thou hast shown us through Thy Son Jesus Christ; and . . . *send us Thy Holy Spirit and kindle in us the fire of Thy divine love; . . .'*[5]

The Holy Spirit was the *power from on high* for the early Anabaptists. He was their power both to live and to die. He was also their power to witness:

I am going to send you what my Father has promised; but stay in the city until you have been clothed with *power from on high*. (Luke 24:49)

Do not leave Jerusalem, but wait for the *gift* my Father promised. . . . But you will receive *power when the Holy Spirit comes on you*; and you will be my witnesses in Jerusalem, and in all Judea and Samaria, and to the ends of the earth. (Acts 1:4-8)

The Holy Spirit was the "sending authority" of the early Anabaptist church, as they went everywhere in fulfillment of Christ's Great Commission. As one forefather, Matthias Binder, told his questioners, God's Spirit was the one who "showed them where to go to and bring their testimony."[6] Like the wind, they were blown by the Spirit all over the known world:

Flesh gives birth to flesh, but the *Spirit gives birth to spirit.* You should not be surprised at my saying, 'You must be born again.' The wind blows wherever it pleases. You hear its sound, but you cannot tell where it comes from or where it is going. *So it is with everyone born of the Spirit.* (John 3:6-8)

This wind, the "rushing mighty wind" who blew into the room at Pentecost, was the same Spirit who transformed our ancestors' lives by birthing a new spirit within them (Acts 2). Conrad Grebel wrote that it was this "inner baptism" who enabled the new believer to live out their faith.[7] Felix Manz agreed with him:

> Upon relating the account of Peter and Cornelius (Acts 10), Mantz concludes: 'Afterwards they too were poured over . . . with water that, just as they had been *purified inwardly* through the *coming of the Holy Spirit*, the affusion with *water externally would indicate the inner cleansing* and *dying to sin.*'[8]

Covenants of Love

Within the State Catholic Church, there was little teaching about the Spirit of God living in human vessels. Instead of the Breath of God blowing into a soul to change a life, it was chiefly the outward forms of sacraments, indulgences, and holy relics which were thought to make a life "holy" (John 20:22 and Job 33:4).

Since believer and unbeliever were mixed together in the State Churches, there was also no clear symbol demarcating when a person came to trust *in the heart*, where the Scriptures say belief occurs:

> That if you confess with your mouth, "Jesus is Lord," and *believe in your heart* that God raised him from the dead, you will be saved. For it is *with your heart that you believe and are justified*, and it is with your mouth that you confess and are saved. (Romans 10:9-10)

For the Anabaptist, water baptism was that sign of the inner change in the heart. It was the first physical act of faith for those who had heard Christ's call and responded by inviting Him to come and dwell in them forever. It was an outward act of an inward covenant with God, symbolizing their spiritual death and resurrection with Christ (Romans 6:4).

In addition to representing the heart covenant made with their Savior, water baptism also represented an entering into covenant with the community of believers, in part because being baptized automatically meant persecution. Joining the brotherhood was essential in order to stand against evil, just as Peter declares:

> Resist (the devil), standing firm in the faith, because *you know* that *your brothers* throughout the world *are undergoing the same kind of sufferings.* (I Peter 5:9)

Through the new convert's baptism, the brethren were committing to share their goods, their honor, and their lives with their new sister or brother, and to care for them in divine love.[9] The message for a new convert was that now they were part of a committed spiritual family in the midst of oppression. Water baptism was considered a sign of their initial entrance into the church.[10] Hans Hut wrote that the covenant symbolized by baptism and communion was:

> . . . (a) place whereby the Christian will be assured and certain that he is received as a child of God . . . a socio-religious *covenant between brothers and sisters* who assemble regularly and *find oneness in the midst of 'malevolent rumors'*. . .[11]

From water baptism forward, Anabaptists would continue to walk together through life. They followed the pattern of the New Testament church which, after Pentecost's Spirit and water baptisms, continued to meet together daily in their homes and in the temple for fellowship (Acts 2).

A Church Led by God's Spirit

Just as the Holy Spirit had completely changed the believers' lives in Acts, the early Anabaptists believed He was the foundation of their own transformed church. He was the one who gathered the church together and He was its leader. Peter Rideman, a Moravian Anabaptist leader, wrote this about the true church:

> 'Therefore is such a people, community, assembly or Church **gathered and led together by the Holy Spirit**, *which from henceforth ruleth, controlleth, and ordereth everything in her* The children of God . . . become his children *through the unifying Spirit*. Thus, it is evident that the Church is **gathered together by the Holy Spirit**: also that she hath being and is kept in being *by Him,* and that there is no other Church apart from that which the **Holy Spirit buildeth and gathereth**.'[12]

There was no other fellowship than the one the Holy Spirit had established. And though the State Churches ruled with "outward power," early Anabaptist Pilgram Marpeck wrote that the Holy Spirit was the Ruler of the true church:

> When outward power is allowed to rule in the kingdom of Christ *it brings an offense to the Holy Spirit, the true Lord and Ruler* without human assistance. . . . [13]

The State Catholic Church took their authority to rule mainly from the pages of their own history. They led by following tradition: by doing things the way they had always been done, generation after generation. Well established mental strongholds caused its leaders to take the Scriptures and fit them into the Church's historical context, rather than asking for the Spirit's interpretation and guidance.

In a measure, the Reformers did likewise, relying heavily on a *mental interpretation* of God's Word rather than being able to hear the Holy Spirit. Theirs was a scrutiny of the Scriptures which was still "manipulating verses into proper theologies" and led to continued errors of interpretation.[14]

Early Anabaptists also turned to the Scriptures for guidance. Yet, as Peter Hoover writes:

> They went "beyond the sacred page" to focus on the *Person
> the Scriptures were intended to reveal* . . . They saw the
> Scriptures as an *"outer word"* that would lead the genuine
> seeker to the *"inner Word,"* which was Christ.[15]

The *Inner Word* gave understanding of the outer Word, just as *inner baptism* preceded the outer baptism. Our early forefathers had already experienced the effects of the State Church's interpretation of Scriptures through veiled hearts that were void of the Spirit's leading. From experience, they knew the Bible could not be interpreted without the guidance of the Living Word. Hans Denck wrote this in regard to this Living Word:

> I value the Scriptures above all human treasure, but not as
> highly as the Word of God which is alive, strong (Hebrews
> 4:12), eternal, and free. The Word of God is free from the
> elements of the world. *It is God himself. It is Spirit and not
> letter*, written without pen or paper so that it can never be
> erased.[16]

Balthasar Hubmaier wrote as well about the written Scriptures, calling them *dead* without the Spirit:

> The Word of God is water to all those who thirst for
> salvation and is made alive in us *through the Spirit of God,*
> without whose work it is only a *dead letter*.[17]

Reformers Ulrich Zwingli and Martin Luther eventually became angry at the Anabaptists' guidance by their "inner conviction" and by the "inner Word." In their opinions Anabaptists were disregarding the Church's "correct interpretation" of the Scriptures. The Reformers also rejected the Anabaptist practice of the *sitzrecht*, or "sitter's right," as explained by Paul:[18]

> And if a revelation comes to someone who is sitting down,
> the first speaker should stop. For you can all prophesy in
> turn so that everyone may be instructed and encouraged.
> (I Corinthians 14:30-31)

Early Anabaptists believed the Scriptures taught that lay people within the church, as led by God's Spirit, had the right to speak in the assembly. Martin Luther condemned them:

> (The Anabaptists) called this the "sitter's right" and calmly implied that they, when moved by inner conviction, had as great a right to speak and to act as any pastor, any priest, any reformer or bishop or pope. This audacity, this 'Sitzrecht from the pit of hell,' Martin Luther and his friends believed, could be dealt with only by fire, water, and the sword.[19]

Menno Simons wrote that we have been anointed,

> . . . not with the external oil of Aaron . . . but with the oil of the Holy Ghost. . . .[20]

He writes that this baptism of "Spirit and fire" is first, and water baptism follows. To Menno, it is the *Holy Spirit* who has enabled us to find the true knowledge of the Kingdom, and it is "through the Spirit of our God," that we are justified in Jesus.[21] The one who has become a believer has . . .

> . . . become confident, satisfied, and joyful *in the Holy Ghost*. They get a joyful spirit and so are made to belong to their Head and Savior...ingrafted *through the Spirit of God* . . . by faith they are *changed in the inner man*, converted and renewed. . . .[22]

Our forefathers knew no church could walk in truth without the Holy Spirit. They also knew no individual could live a faithful life without God's presence and power, because obedience required not only dying to self within the community of believers, but possibly even physical death through persecution.

We Are Still Asking

In a later chapter we will address some of the heresies about the Holy Spirit and His gifts which were prevalent during the times of our ancestors. These heresies caused great harm to our forefathers, because for decades State Church leaders associated them with *all* Anabaptists, making authorities even more determined to annihilate our ancestors.[23] Because of these and other tremendously negative experiences with the Holy Spirit, many of us have become wary when we hear teaching about His presence in our churches.

At the same time, we also recognize our *need* for God's presence. We all understand the inner "tug of war" that happens when we are forced to make a choice between two paths. It may be something as simple as choosing whether to go to an auction we *really* want to attend, or staying home to finish pressing work. Whatever the choice, we recognize the internal struggle that occurs. That is the same struggle many feel about the Holy Ghost. We are hesitant, but we also *want* fellowship with God's Spirit. We desire the covenant our early ancestors experienced with the Living Word, but we also want to know we will not wander off into excess or heresy. We want to know we will be *safe* if we welcome God's Spirit to come in His fullness and as He desires to come.

Because we recognize our need for His presence in our midst, we have been asking Him to come since the early generations of Anabaptism. In *Our Heritage, Hope and Faith*, a translation of German prayers, hymns and meditations used by today's Amish churches, editor Mary Miller puts it well when she writes:

> Our fondest wish is that others too may be touched (by these translated writings) and that **the same Spirit that was the very life blood of our forefathers** may still find room in our hearts today.[24]

Several old prayers are translated which are still used during services within today's Amish church. This portion is from a prayer for Ascension day:

> . . . do Thou open thy gentle (charitable) hand and pour down on us Thy ascension gifts from on high; **give Thy Holy Spirit, whom Thou has promised** to Thy church . . .[25]

Another prayer translated from *Christenpflicht* calls out for God
to make his home with us through His Spirit's presence:

> Oh, Thou holy Trinity! Come and *make Thy abode with us*;
> fill us here with Thy grace, and there with Thy eternal glory.
> ***Hear our prayer, and give us Thy Holy Spirit*** . . .[26]

The passion of our ancestors was to see the church return
to the model of the apostles' church in Acts.[27] As one more
recent Anabaptist writer put it, they believed this *true church*
was built on . . .

> . . . perpetual *spiritual re-creation* which derives its author-
> ity from the *work of the Spirit* among men thereby united,
> and not from ecclesiastical structure . . . [28]

The New Testament church met together in one heart and
mind and shared the whole of their lives together. The Holy Spirit
filled them again and again, as evidenced not just by Pentecost,
but also in this passage in a later chapter of Acts:

> Now, Lord, consider their threats and enable your servants
> to speak your word with *great boldness*. Stretch out your
> hand to *heal and perform miraculous signs and wonders*
> through the name of your holy servant Jesus." After they
> prayed, the place where they were meeting was shaken. ***And
> they were all filled with the Holy Spirit*** and spoke the
> word of God boldly. All the believers were *one in heart and
> mind*. No one claimed that any of his possessions was
> his own, but they *shared everything* they had. With *great
> power* the apostles continued to testify to the resurrection of
> the Lord Jesus, and *much grace was upon them all*. (Acts
> 4:29-33)

Much grace was upon their church, as the Holy Spirit's presence
was manifested through all these attributes:

> . . . great boldness of witness, healing, miraculous signs,
> wonders, unity, generosity, and great power.

As we consider the vision of our ancestors to emulate the early church, we can be so grateful for their righteous desires to follow God with their whole hearts. This prayer, written as an introductory greeting in our ancestors' first confession of faith, the *Schleitheim Confession Of Faith,* sums up well the grace and presence of God's Spirit in their midst. He and His gifts were sent from the *Father,* through the *Son,* "to all believers":

> May joy, peace, mercy from our Father, through the atonement of the blood of Christ Jesus, *together with the gifts of one Spirit—who is sent by the Father to all believers to give strength and consolation and constance* . . . be with all who love God and all children of light, who are scattered everywhere…wherever they might be gathered in *unity of spirit* in one God and Father of us all; grace and peace of heart be with you all. Amen.[29]

Thank You, Father, for our ancestors, who knew Your Presence within their hearts. Thank You for giving them both an inner and outer baptism. Like them, I want to know more of You.

I confess, I have not always welcomed Your Holy Spirit. I've seen and heard of people within the church misusing His gifts. I've seen and heard of the harm done by their error. Yet, Father, You tell me to ask for Your Spirit.[1] You want to live in me and to have fellowship with me.[2]

Heal my heart wherever I have been afraid of inviting Your Spirit into my life. You're my Comforter and the power I need to live the Christian life. You're my Inner Word, who reveals the meaning of the outer Word. You promised You would come to Your children, and through Christ's blood I am Your child.[3]

Forgive me for not always welcoming You. Forgive me for when I've rejected Your Presence. I choose now to change my mind. Holy Spirit, I invite You, come and fellowship with me. Come and live in me. Father, just as Peter promised, give me the "gift of the Holy Spirit."[4] I ask for myself, and also for my children and their children, according to Your promise.[5] Fill us with Yourself and give us Your inner baptism of fire.

You have promised Your Spirit would lead me into all truth.[6] I ask You, keep me from error and expand my understanding of what it means to walk by Your Spirit.[7] Teach me about the gifts You desire to give to me through Your Spirit.[8] Help me to receive all You have for me because You are my God, and I can trust You completely.

Wherever my family and my church congregation have resisted Your Presence, forgive us. When we've been afraid of You, Holy Spirit, forgive us. Demolish all the strongholds, arguments, and pretensions of our thinking that have prevented our complete trust in You. Come and blow a new breath of Your presence into our congregation and fill us like You filled the New Testament church.

Give us ears to hear "what the Spirit says to the churches."[9] Show us how to handle human error and excess. Teach us to trust You in the learning process, and not to "close down" in fear when things aren't perfect or when people make mistakes. Build in us a holy rest as we grow together.

Where disagreements about Your Presence and the gifts of Your Spirit have divided Your church, please forgive us. In Your mercy, restore unity. Have Your way, Father, and change our hearts.

Thank You that when I ask, You promise to answer my prayers.[10] Thank You for all that has been provided through the blood of Jesus. Cover me now in Your blood, according to Your promise.[11]

I ask all these things in the Name of Your Son, Jesus. Amen.

---

[1] Luke 11:9-13; [2] John 14:16-21; [3] Romans 8:14-17; [4] Acts 2:38; [5] Acts 2:39; [6] John 16:13; [7] Romans 8; [8] I Corinthians 12 and Ephesians 4; [9] Letters in Revelations 2 and 3; [10] Jeremiah 33:3; [11] Hebrews 9:12-14.

Here are some additional Scriptures for study concerning the Holy Spirit:

Mark 1:8; Luke 4:1; Luke 10:21; Luke 11:13; Luke 12:10; Luke 12:12; John 14:26; John 20:22; Acts 1:5-8: Acts 2:38; Acts 4:31; Acts 5:32; Acts 6:5; Acts 8:15-16; Acts 9:31; Acts 10:44-48; Acts 15:28; Acts 13:52; Acts 19:1-6; Romans 5:5; Romans 8; Romans 14:17; Romans 15:13; I Corinthians 6:19; II Corinthians 13:14; Galatians 5:18; Ephesians 1:13; Ephesians 4:30; I Thessalonians 1:5-6; Titus 3:5-7; Hebrews 2:3-4; Hebrews 10:15; II Peter 1:21; Jude 1:20.

~ 8 ~

BROTHERLY LOVE
AND COMMUNITY

When heavy and prolonged rains settled over the Mississippi and Missouri River basins of America in 1993, area dams were opened wide out of fear that they might break.[1] As a result, hundreds of protective levees failed along the banks of more than one hundred and fifty major rivers. Flooding was massive. Tens of thousands of people from the region were evacuated and as many homes destroyed. Fifteen million acres of farmland were affected. In its wake the floodwater left behind an estimated fifteen billion dollars' worth of destruction.

Immediately, Anabaptists poured into the area to begin cleaning up and rebuilding property and lives. Over a period of almost two years following the flooding, six thousand Anabaptist volunteers gave a total of twenty-three thousand workdays towards the project.

Volunteers who participate in this type of disaster recovery come from every "tribe" of Anabaptism. Many are Amish or Mennonite, both new order and old order, or Brethren. Some are women, some men, some white or Hispanic, or other ethnic groups. Some are Hutterites and others no longer use an Anabaptist name for their congregations. But all who come, "eat at the same table, are constrained by the same God of love, and throb with the same Spirit."[2]

This particular gathering of Anabaptists around the table of others' needs was organized by Mennonite Disaster Service, a

non-profit organization begun in 1951.[3] Today, MDS operates
in America and Canada, aiding with financial resources and man-
power in response to every disaster imaginable. From hurricanes
to civil disorder, ice storm damage to tornadoes, arson fires, winter freeze crop damage or forest fire destruction, Anabaptists
respond when there is a need.

Its international counterpart, Mennonite Central Committee, aids in all these and much more.[4] In addition to disaster relief, MCC [5] provides millions of dollars worldwide in rice, flour,
meat, and other foods, as well as supplying material resources
like medical supplies, quilts, blankets, and school and health kits.
Support through their Global Family Program also sponsors the
education of almost four thousand children and young adults in
thirty-eight countries. MCC is deeply involved in the African
HIV/AIDS crisis and in helping innumerable children and adults
affected by civil war, famine or other natural or manmade
destruction all over the world, including the recent tsunami which
devastated countries on three continents. More than seven
hundred international MCC contacts coordinate humanitarian aid
in fifty-five countries, with an annual budget exceeding thirty-
five million American dollars.[6]

I have described these particular organizations because I
happen to be most familiar with their work. But there is also
much relief work done under the auspices of other Anabaptist
denominations, like Brethren groups and the Amish churches,
and others. For example, annual relief sales from various groups
raise hundreds of thousands of dollars towards helping the poor.
Small groups of believers within these denominations meet
regularly to create comforters or assemble relief kits to send all
over the world. The gift of helping others is found wherever
Anabaptists have gathered in community.

Helpers From the Start

From our beginnings, Anabaptists have been a people
whose lifestyle automatically included helping the needy. Im-

mediate persecution quickly wrote into our ancestors' hearts the biblical mandate of caring for our neighbor. As financial providers of families fled to avoid arrest, were incarcerated, or left home to preach the gospel, Anabaptist communities lovingly assumed responsibility for those who were left behind. Their families were cared for as,

> . . . their wives and little ones would be parcelled out with other members of the fellowship.[7]

The concept of caring for one another was part of their perception of the *true church*. As new believers were brought into the fellowship of the brethren, they were fed spiritually from the Scriptures and also helped with any physical needs. The goal was to "make *disciples* of all nations"—meaning those who applied their faith—rather than merely *converts* (Matthew 28:19). To them, the true church was,

> . . . a voluntary community of committed Christians bound together by God's Spirit, who lived in peace and love and shared one another's burdens.[8]

Menno Simons pointed out that though the Anabaptists of his day had an unusually high number of needy ones, they were all provided for by the community:

> . . . not one of the devout who have joined themselves to us, nor any of their orphaned children, have been left to beg their way. . . . This mercy, this love, this community of goods we do teach . . . the Scriptures say plainly enough: 'whosoever hath this world's goods and seeth his brother in need and shutteth up his compassion for him, how dwelleth the love of God in him?'[9]

True Christian love held onto temporal possessions loosely, with a ready heart to share as God directed. Believers were to give as He had given, caring not only for their own needs but also for the needs of others beyond their own walls and gates.

Concern for the less fortunate was considered love in action. It was Balthasar Hubmaier who testified:

> . . . a man must at all times be concerned for his fellow man, in order that the hungry may be fed, the thirsty given to drink, the naked clothed. For we are verily not lords over our own possession, only administrators and dispensers.[10]

This strong sense of reaching out to the poor was obvious to all, even to our enemies. Anabaptists were praised for their "piety" and "consecration" of lifestyle by early Catholics and Reformers alike. One Reformed Dutch author wrote in 1698:

> While we should be on our guard to shun the errors of these people, we may nevertheless learn from them much that is good, namely humility, contentment, moderation, and espe-cially *mercy toward the needy . . . this virtue is particularly characteristic of these people.*[11]

One of the greatest offenses to early Anabaptists was the apparently large discrepancy between the lavish lifestyles of clergy members within the State Churches, and the poor and needy who were forced to beg for food on the streets. One Anabaptist pioneer compared the wealthy church-goer and the needy in God's eyes:

> The man who doesn't need (money), be he clergy or lay person, and practices usury . . . or lays up more goods than he needs in order the more royally to take care of his fat belly, such a man, when compared with a man . . . who steals because of poverty, in an effort to find a way out for himself and his little ones, such a man is no better in God's sight than the man who steals out of poverty.[12]

For most, living in community did not mean living *com-munally*: only the Hutterites of Moravia actually practiced the sharing of all goods and property in common. During the years they flourished, they were praised even by their critics as being from God:

Many were convinced . . . that it (the community) must have
been established by God. It would otherwise have been impossible for so many to live together in such unity, whereas
among others, where only two, three, or four live together,
they are daily in each other's hair and dissatisfied until they
finally leave one another.[13]

Community Today

The sense of community caring which thrived among the
early Anabaptists has been mostly lost in today's Western societies, impacting even the present-day church. Many homes have
been split by divorce, and family schedules have become so filled
with outside activities that members rarely see each other. And
though at one time friends and family members lived close to
each other, today's increased mobility has spread them all over
the globe. A fierce independence has crippled our *inter-depen-
dence*.

But look around at town and countryside in the Amish
areas of America, and you will see extensions added to houses
as families expand to care for elderly parents. And each night
after the chores are completed in these agrarian regions, heads
still bow around a common evening meal to give thanks. Married family members still settle nearby and friends gather for
house church meetings on Sundays. This sense of inter-related-
ness which is lacking elsewhere in society and in much of the
church-at-large, has been kept intact in many Anabaptist groups.

As the world becomes a "global community," we have
expanded our borders to care for national and international
"neighbors," regardless of race, faith or standing in society. Our
gifts of giving, service and mercy have extended to help others
as we obey Jesus' command to love our neighbor as we love ourselves (Luke 10:27). Like the despised Samaritan who carried the
beaten stranger to a nearby inn and paid for his care, Anabaptists
have demonstrated love through our actions and our words.

In recent years the tireless rebuilding efforts of
Anabaptists in one flood-destroyed community had such an

impact on the townspeople, that some were drawn back to attending church and others rediscovered the "abundant life." Residents said that by seeing "Christian love in action" they came to understand the reality of Jesus' words, "If you have done it unto one of the least of these, you have done it unto me" (Matthew 25:45).[14]

We have much to offer as we recognize these gifts which have been laid in us by God's will:

> We have different gifts, according to the grace given us. If a man's gift is prophesying, let him use it in proportion to his faith. *If it is serving, let him serve;* if it is teaching, let him teach; if it is encouraging, let him encourage; if it is *contributing to the needs of others, let him give generously*; if it is leadership, let him govern diligently; *if it is showing mercy, let him do it cheerfully*. (Romans 12:6-8)

Our gifts are needed both in the world and in the greater body of Christ. In the body, the gifts of the Anabaptists can be used to foster a heart of service in other fellowships and denominations. Just as we can learn from their strengths, we can offer the church our abilities in training, educating, and developing the gifts of service, mercy, and giving. In the world as we share our gifts, the gospel message is confirmed through our feet and hands. In very practical ways, we represent Christ every time we give flour for food, pencils for education, or wood for housing.

As the Scriptures indicate, each person is given spiritual gifts (I Corinthians 12:7). Not every individual from Anabaptist heritage will necessarily be strong in the particular gifts of service, mercy, or giving. Some will excel more in other gifts, as apostles, prophets, teachers, evangelists, and so on (Ephesians 4:12-13). Yet, overall the particular gifts of helping others have been deposited into the fabric of our heritage, and we can offer them to others, just as Christ offered Himself to us as a gift.

At the end of the age, those who have been compelled by God's love to lay their lives down for others, will be welcomed by the King Himself. He will then hand to them the Father's Kingdom as their inheritance:

> Then the King will say to those on his right, 'Come, you who are *blessed by my Father; take your inheritance, the kingdom* . . . For I was hungry and *you gave me something to eat*, I was thirsty and *you gave me something to drink*, I was a stranger and *you invited me in*, I needed clothes and *you clothed me*, I was sick and *you looked after me*, I was in prison and *you came to visit me.*'. . . I tell you the truth, **whatever you did for one of the least of these brothers of mine, you did for me.'** (Matthew 25:24-40)

Father in heaven, thank You that my ancestors built upon a good foundation of active love for others. Thank You for their examples of reaching out to meet the needs of the poor and oppressed.

Please give to me an increasing measure of these gifts which were so much a part of my heritage. Holy Spirit, place in me Your compassion for the needy and the poor. Help me to be generous with the resources You've given to me, and to trust You to replenish and even increase what I give away in obedience to Your leading.

And Father, thank You for the revelation about community life that my forefathers possessed. Please pour into me an understanding of what it means to live in community with other believers. Give me this wonderful gift of my heritage.

Forgive me for times when I have separated myself from others in the body of Christ, preferring my independence more than relationship. I repent. Teach me how to be interdependent rather than independent. Take all my unhealthy independence into Your death on the cross, and bring to life in me the kind of loving community You lived with Your disciples. Show me how to be real with others and how to love my neighbor and to love myself, as You have commanded.[1]

Give me Your heart for those who are hungry, thirsty, strangers, naked, sick and in prison. Show me who these are in my life and where I am to apply the gifts You have given to me. I'm willing to be Your hands and Your feet, if You fill me with Yourself so that I can love truthfully and honestly.

Thank You for giving all for me. I give myself to You. Lead me in paths of righteousness, for Your Name's sake.[2] *Thank You, Jesus. You are my all in all, the Shepherd of my soul, my Brother.*[3]

I ask these things in Your loving Name, Amen.

---

[1] Matthew 22:39; [2] Psalm 23:3; [3] I Corinthians 15:28 and Psalms 23:1 and John 20:17 and Romans 8:29

WE HAVE A TALENT

We are a talented people. In the Anabaptist-rooted area where I live, tourists come just to be in the midst of our verdant farms with lush, green fields. They admire our beautiful flower beds and well manicured lawns and gardens and they buy our colorful quilts and our handmade furniture and crafts. They drink our milk, eat our "whoopie pies" and "shoo-fly" pies, and feast at our in-home cookeries or smorgasbords.

We have been given an uncanny ability to make a living by our own hands. If there is a market for log homes, we begin a log home company. If there is need of a health food store, we provide one. If welding is in demand, we start a welding business. We sell our wares and our garden produce at roadside stands, farm markets, and private businesses. We are true entrepreneurs.

An Historic Reputation

Since ancient times we have been known for these gifts. It was the natural farming skills of our Swiss forefathers which gave them a place to settle when they were fleeing persecution. Because of the Thirty Years War, the ruling elector and regional lords of the Palatinate area north of Switzerland desperately needed farmers to restore their devastated towns and countryside. As Swiss Anabaptists moved into the area, they were allowed to stay there in spite of their "heretical" faith, because they had a good reputation as farmers who could take harsh land and make it profitable.[1]

During the same era, the Protestant Ribeaupierre family of Alsace, France, invited Bernese Anabaptists to farm the Vosges Mountain regions which had also been impoverished by the war. Those who responded soon distinguished themselves and were chosen to farm for the nobility.[2]

Wherever they settled, Anabaptists were able to carve out a niche of provision. When the first Mennists (Mennonites) arrived in North America in the early 1700s, they quickly developed a reputation as excellent farmers who were willing to tackle the hard work of clearing virgin forests filled with sizeable trees. By the late nineteenth centuries, they were regarded as prosperous homesteaders even west of the Mississippi in Kansas, and to the north in communities of Manitoba, Canada.[3] As more arrived in North America in ensuing years, they expanded into other trades like fur trading, millwork, and other occupations.

Artists, Artisans And Scholars

Working the land was only one of many God-given abilities for which our forefathers were noted. The Hutterite Communities of Moravia were proficient as farmers, yet were also skilled in making all sorts of fine crafts and goods. They were known far and wide for their pottery and ceramics and for handmade carriages, cutlery, furniture, and even clocks. They were also prolific writers and were sought out because of their excellence as gifted physicians, surgeons, and teachers.[4]

Many of our earliest ancestors were scholars and theologians. Hans Denck was a teacher, writer, and translator of the Scriptures. Conrad Grebel excelled in the study of Latin literature, liturgical music, and logic. Balthasar Hubmaier received a doctorate in Theology and was a gifted orator. Michael Sattler was a writer, as was Menno Simons.[5] Others were song writers, poets, and artists. *Martyrs Mirror*, a book of testimonies of the heroic faith of our ancestors, demonstrates their artistic giftings with pictorial engravings that "tell a thousand words."

We All Have a Talent

God has given us our talents and He has also given us the ability to provide a living for ourselves and our families. It is He who has placed in our lives the gifts of artisan or writer or singer or worker of the soil. He proclaims these truths in the Bible:

> You may say to yourself, "My power and the strength of my hands have produced this wealth for me." But remember the Lord your God, for it is he who *gives you the ability to produce wealth*, and so confirms his covenant . . . (Deuteronomy 8:17-18)

> And he has *given (them)* . . . *the ability* to teach others. He has *filled them with skill* to do all kinds of work as craftsmen, designers, embroiderers in blue, purple, and scarlet yarn and fine linen, and weavers—all of them *master craftsmen* and *designers*. (Exodus 35:35)

Just as our Father in heaven is the *Creator*, so He has made His children—"His offspring"—in His image, to be *creators*. (Acts 17:28-29).

> So God *created man in his own image*, in the image of God he created him; male and female he created them. (Genesis 1:27)

We have a healthy and natural desire built into us to take the raw materials He has provided on earth and to do something with them. Each and everyone of us has a talent, both spiritual talents of the Kingdom and natural talents which are human. For example, in my own family my husband is a musician and an artist. My mother and sister create crafts, and another sister is an artist. My father and brother have excelled in working with their hands in carpentry and mechanical skills.

In the parable of the talents, Jesus tells us to *use* our talents and not to waste them because of fear (Matthew 25). Proverbs challenges parents to help a child uncover these spiritual and human talents and to foster them, being diligent to understand and draw out the specific gifts which each child possesses:

Train up a child *in the way he should go*: and when he is
old, he will not depart from it. (Proverbs 22:6 *KJV*)

Though we have often associated this verse with raising
children in the Christian faith, there is a deeper meaning as we
realize God has created every child uniquely. Each child has a
way he or she should go. It may be different than the parents'
way or the parents' occupations, because it is a God-given way
designed to fit the personality of that particular child.[6] And no
matter where the way leads, it will always include an element of
some creative gift.

Creating Beauty

There are many reasons we have been gifted with
creativity. One reason is simply that we create by reason of
improving the function and form of our lives. Mechanics, weld-
ers, and builders create practically in this way. Another reason is
to display beauty. The Scriptures proclaim that *beauty* is part of
God's character and part of His dwelling place. Beauty is also
part of us, who have been made in God's image:

One thing have I desired of the Lord, that will I seek
after; that I may dwell in the house of the Lord all the
days of my life, to behold the *beauty of the Lord*, and to
enquire in his temple. (Psalm 27:4 *KJV*)

Out of Zion, the *perfection of beauty*, God hath shined.
(Psalm 50:2 *KJV*)

Honor and majesty are before him: *strength and beauty*
are in his sanctuary. (Psalm 96:6 *KJV*)

The Lord their God will save them on that day as the flock
of his people. They will sparkle in his land like jewels in
a crown. *How attractive and beautiful they will be!*...
(Zechariah 9:16,17)

He has made *everything beautiful* in its time. He has also
set eternity in the hearts of men . . . (Ecclesiastes 3:11)

Why do we enjoy planting, arranging and displaying flowers of all types and colors? Because we are made like our heavenly Father, to beautify our dwelling places. Why do we make quilts with intricate designs, patterns, and hues? Because we are made in our Father's image, to enjoy beauty. Why do we add scrolling or inlay to our furniture? Because we want the finished product to be pleasing to our eyes and beautiful to behold.

Beauty refreshes us, strengthens us, and exalts God who is the author of everything good (James 1:17). When God finished each aspect of His creation of earth, He saw that "it was good," and enjoyed the creativity of His own hands! (Genesis 1). Like God, we are able to enjoy the creations of our own hands and call them good.

Gifts That Have Been Preserved

Take a survey of the world today and you will quickly understand that creative ability is innate in all humankind. How then, can we define a special gift or call that has been preserved just for Anabaptists? Part of the answer lies in the fact that everyone has special giftings, but not every people group retains or develops those giftings. But in generation after generation, Anabaptists have developed many of our skills and passed them along to our children. And, because of the unique interdependence of our community life, we have been able to retain what has been lost by many other people groups as they have been dispersed throughout society.

Anabaptists have even taken our gift of "producing wealth" by our creative hands and shown others less fortunate how they can do the same. Today, through an organization called *Ten Thousand Villages*,[7] Anabaptists, along with other contributing church denominations, help impoverished artisans make a living by purchasing their crafts, jewelry, and works of art at fair trade prices. These goods are then resold in stores located in the United States and Canada. As its name indicates, Ten

Thousand Villages enables many thousands of artisans in more than thirty-five different countries to provide for their families by earning a viable income. Over the last year alone, purchases of artisans' crafts totaled more than six million dollars in U.S. currency.[8] From Sri Lanka to India, from Mexico to Nepal or the Philippines and Uganda: all over the world, Anabaptists are applying their creative know-how to help better the lives of the poor.

Another talent of our heritage which we have shared through missions outreach is our knack for farming well. Through Mennonite Central Committee (MCC) we have developed programs to help farmers in third world countries increase crop yields through soil conservation, better irrigation techniques, and other improvements.[9] We offer education, training, and support, passing on what we have learned so they can raise their incomes and their quality of life.

Programs like the Maasai Food Security Program (MFSP) have improved basic food and water supplies in drought-stricken areas. MFSP increased the production of food and water for approximately 26,000 Maasai near Nairobi, Kenya, through better farming techniques and environmental solutions.[10] In Cambodia, farmers were instructed on irrigation, reforestation, small animal husbandry, and other farm-related skills.[11] In resource-deficient Haiti, agricultural education is offered, as well as financial support for initiatives like community-based tree nurseries.[12]

These are just a few of many projects which have taken the natural gifts of our heritage and applied them to improving the lives of people in third world countries. They are a small sampling of all that God is doing through Anabaptists' talents. We can be thankful for our ancestral giftings because we have learned much as father and mother pass on their own experience and training to their children, their grandchildren, and forward through the generations.

I have a sense as I write these words that God is incredibly pleased with our many outreaches to the needy. We are practicing "true religion" by providing for the "orphans and widows" of the world (James 1:27). Through sharing both the spiritual and natural abilities God has placed in us, we have demonstrated His love and His heart in the earth and opened doors to share the gospel of Jesus with the poor.

Every person's gifts are valuable and each one has a place where they can be used to bless other people. Gifts were meant to be shared. May God reveal the fullness of our own natural creative abilities, and fan into flame in us the spiritual gifts we carry for others!

Thank You, my Creator, for creating me.[1] You have said that I am "wonderfully made."[2] Thank You for placing in me both spiritual gifts and creative gifts.[3] And thank You for the natural abilities of my heritage.

Father, You know me completely.[4] You know I have not always felt very gifted or creative, but You have said otherwise. You have told me I am gifted. Forgive me for the times when I have hidden or denied my gifts. Help me to accept them and not to bury my talents.[5] If I have gifts that I have not yet identified, give me eyes to see them. Show me by Your presence within me what they look like, and how to use them. Help me to practice, strengthen and develop my gifts so they can be used with excellence.[6] And give me grace to be patient and to persevere while I am in the learning process.

I offer all my abilities to You. Like Jesus, help me to see what You are doing, Father, and to do the things which will bring You blessing.[7] Give me boldness and courage to be the person You have created me to be.[8] Thank You that You delight in who I am.[9] Help me to know Your delight deep within my being, that I may walk as one who knows I am pleasing to You. Show me the "way I should go" and finish the work You have started in my life.[10]

Father, awaken within me the gifts of my family and my heritage, both spiritually and creatively. Wherever those gifts have been laid aside, restore them according to Your promise, for You are able.[11] *I agree with You that, "I am like an olive tree flourishing in the house of God; I trust in God's unfailing love for ever and ever. I will praise You forever for what You have done; in Your name I will hope, for Your name is good. I will praise You in the presence of Your saints."*[12]

In Jesus' Name, Amen.

---

[1] Psalm 139:13; [2] Psalm 139:14; [3] I Corinthians 12:11 and Ephesians 2:10; [4] Psalm 139:1; [5] Matthew 25:24-25; [6] Colossians 3:23-24; [7] John 8:28; [8] Psalm 34:4 and Joshua 1:9; [9] Isaiah 62:4; [10] Proverbs 22:6; [11] Joel 2:25-27 and Ephesians 3:20; [12] Psalm 52:8.9.

~ Interlude ~

Before we pick up the keys and unlock part two of this book, we'll unearth a precious treasure which has been hidden for some time from the hearts of many Anabaptists. That treasure is . . .

OUR WORTH TO GOD

God sits enthroned above the earth and makes the heavens
His tent. The people of the earth are tiny; called "grasshop-
pers" in His eyes. (Isaiah 40:22)

I used to wonder how such a great and magnificent God
could possibly have time for one little "grasshopper" like me.
I couldn't fathom that He would be interested in hearing my
thoughts, because there are so many other things in the universe
which demand His attention and time. Eventually, God showed
me that my stumbling block was that I was thinking too small.

God is BIG. He has ". . . measured the waters in the
hollow of His hand . . . and calculated the dust of the earth in a
measure . . ." (Isaiah 40:12 *NKJV*). That means all of the water
in the depths of the oceans, all of the great rivers, all of the vast
seas and all of the great lakes, all of the streams and ponds, and
all of the underground water sources of the entire earth can be
held in the cupped palm of God's hand. It also means He knows
how much "earth" there is on earth. He knows the exact amount
of rock and ground and has calculated the size of the continents
in a measure.

He has named every single star, not just the millions in
our own galaxy, but in all the galaxies (Psalm 147:4). Considering that scientists have calculated that each galaxy contains
billions of stars and that there are millions of galaxies, naming
each one is a pretty incredible feat! God's understanding has *no
limit*. No one can fathom His greatness (Psalm 147:5; Psalm
145:3). Absolutely nothing is too hard for God (Jeremiah 32:17).

One day in prayer, I was pondering the fact that there are probably at the very least, a few thousand Christians on earth who are all praying to God at the same time. I couldn't understand how Jesus could really pay full attention to each one while *also* hearing all the prayers of the others. In addition, with thousands of people talking to Him at any given moment of the day, He also has to attend to the affairs of the whole earth, causing everything to work out according to His will (Ephesians 1:11).

The answer was in His size. As I prayed, God showed me that my thinking about Him was much too limited. It is because God is so vast and so great that He has the capacity to give full and complete focus to all things simultaneously. God can be ***one hundred percent intimate*** with each and every person who has ever been born—those who are already in heaven and those who live on earth—all at the *same time*, while He is *also* perfectly orchestrating everything on earth and in eternity. He has an infinite capacity to always pay full attention to every detail of His creation. He is truly a GREAT God, beyond any greatness our human minds can conceive. When the Scripture says that His understanding has no limit, it means exactly that: His understanding has *no limit*!

This great God is also our intimate heavenly Father. He actually created so many humans because it gave Him more children to whom He could express His love, since He has an infinite capacity to love (Romans 8:29; I John 3:1; Jeremiah 31:3). And He created each person uniquely, in order to give His love to meet our specific needs. God's vastness, combined with His love means that He can love each and every person with the perfect, individual attention they need. Jesus tells us God knows how many hairs are on the head of each and every human being (Luke 12:7). He knows us to the minute detail of cells and corpuscles within our bodies (Psalm 139). He knows our all innermost thoughts and desires (I Chronicles 28:9). This is our amazing, holy and very approachable Father-God.

Desiring Worth

As human beings, we all want to know we matter to someone. We want to feel like we belong and that we have an important place in our family and with our friends. When we marry, we hope we will find a man or woman who loves us and likes us for who we are. As Christians, we also want to know that we are important to others in our churches.

But more than all our human desires for acceptance and worth, there is only one relationship where deep in our inner being, we want to *know* we matter. That is in our relationship with our heavenly Father. As we stand in His presence, we want to know that not only are we His child, but that we are precious and valuable to Him. We all want to be the favorite son or daughter of the Lord. We all want to see His look of adoration. We want to know that if we had not been born, God would have felt like something very important had been left out of the plan of earth. We want to know that He considers us—His 10 millionth spiritual child to be born—as *necessary* for His fulfillment. We want to grasp that God Almighty created us because He did not want to exist without our existence. We want to know that having us as His child makes Him feel rich beyond measure. We want to *know* His perfect love.

Remembering the vastness of God's ability to love each one of us with complete intimacy, we can allow ourselves to believe that every one of these hopeful desires is absolutely true. That is, if our hearts will believe. Unfortunately, most of us have never been able to embrace the reality of this sort of deep love from God because of our doubts and fears.

Inclined Towards Unworthiness

Knowing we stumble and err, our hearts are much more inclined to believe we're unlovable and offensive. We think we're just too sinful for God. Part of our belief is associated with an erroneous teaching throughout the larger body of Christ, having to do with the sin of Adam and Eve. Many have been taught that because of "original sin", all humans are evil, or bad —our bodies are bad, our souls are evil—we are bad down to the very core of our beings.

The truth is, every single human being *has* been corrupted through the fall of man which occurred in the garden of Eden. We have all sinned and fall short of God's glory (Romans 3:23). But, there is a profound difference between being corrupted and being "bad" or "evil" to the core. Let me explain, using a modern day parable.

I am writing this book by typing my thoughts into a computer. In this age of technology, if you haven't used a computer, you have at least heard of their use in business offices for keeping records and creating letters and documents. So far, I have spent thousands of hours and much energy in writing. I've also shared much of my own heart through the words on its pages. As a result, the chapters stored on the computer are very valuable to me because of all that I have invested in their creation.

If suddenly a "virus" from the internet corrupted my files and I was no longer able to retrieve them for use, I would be heartbroken! I would not instantly despise the chapters I have written because they became defiled. I would not hate those files or be angry with those files or disgusted with those files. I would not see those files as worthless or throw them away because I decided the things I had written were suddenly undesirable. Rather, the computer files would continue to be very valuable to me even though they had become corrupted. Most likely, I wouldn't sleep until I had called in every expert who knew any-thing about computers, in order to find some way to restore the files. I would be desperate to recover the many months of hard work and heartfelt creativity which were lost through the corruption caused by the computer virus.

Transferring this analogy to our relationship with God, the book files represent our lives and the writer of the book is God. The computer "virus" represents our sin. God has created us *in His image* and we are very valuable and of much worth to Him (Genesis 1:26). The Father loves us as much as He loves Jesus (John 17:23). Though the virus of sin has corrupted us, we are still incredibly valuable to Him. He does not see our sin and despise us or hate us or become angry or disgusted with us. We do not become "bad" or worthless in His eyes.

Rather, He was so concerned, so pained over the effects of our corruption, that He immediately set about to restore our "files" and save His precious creations who were lost. Our worth is so great in His eyes, He sent *Himself* to take on our corruption so that we would no longer be corrupted, but completely restored to the purity of pre-corruption and to open fellowship with Him. He *values* all human beings immensely, even corrupted ones!

> But God *demonstrates His own love toward us,* in that *while we were still sinners*, Christ died for us. (Romans 5:8)

We are His "offspring" and we are "fearfully and won-derfully made" (Genesis 1:26; Acts 17:29; Psalm 139:14). One saying that circulated a few years ago said it like this: "God doesn't make junk." He gave us an eternal spirit and soul made like Him. He made us creative as He is creative. Our bodies have been lovingly fashioned by God and He delights in how He has formed each and every one of us. He *likes* His children, His creations!

Beloved Prodigals

Jesus tells us about the favor of our God in Luke, chapter fifteen, using the story of the prodigal son. There are three characters in His parable: the prodigal, the father, and the older brother. For now, we will only discuss the relationship of the prodigal with his father. We all know the story and in our minds we have probably associated it with a person coming to salvation for the first time. But its can also be applied to us, since we have all struggled with feeling like an unworthy prodigal as we approach our Father.

The story begins as the prodigal demands his inheritance from the father and leaves home, spending every penny on riotous living. When a famine hits, his life turns sour and he is forced to feed pigs (an animal despised by the Jews). He finally comes to his senses and decides to return to his father's household, hoping at best, to be allowed to serve there as a hired hand for the rest of his life:

> And he arose and came to his father. But when he was still a *great way off*, **his father saw him** and **had compassion**, and **ran** and **fell on his neck and kissed him**. And the son said to him, 'Father, I have sinned against heaven and in your sight, and am **no longer worthy to be called your son.**' But the father said to his servants, 'Bring out the *best robe* and put it on him, and put a *ring on his hand* and *sandals on his feet*. And *bring the fatted calf* here and kill it, and *let us* eat and *be merry;* for this my son was dead and is alive again; he was lost and is found.' And they began to be merry. (Luke 15: 20-24)

The son (it could have just as easily been a daughter) felt that in his sinfulness, he was *no longer worthy* to be a son. Many of us have felt the same way: unworthy to be a son or daughter of God the Father. We find salvation, but we continue to feel condemned by our sin, as though it has permanently stained us and it cannot be removed by the blood of Jesus. Our hearts sincerely desire to follow God, but since we continue to stumble and sin *after* we have received salvation, we assume we are too defective to be a fully accepted child of God.

But, what is the heart of the prodigal's father? He has been watching and waiting eagerly for his son's return. When he saw him, he was *filled with compassion* and ran, *falling on his neck and kissing him*. What a loving father! Our heavenly Father responds to us in the same way. Each day He watches for us to come to Him. He has compassion for us when He sees us and He runs to meet us as we approach Him. He falls to the ground and lifts up our broken heart, hugging us and kissing us with a kiss of fatherly love.

In the beginning of my faith as a Christian, my first reactions to what I read in the Bible were reactions of the religious heart. I felt terribly unworthy before the God of the universe. Most of the words in my Bible seemed to condemn me and if there were any encouraging words written in its pages, I found it difficult to believe they could possibly be for me. I would cry out to God, asking for peace but feeling mostly unrest.

Yet, as time progressed and I began to recognize and repent of the judgments and the heart vows I had made and of the bitterness of my own sins of unforgiveness, I began to experience His love, *even while I was being corrected* by His Spirit. Each time I turned to Him with yet another area of judgment or sin, I felt His affirming, loving forgiveness, and his tender comfort. He knew I was made of dust, and He felt pity and compassion for me, His child:

> He has **not dealt with us according to our sins,** Nor *punished us according to our iniquities. For as the heavens are high above the earth,* **so great is His mercy** toward those who fear Him; As far as the east is from the west, *so far has He removed our transgressions* from us. **As a father pities his children, so the Lord pities** those who fear Him. For *He* **knows** *our frame;* **He remembers** *that we are dust.* (Psalm 103:10-14)

Just as the father of the prodigal embraced and received his errant son, God is thrilled to receive us as we come to Him. He has called us worthy sons and daughters. He completely forgives our sin and embraces us with a hearty hug. We bring Him much joy, even though we will continue to need to come to Him in repentance (during times of refining, we will come more often!).

But, there's more. The prodigal's father, after a warm and full embrace, jumps up and yells excitedly to his servants, "Bring out the best robe . . . and put a ring on his hand and sandals on his feet!" God does the same with us. Though we have squandered God's gifts: though we have avoided God and run away from Him: though we have recognized our sinfulness and we fall at His feet and proclaim we are not worthy, our Father cries out, "Give my child the best robe of the house! Give Him the robe of righteousness! (Isaiah 61:10) And put a ring on his finger! Give him a ring of authority as my child (Galatians 3:26)! And put sandals on his feet, that he may arise and walk the land I am giving Him (Genesis 13:17; Jeremiah 3:19)!"

As we have run to Him in repentance, God gives us much through our restoration at the cross. He gives us not just *a* robe, but the *best* robe in His house. That robe of righteousness is a robe of kingly authority and stately bearing as His heir. He restores to us our perfect standing in the Father's Kingdom, not as a servant or hired hand of the property, but as a son or daughter of His estate and of His Kingdom.

He gives us a ring, like the signet ring which a King bestows to His heirs, to carry His seal of approval and His seal of authority (Matthew 10:40; Luke 10:16). He gives us sandals for our feet, the "good news of the Gospel of peace" (Ephesians 6:15). We walk in His peace and we walk with confidence as the sons and daughters of the Owner of all things. We walk as His ambassadors (II Corinthians 5:20).

Then, the celebration begins! The prodigal son receives his gifts and is taken into the father's house for a great feast. Our Heavenly Father does the same for us. He celebrates our life in Him, rejoicing over us with singing. He takes *great delight* in us, quieting our protests of unworthiness with His love (Zephaniah 3:17; Isaiah 62:5). At the end of this present age, one of the great joys in heaven both for us and for God will be a celebration feast, held for all those who are in the family of God (Luke 13:29).

Receiving our Place as Heirs

In telling the parable of the prodigal and his family, Jesus was illustrating the heart of God towards a sinful but repentant mankind. To some of our own hearts though, the story might have progressed a little differently if we had written it from our perspectives of feeling unworthy. What if the prodigal son had not been able to receive his father's gifts and his father's full restoration into the estate? What if he had said, after his father had given orders to bring out the robe and sandals and ring, "No, Father! I will not accept these gifts and I will not accept a celebration! And especially, I can never accept that I am your son. I will only accept a place as a servant, because that is all I deserve." The father would have been greatly grieved at his son's reaction. He would have protested and explained his heart's intent to his son again and again and again: that he *had* to celebrate because he was receiving him alive again as though returning from the dead. If the son continued to firmly deny his sonship the father, though saddened and grieved, would have been unable to do anything other than allow him to work as a servant, living with his errant thinking in the servant's quarters.

So it is with many of God's children. We have felt too unworthy to believe or receive the truth about ourselves and our standing in His Kingdom. We have approached our heavenly Father timidly with a slave mentality, our hearts denying all that He has given us, and unwilling to ever consider the spiritual wealth or position of our favor in His sight.

But, the Bible promises that we are His *completely restored* children:

> But when the time had fully come, God sent his Son, born of a woman, born under law, to redeem those under law, that we might receive the *full rights of sons*. Because you are *sons*, God sent the *Spirit of his Son* into our hearts, the Spirit who calls out, "Abba, Father." So you are *no longer a slave, but a son*; and since you are a son, *God has made you also an heir*. (Galatians 4:4-7)

God has given us the *full rights of sons*. He gives us Himself through His Spirit and declares, ". . . you are no longer a *slave, but you are my son* (my *daughter*). He finishes by promising that since we are full-fledged sons, we are also heirs. We are heirs of the wealthiest and most overwhelmingly generous eternal Father, and we will inherit His Kingdom.

Let's look at just a few of God's promises concerning our position as His inheritors. During the eternal "Kingdom age" which will follow the present age, it is God's *saints* who will receive His Kingdom. That's us! We are His sanctified saints (Colossians 1:12). The Father's plan is to hand the Kingdom over to the possession of the saints, with their Bridegroom, Jesus:

> But the *saints of the Most High shall receive the king-dom, and* **possess the kingdom** forever, even forever and ever.

> . . . until the Ancient of Days came, and a judgment was made in favor of the *saints of the Most High, and the time came for the saints to* **possess the kingdom.**

> Then the *kingdom and dominion, And the greatness of the kingdoms under the whole heaven,* **shall be given to the people, the saints of the Most High.** His kingdom is an everlasting kingdom, And all dominions shall serve and obey Him. (Daniel 7:18, 22, 27)

> (Jesus is speaking) To him who overcomes I will grant to **sit with Me on My throne**, as I also overcame and sat down with My Father on His throne. (Revelation 3:21)

> Do you not know that the **saints will judge the world**? And if the world will be judged by you, are you unworthy to judge the smallest matters? *Do you not know that* **we shall judge angels**? How much more, things that pertain to this life? (I Corinthians 6:2-3)

We are kings and queens. Though we have felt unworthy, we are worthy. Though we have felt condemned, we are loved and embraced. Though we have denied our authority, God is waiting for us to perceive the truth and to agree with His Words spoken about us. When we start to believe Him in this area, the world will turn their heads and notice that the church is beginning to *look* like royalty, and they will then be drawn to us as they see the Father's glory shining out from the midst of his royal heirs.

God considers *us* His rich inheritance and has a wonderful "hope" for those who will **receive** all He desires to give:

> I pray also that the eyes of your heart may be enlightened in order that you may *know* *the hope to which he has called you,* **the** *riches of* **his** *glorious inheritance in the saints...* (Ephesians 1:18)

My Father, thank You that You have loved me all along with a complete love. Thank You that even when I sin, You love me.[1] When I fail or I'm weak, You love me.[2]

I want to receive all You have for me, Father. Help me to know my worth in Your eyes. Give me revelation about how deeply You esteem me. Give me understanding about being Your royal heir in the spiritual realm.[3] Help me overcome my unbelief in this area.[4] Though many times I've felt like an unworthy prodigal, I choose to receive Your loving embrace. I choose to believe that You watch and wait for me to come to You. I accept the royal robe of righteousness You give me. I receive Your ring of authority as Your child and as Your heir. I take the sandals You give me, that wherever I go I may walk as Your ambassador.

Thank You for celebrating my life. Thank You for taking great delight in me.[5] Thank You that You generously share Your Kingdom with me, along with all my brothers and sisters.[6] I choose to believe I am one of Your chosen ones: that "I am a royal priest, and included in Your holy nation of saints."[7] Renew my mind to agree with Your truths. Take my old patterns of thinking about myself into Your death at the cross, and bring to life new ways that are truth, because You have promised the truth will set me free.

Thank You that everything You have made is good, including me.[8] Wherever I have believed that I am evil or bad, forgive me. I repent for condemning what You have called "good" and for judging myself to be unworthy. I repent from these harsh judgments and ask You, take them to the cross where You died. Forgive me for believing wrongly about who I am in Christ, and for believing error about how You perceive me.

Forgiving others:

I choose now, to forgive every person who has taught me incorrectly about my worth and about how You see me. I forgive those within my denomination, my church fellowship and my family (take time to forgive each name that comes to mind). I forgive _____. Father, forgive them. They didn't realize what they were doing. Bless them with Your mercy.

Heal my heart from the errors I was taught. If I have judged anyone concerning these errors, I now repent for condemning them. You are the Judge, not me, and I'm sorry for the times I held judgments in my heart. Thank You Jesus, that You died to carry these judgments on my behalf. Cleanse me because of Your forgiveness, through Your sacrifice.

Thank You, God for hearing my prayer and for answering me. You do all things well.[9] Thank You for your compassion, and thank You for Your kindness towards me.[10] Thank You, Abba, Father. Hide me now in the shelter where You dwell, and keep me safe as You have promised.[11]

In Jesus' Name, Amen.

---

[1] Lamentations 3:21-23; [2] II Timothy 2:13; [3] Romans 8:17; [4] Mark 9:24; [5] Zephaniah 3:17; [6] I Thessalonians 2:12; [7] I Peter 2:9 and Revelation 21:7; [8] Genesis 1:31; [9] Mark7:37; [10] Luke 15; [11] Psalm 27:5.

Part Two

Mining for Spiritual Treasure

*My father worked as an underground miner, so I am aware that digging for precious metals, or in my father's case, iron ore, is **hard work**. It requires blasting with explosives, large machines to haul away the rock, and a great deal of physical exertion. In part two of this book, we will mine for spiritual treasure and it will take energy. We will use the muscles of our spirit, our heart, our mind, and our will. But just as the physical hard work of mining brings a reward of precious metals, our efforts will bring us **spiritual riches**. Of greatest worth will be our deepened friendship with God, the most valuable and costly treasure we could ever seek.*

EXTRACTING THE TREASURE

In part one of this book, we looked at some valuable treasures of our heritage. In this second section, there is *much more* treasure to unearth! But these particular treasures are embedded within other materials, just as gold and silver are usually embedded within plain old rocks.

God told Jeremiah to separate out what is precious, costly and prized, from what is worthless and vile (Jeremiah 15:19). As each of the following chapters unfold and you are turning over in your mind the concepts I've written, *look for the gold.* When a gold digger looks at a rock, he's not focused on the rock itself. He's looking for any hint of a shiny metal that catches his eye. In each piece of the "worthless" throughout these next chapters, you'll catch a glint of what is precious. *That's* what we're searching for!

As Paul wrote, the goal of this instruction is *love*:

> But the goal of our instruction is *love* from a *pure heart* and a *good conscience* and a *sincere faith*. (I Timothy 1:5 *NASB*)

The goal of identifying what is spiritually worthless is always to come back to love: God's love, Christian love between brothers and sisters, and love for those in the world who are spiritually lost. As the worthless is pulled away to reveal the costly prize we're seeking, we will then be able to give and receive love more purely, with a good (useful, pleasant, excellent[1]) conscience, and with a faith that has no hypocrisy.[2]

Cleansing and repentance are a necessary part of our search to recover our spiritual treasure. It is by repentance that we return back to the Father, and are able to *receive* all of His many, many blessings (chapter six). But *too much* heaviness can weigh down our spirits:

> A merry heart makes a cheerful countenance, but by sorrow of the heart the spirit is broken. (Proverbs 15:13 *NKJV*)

There *are* biblical calls for times of repentance where we are sorrowful, but we must not stay in a place of sorrow after we have fully turned back to the Lord. As we'll learn later in chapter fifteen, true and godly sorrow will always lead us back to *joy*. So, when we follow James' advice to repent, or change our minds, we need to let God *lift us up*:

> Come near to God and he will come near to you. Wash your hands, you sinners, and purify your hearts, you double-minded. *Grieve, mourn and wail*. Change your *laughter to mourning and your joy to gloom. Humble yourselves* before the Lord, and *he will lift you up*. (James 4:8-10)

As you consider these areas of what I call "negative heritage," your heart may become heavy. In the midst of pondering what has been written, I encourage you to take time to breathe, take a walk, or pull away once in awhile to relax and refresh your soul. Let God lift you up!

Reaping The Fruit We Sow

We turn now to our ancestors. As grateful as we are for our wonderful Anabaptist roots, it would be unwise to assume that our heritage is perfect. John writes, if we claim we have not sinned we are calling God a liar (I John 1:10). In the same way, we are deceived if we ignore the fact that our ancestors made mistakes, or *missed the mark,* as the word "sin" is often translated in the Bible.[3]

We can understand how our ancestors responded with a mixture of attitudes towards the State Churches, ranging from Christlike forgiveness on one end of the pendulum swing, to outright violence on the other. One example which we will visit in a later chapter is the impatience and resentment of young Swiss Anabaptists Conrad Grebel and Felix Manz towards their Reformed mentor, Ulrich Zwingli. In the more radical vein, a few people who were loosely connected to the early Anabaptists became involved in actual fighting and more active protests, the most obvious historical example being the debacle of the peasant's revolt in Münster (1534-1535), which resulted in thousands of deaths.[4]

There *were* Anabaptists who kept good attitudes towards the State Churches. But wherever our Anabaptist forefathers held unforgiveness, judgments, unrighteous anger, or similar attitudes, repentance was the pathway to walking in God's best for their lives.

God knew that eventually, unforgiveness would allow *bitterness* to become established in the hearts of our ancestors, and He did not want them to be defiled:

> See to it that no one misses the grace of God and that no **bitter root grows up** to cause trouble and **defile many**. (Hebrews 12:15)

> And do not grieve the Holy Spirit of God, with whom you were sealed for the day of redemption. *Get rid of all bitterness*, rage and anger, brawling and slander, along with every form of malice. (Ephesians 4:30-31)

He also wanted them to sow only *good* spiritual seed in their lives, so they wouldn't reap harmful fruit by fleshly reactions:

> Do not be deceived, God is not mocked; *for whatever a man sows, that he will also reap.* For he who *sows to his flesh* will of the flesh **reap corruption**, but he who sows *to the Spirit* will of the Spirit *reap everlasting life.* (Galatians 6:7-8)

In nature, sowing corn seeds always yields corn stalks and not barley or wheat. Spiritually, sowing fleshly attitudes like bitterness will always yield bitterness. We will be judged in the *same way* that we judge others:

> Do not judge lest you be judged. "For *in the way you judge, you will be judged*; and *by your standard of measure, it will be measured to you*. (Matthew 7:1,2, *NASB*)

God understood that wherever our ancestors held an attitude of angry judgment against the leaders of the State Churches, they would *reap* the sin of their judgments back into their own lives and also into their churches. That is why even though the State Churches taught false doctrine, and many leaders were corrupt and hypocritical, our forefathers were still to walk in forgiveness. God's call is never less than that, as He writes in Matthew 5:44-45:

> But I say to you, *love* your enemies, *bless* those who curse you, *do good* to those who hate you, and *pray* for those who spitefully *use you and persecute you*, *that you may be sons of your Father* in heaven; for He makes His sun rise on the evil and on the good, and sends rain on the just and on the unjust. *(NKJV)*

Like many of you, I have read the testimonies in books like *Martyr's Mirror* and have been greatly affected by the deep mercy, compassion, and grace of our Anabaptist ancestors, even as men like Dirk Willems gave his own life to save the one who was pursuing him.[5] I have been stirred in the same ways you have been stirred, not discounting the godliness of those who died in victory. Yet, we need to understand and examine the *whole* of our heritage, perfect and imperfect, in order to answer important questions about our current day spiritual needs as Anabaptists. It is the way to recover the power of the Lord, and the blessings of the gifts and the call that they received. And so, I encourage you to bear with me as we search out what is hidden in order to recover the full strength of our heritage.

Doctrinal Error

Though the Reformers and Anabaptists both made great strides in coming to spiritual light out of the Dark Ages, they would not become perfect in their quest for the truth. The Reformers were not able to see many of the revelations given to the Anabaptists and as a result, persecuted our forefathers. And though the Anabaptists received much spiritual understanding, doctrinal error would continue to trickle down through their very own ranks. Men like one of our most honored founding fathers, Menno Simons, taught errors mixed right alongside his discoveries of truth. For example, Menno taught, along with Melchior Hoffman and others, that when Jesus was born He never touched Mary's physical body, because to do so would have contaminated His holiness as God.[6] Other Anabaptists entered into an overemphasis of dreams, visions, and end times preaching. Though God breathed into the lives of early Anabaptists so that the face of Europe was changed by their evangelistic zeal, not one of them was infallible as they followed their Savior, even to death.

Sins To The Third And Fourth Generations

The Scriptures tell us the sins of a father are visited to the third and fourth generations of a family (Exodus 34:7; Exodus 20:5; Numbers 14:18; Deuteronomy 5:9):

> The Lord is slow to anger, abounding in love and forgiving sin and rebellion. Yet he does not leave the guilty unpunished; *he punishes the children for the sin of the fathers to the third and fourth generation.* (Deuteronomy 5:9)

How does this transpire? One way is through the passing on of sins within the heart, like the judgments and bitterness we've been discussing. A bitter father or mother will speak with a bitter tongue and act with bitter actions, and by their own examples and words, train their children. That is why we are told to keep our heart with "all diligence, for out of it springs the issues of life" (Proverbs 4:23 *NKJV*).

If the child's response to his parents' bitter treatment is to *judge*, the child will then *reap* bitterness, until he repents and turns to the Lord in that area of his life.[7] And so the cycle starts all over again, as that child grows up and becomes a father, and trains his children through his own bitterness. Now, the sin follows through to *his* third and fourth generation. That is how the pattern continues from one generation to the next, each generation affecting several generations to follow, unless someone in the family line is able to recognize the error of their ways and "change their mind" by forgiving.

A Present Day Example

An honest reflection on the lives of people around us or even of our own lives, will confirm the truth of this principle. For example, think about the immense and growing problem of divorce in our Western societies. A father has moved out of the house and "abandoned" his child through divorce. If the child holds unforgiveness, that "bitter root" finds a place in his heart to grow. When he becomes an adult, it bears harmful fruit in his life through his own cycle of marriage and divorce, or through abandoning his own son or daughter. And so, the cycle continues from one generation to the next, as a father deserts his child, and that child grows up to desert his own child, to the point where in just a few generations, divorce has become a common phenomenon. Sowing and reaping to the third and fourth generation and beyond, is one of the reasons more than half the marriages in America now end in divorce.

Though the reaping of the sin may look slightly different in the life of each succeeding generation, it will be with the *same manner* of judgment and with the same measure or strength of judgment, as the scripture in Matthew 7 illustrates. It will probably be even *greater*, since seeds that are sown reap an *increase* of seed.

The *good news* is that as a family member repents and the sin is cleansed through the blood of Jesus, the pattern of that sin is no longer transferred to their children. Rather, the *blessings* of God begin to flow through the righteous heart of the parent to bless his children, since the law of sowing and reaping applies to blessing as well as to sin.

Repenting for Past Sins

Jesus' sacrifice on the cross has cleansed us from all sin, so that in *spiritual position,* believers stand boldly and purely before the throne of God (Hebrews 4:16 and Hebrews 10:14). Yet there is still an ongoing work of repentance in which we "work out our salvation" with God's help and grace, so that while we are on this earth nothing comes between His Spirit and our heart (Philippians 2:12-13). This outworking applies both to individuals and to groups of people, since in the Scriptures God calls individuals to repentance and also churches and even nations.[8]

Part of repentance also includes a confession of *past sins* as well as present sins. As we understand the sins of generations being passed down from father to son to grandson and so on, it is not too difficult to see how sins done by someone who lived ten or fifteen generations ago can still impact present day generations if they are not cleansed through repentance. Repeatedly, the Scriptures indicate that in order to be fully cleansed and healed from the effects of sin, it is necessary and valuable to confess not only our own sins, but also the sins of the fathers who went before our generation. In the following Bible references, the translations of the Hebrew and Greek all indicate former sins, including even ancestral sins:

'So those of you who may be left will rot away . . . also because of the *iniquities of their forefathers* they will rot away with them. If they *confess their iniquity and the iniquity of their forefathers,*...then *I will remember My covenant* with Jacob, and I will remember also My covenant with Isaac, and My covenant with Abraham as well, *and I will remember the land.* (Leviticus 26:39-42 *NASB*)

Do not remember against us the *iniquities of our forefathers*; let thy compassion come speedily to meet us, for we are brought very low. (Psalm 79:8 *RSV*)

(Daniel is praying) O Lord, in view of all your righteous acts, let your anger and wrath, we pray, turn away from

> your city Jerusalem . . .; *because of our sins and the in-iquities of our ancestors*, Jerusalem and your people have become a disgrace among all our neighbors. . . . While I was speaking, and was praying and *confessing my sin and the sin of my people* Israel, . . . the man Gabriel . . . came to me . . . (Daniel 9:16-21 *NRSV*)

> (Jesus is speaking to the Pharisees) So you testify against yourselves that you are the descendants of those who murdered the prophets. *Fill up, then, the measure of the sin of your forefathers!* (Matthew 23:31-32)

Reaping The Fruit Of Righteousness

God realizes the task of turning back in repentance is not an easy one. Once, as I was "looking to the rock from which I was hewn" and facing the sinfulness of my own heart's judgments, God quietly whispered that He thought I was being very brave (Isaiah 51:1). I was caught off guard by the thought that my Heavenly Father would call my repentance bravery, yet comforted by His Spirit's affirmation.

He never condemns us or scolds us (Romans 8:1; James 1:5). He knows our discipline is *painful*, or grievous and sorrowful, as it is also translated:[9]

> No discipline seems pleasant at the time, *but painful.* Later on, however, it produces *a harvest of righteousness and peace* for those who have been trained by it. Therefore, *strengthen your feeble arms and weak knees!* "Make level paths for your feet," so that the lame may not be disabled, *but rather healed.* (Hebrews 12:11-13)

He also knows that as we repent, we will begin to reap on earth the *harvest of the righteousness* we are meant to walk in through the exchange which occurred on the cross of Jesus. And as we allow the pain of correction, we will reap *good* fruit: a harvest that is pure and precious and priceless. We will also begin to experience His peace—a great peace that will stand in the midst of any storm of life which comes our way (John 14:27).

God encourages us to "strengthen our feeble arms and weak knees" as we face this process, making level paths for our feet so that we may be healed, no longer disabled in any way. He wants to see us rise up in strength and glory as His children and His royal heirs, carrying the precious treasures we have extracted, and sharing them throughout the world!

Heavenly Father, thank You for Your Spirit of truth.[1] *Come now and restore my soul as I pray.*[2] *You alone know the truth of my heritage, both the blessings and the sins. If there has been any reaping of unforgiveness, bitterness, or judgment through the generations, I choose to stop the pattern for myself and for my family.*

Repentance:

As Daniel prayed for his people, I now pray for my people. As a representative of my church congregation, my family line and myself, I choose to forgive these two State Churches for persecuting and torturing and hunting down my spiritual forefathers. I forgive them for jailing my ancestors, and for killing them. I forgive them for taking our property and for taking our children away. I forgive them, just as You forgave me.

I forgive them for teaching doctrinal error and for forcing us to obey these doctrines. I forgive them for their hypocrisy and their corruption and their extortion. I forgive them, knowing that my own great debt of sin has been forgiven by the shedding of Your blood.

Remembering that You tell me to confess my sins and the sins of my "fathers."[3] *I now confess these sins: where my forefathers, my family, my people, or I may have judged the State Catholic church and the State Reformed*

Church for their sins against us, forgive us for those judgments. I confess every judgment against them for persecution, torture and murder, for error and corruption, and for extortion and stealing. As a representative of my family line, I repent, asking You to please take every judgment associated with our unforgiveness to the cross, where Jesus died. Cleanse me and my family and my people from our sins and the sins of our ancestors.

Blessing and cleansing:
You tell me to love and pray for those who have persecuted and spitefully used us, and to bless those who have cursed us.[4] So, as a representative of my family line and my people, I pray for today's Reformed churches of the world. Bless them with Your life, and bless them with a deep revelation of Your love. Bless them with every spiritual blessing in Christ.[5] I pray for those who worship within the Catholic church: draw them to Yourself and bless them with great spiritual life and truth. Bless them with Your presence. Forgive them, Father, just as Stephen prayed in Acts, and I ask You not to hold the sins of their forefathers against these descendants.[6]

In Your Name, Jesus, I now cut off every generational sin of unforgiveness or bitterness which has been connected to my family line through my ancestors, and ask You to hold all our judgments to Your cross. I receive Your forgiveness. Thank You that Your sacrifice cleanses us from all unrighteousness. Fill us with Your Presence and renew our minds concerning our past.

Thank you that you are the God of all comfort.[7] I ask for Your healing and comfort to be poured out into my family and to the Anabaptists, and into my own life. Help me to completely change my mind to agree with the mind of Christ, and be my Shelter and my Strong Tower.[8]

*I ask these things in the name of Your Son, Jesus Christ.
Amen.*

---

[1] John 16:13; [2] Psalm 23:3; [3] Leviticus 26:40; [4] Matthew 5:44-45; [5] Ephesians 1:3; [6] Acts 7:60; [7] II Corinthians 1:3; [8] Psalm 61:3.

Promises for you taken from Jeremiah 15:19:

Because you have chosen to extract the precious from the worthless, God has *promised* to restore you. You will stand before His very presence. You will be one He can trust to speak to others, the things He would like to say to them. He will bless you in all these ways, because you have turned to Him!

FALSE PEACE: INABILITY TO WITNESS

If you have ever been really excited about something, you know one of the first things you want to do is tell somebody about it. When I became engaged, my heart was *filled* to overflowing and my words spilled out to friends and family. Most of my thoughts and conversations centered around my fiancé and our upcoming life together. I couldn't stop talking about him!

So it was with the early Anabaptists: after the long spiritual drought of the Dark Ages, they exploded with enthusiasm as they took a cool drink of God's Living Water. Their conversations and thoughts centered around Him and they couldn't wait to share with others what God had done in their lives. Their witness was unstoppable as they talked to everyone and anyone about their First Love.

But as time passed, our ancestors became weary in persecution and tired of suffering. Something changed and they no longer carried an unquenchable passion. During the later years of oppression, many of our ancestors made agreements not to witness to others within the societies where they lived. They did so in order to settle down and live in the land: to have a place where they could be relieved of harassment by pursuers who had dogged their steps for so many years.

In my research for this book, I found at least three places where historians denote an actual agreement with lords or rulers of the land. One such agreement was made with the Ribeaupierre family of Alsace, France, around the middle of the seventeenth century. Anabaptists coming from the Bern region of Switzerland were given privileges like military exemption and invited to farm, *if they promised not to proselytize* others with their "heresy."[1]

Another agreement occurred in the Ukraine under the rule of Catherine II and Paul I, around the beginning of the nineteenth century. A Dutch historian had this to say about Anabaptists moving to the Ukraine:

> ...they were not only allowed free settlement, but also guaranteed "everlasting freedom" to live and believe according to their own view. However, there was *one strict condition: They had to be silent citizens* and could proselytize neither among the members of the Orthodox Church, nor among Lutherans or Roman Catholics who lived near the Mennonite colonies. [2]

Anabaptists in the Palatine area of Germany also agreed to silence in order to be able to stay there and farm their land. By the mid-seventeenth century, families who had emigrated there from Switzerland were championed as excellent and hardworking farmers. In exchange for being allowed to remain on the land, these Anabaptists agreed that there would be no witnessing to non-Anabaptists who lived nearby.[3]

These agreements meant our ancestors were able to provide for themselves and their families. They could also establish their own independent lifestyles and community life. In some places, like the Palatinate, they were even allowed to meet together in small groups. After years of being put to death or imprisoned for their faith, a measure of rest from more intense persecution seemed worth the cost of agreeing to be silent in their witness.

Not every agreement to stop evangelizing was as obvious as those made in France, Germany, and the Ukraine. But these specific examples demonstrate the broader weariness of our ancestors and the eventual internal attitudes of silence which became normative in most of Anabaptism as it continued through the centuries.

Sharing Our Faith

The Scriptures teach that *even in times of persecution,* we are to continue a bold witness. As we examine the context of this passage from Matthew 10, we'll realize the Lord Jesus actually told His disciples to preach the gospel as they were fleeing from one place to the other!

> **When you are *persecuted in one place, flee to another.* . .** If the head of the house has been called Beelzebub, how much more the members of his household! So *do not be afraid of them.* There is nothing concealed that will not be disclosed, or hidden that will not be made known. *What I tell you in the dark, speak in the daylight; what is whispered in your ear, proclaim from the roofs. Do not be afraid* of those who *kill the body* but *cannot kill the soul.* Rather, be afraid of the One who can destroy both soul and body in hell. Are not two sparrows sold for a penny? Yet not one of them will fall to the ground apart from the will of your Father. And even the very hairs of your head are all numbered. *So don't be afraid;* you are worth more than many sparrows. *Whoever acknowledges me before men,* I will also acknowledge him before my Father in heaven. But *whoever disowns me before men, I will disown him before my Father in heaven.* (Matthew 10:23-33)

Three times Jesus commands, "Don't be afraid," telling us to "proclaim from the roofs" the things we have heard Him sharing with us in our secret times in His presence. Then, He adds a blessing and a warning. Jesus promises to acknowledge us as we stand before His Father in heaven, because we have *acknowledged Him before men.* He will be our Advocate in the court of the Father's house! Yet, at the same time, if we have *disowned or denied Him before men,* He will disown and deny us as we stand before the Father in eternity.

The apostle Paul affirms Jesus' call to a bold witness during persecution by telling Timothy to unashamedly testify about the Lord, though it meant suffering for the gospel:

> For God *did not give us a spirit of timidity (fear),* but a spirit of power, of love and of self-discipline. *So do not be ashamed*

> *to testify about our Lord*, or ashamed of me his prisoner.
> But *join with me in suffering for the gospel, by the power of
> God* . . . (II Timothy 1:7,8)

The literal translation of the word "timidity" in this scripture is
cowardice. God has not given us a spirit of cowardice, but by
His Spirit, we have bold courage.

In the book of Acts, our witness is tied to our *obedience*.
The ruling Jewish council, the Sanhedrin, had ordered the
apostles not to preach. Peter gave this answer for their actions:

> We (the Sanhedrin) gave you strict orders not to teach in this
> name," he said. "Yet you have filled Jerusalem with your
> teaching and are determined to make us guilty of this man's
> blood." Peter and the other apostles replied: '*We must obey
> God rather than men!*' (Acts 5:28-29)

Called To Preach

In the 1500s, many Reformers believed the Great Commission had already been fulfilled by the apostles. They taught
that the State Church system had taken the place of an evangelistic witness, and only those ordained by the civil authorities
were called to "preach the gospel" within their own Church
domains.[4] Their predecessor, the Church of the Middle Ages,
also believed the call to preach was only to be carried out by
princes and specially chosen professionals.[5]

The Anabaptists disagreed. To them, every person joining the *True Church* was making a commitment to witness:

> . . . the promise to *go where sent* was part of the ceremony of
> admission to the True Church. They 'went freely under the
> cross' where the representatives of the state churches dared
> not go, and for the Gospel's sake were made pilgrims and
> martyrs throughout the known world.[6]

Becoming A Secluded People

How then did our heritage change, so that today's Anabaptists have become known as the "quiet in the land"? What happened to weaken the broad scope of our evangelistic gift? There is no simple explanation, but for various reasons our priorities changed and our zeal faded:

> Under the impact of martyrdom, internal divisions, and accommodation to their environment, *the strength of original Anabaptism had gradually been lost* in the four generations from 1525 to 1650.[7]

Our strength was lost and our fire grew cold. As time progressed, in order to avoid oppression in some places, leaders placed emphasis on appearing as harmless as possible by trying to look like other Protestant groups.[8] And in Russia, by the early nineteenth century being a Mennonite had become more a description of ethnic background than of faith. The spiritual life of the group had "lost its salt":

> . . . a slow stagnation crept into the intellectual and spiritual life of the group. When missionary David Schlatter visited the colonies in 1825, he reported that the church had *lost its salt*. But the *spiritual life* was to *sink even lower* during the next two decades. What impact could have come from the Russian culture was lost since the *settlers did not know the Russian language.* . . . Continued intermarriage within the group led to a unique self and group consciousness. *To be a Mennonite meant not primarily religious but ethnic relations.*[9]

By the nineteenth century our historic witness had virtually ceased and the Anabaptist church as a whole had no real desire or sense of missionary call. Instead, our focus had turned inward, as one Dutch Anabaptist described the Mennonites in Europe:

> The situation we find in the nineteenth century is entirely different. Then we find *no longer* in the Netherlands, nor in Switzerland, Germany, France, or Russia a Mennonite *missionary* congregation, but we find *secluded* Mennonite congregations—congregations in which the missionary zeal is dead . . . *Preaching of the gospel to nations . . . is strange*

to them. The congregation has become what I call a closed congregation. The *goal of the congregation is*, as described in the constitution of one of our Dutch congregations, *the reinforcement of the religious feelings and images of its members*.[10]

Though Anabaptists in both the first generations and these later generations experienced oppression and harassment, their response to suffering was vastly different. The former generations rejoiced and witnessed regardless of governmental orders. The latter generations withdrew into communities set apart from the masses, in order to survive. Anabaptists began to choose separation from society as a form of self protection from persecution.

To this day, one of the wonderful strengths of Anabaptism is a strong and devoted local community. Church members bless one another through fund raisers or barn raisings or numerous other acts of service. Anabaptist believers meet together regularly in fellowship and corporate worship. But when community life becomes exclusive, it is no longer completely healthy.

As our ancestors agreed to stop witnessing and began to separate themselves from "outsiders," they became *spiritually introverted*. Over time, our introversion led to an inability to relate to those in the world who needed Christ. For example, in 1992, Russian Mennonite communities neither spoke the Russian language nor related to the Russian culture of those around them.[11] Separation from Russian society had been a part of their foundation as a whole, when they first settled in the region in 1788.[12] And though some outreach had occurred throughout the years, many still held fast to old ways of seclusion. On another continent in early American life, Mennonites and Amish who had come to the new world mostly chose to be separate and to avoid relating to others.[13]

Through our withdrawals we could no longer "become as they are" in order to reach out and share Christ, as Paul writes to the Corinthians:

> Though I am free and belong to no man, *I make myself a slave to everyone, **to win as many as possible***. To the Jews *I became like a Jew*, to win the Jews. To those under the law *I became like one under the law* (though I myself am not under the law), so as to win those under the law. To those not having the law I *became like one not having the law* (though I am not free from God's law but am under Christ's law), so as to win those not having the law. To the weak *I became weak*, to win the weak. ***I have become all things to all men so that by all possible means I might save some***. I do all this *for the sake of the gospel*, that I may share in its blessings. Do you not know that in a race all the runners run, but only one gets the prize? *Run in such a way as to get the prize*. (I Corinthians 9:19-24)

Paul was willing to become like Jews or like Gentiles or like the weak, in order to speak about Jesus. He became "all things to all men," in order to win some. By God's grace we should be able to do the same—to go out and even acclimate to other cultures in order to win some of the people in that culture, as we identify with their needs.

But because we became so spiritually introverted as a people group we came to expect, either consciously or unconsciously, that if someone desires to know Jesus they must first become like us. *Then* we would welcome them into fellowship with the Lord and with our communities. As a result, in many Anabaptist communities we have closed off our hearts to those around us who are different than we are, and it has cost us an effective witness.

Another ramification of our gradual change to spiritual introversion was that we became afraid of reaching out to the unsaved because we feared being contaminated by their sin. In later chapters, we'll look more closely at the causes of these fears. For now, we only need to understand that God *has* commanded us to reckon ourselves as dead to sin, but He never commanded us to avoid the people of the world who sin (Romans 6:11). We are to hate the sin but walk in an attitude of love for the sinner. Jesus hated sin, yet He repeatedly demonstrated His love for sinful people through eating with them and through healing, teaching, comforting, forgiving, and finally, through dying on their behalf.

The apostle Paul spent much time with the people of the world as he presented the gospel. He reasoned with them and met with them wherever he traveled. He admonishes the church in Corinth regarding their judgments of both brothers and "outsiders" with these words:

> I have written to you in my letter *not to associate* with sexually immoral people—*not at all meaning the people of this world who are immoral, or the greedy and swindlers, or idolaters. In that case you would have to leave this world.* But now I am writing to you that you must not associate with anyone who calls himself a brother but is sexually immoral or greedy, an idolater or a slanderer, a drunkard or a swindler. With such a man do not even eat. *What business is it of mine to judge those outside the church?* Are you not to judge those inside? (I Corinthians 5:9-12)

The Corinthians were not to dissociate themselves with sinners, but with those who called themselves brothers and still walked in these sinful practices.

Just as Jesus ate with "tax collectors and sinners," we do not need to fear the people who are in the world, even though we recognize their sin and their need to be "cleaned up" by the Master. When Jesus prayed for us, He did not pray that we would be taken out of our contact with those in the world. He actually sent us *into the world:*

> I *do not pray* that You should take them *out of the world,* but that You should keep them from the evil one. They are not of the world, just as I am not of the world. Sanctify them by Your truth. Your word is truth. *As You sent Me* into *the world, I also have sent them* into *the world.* (John 17:15-18)

It is true, our overall witness as Anabaptists has increased in recent years. Many denominations have begun to grow once again in outreach and in our willingness to go into all the world and preach the gospel. Yet too often, mission work is thought of as being for a select few. We now support other missionaries who go out, rather than grasping our ancestors' revelations that *all* who know and love Jesus are missionaries. And many of us still avoid those in society around us, either because we can no longer relate to their needs, or because we are afraid of their sin.

Our First Love

It is not by our own strength that we will be able to return to the zeal of our early forefathers. Much of their witness came from a deep love of God. Likewise, the power of our own witness will only come as God changes our hearts. Men and women like Hans Denck, Michael Schneider, Anneken Jansz, Christina Michael Barents, Balthasar Hubmaier, Michael Sattler, and so many other Anabaptists, *knew* Christ's love. It spilled out in their words, their writings, their witnessing, and in the blood they shed as they died martyrs' deaths.

Their witness was not out of obligation. It was a privilege. So with us, our witnessing is not a religious practice where we force ourselves to go out and knock on doors because God has commanded us to preach. Witnessing is an honest, open speaking about what God has done in our lives. Where He has helped us, we tell others. Where He has healed us, we share His healing power with others. Where we have discovered His love as a comfort, we openly explain about His love for us as we interact with others. Witnessing is simply an outgrowth of who we are and of what God has done in our lives.

It will be much easier if we are filled with love. If we don't have much to say to others about how God has met us personally, perhaps the place to begin then, is in asking God to return us to our First Love, that we may again be passionate. In His letter to the church of Ephesus in Revelation, Jesus lists all the wonderful *works* the Ephesians have done for the Kingdom of God, but calls them to repentance for losing their first love:

I know your works, your labor, your patience, and that you cannot bear those who are evil. And you have tested those who say they are apostles and are not, and have found them liars; and you have persevered and have patience, and have labored for My name's sake and have not become weary. *Nevertheless I have this against you, that you have left your first love.* Remember therefore from *where you have fallen; repent* and do the first works, or else I will come to you quickly and remove your lampstand from its place—unless you repent. (Revelation 2:2-5)

It is a spiritual response of our love and dedication to the One who has first loved us, to place Him as preeminent in our lives (I John 4:19). At the cross, Jesus demonstrated His love and loyalty to humans. He laid down everything and suffered a gruesome and brutal death to bring us into His family, because He loves being with us. His request then, is that we also put all things below Him in terms of our loyalty. As He has loved us more than His own life, we are to love Him more than anything in our lives (Matthew 10:37-42). He promises that if we do, we will find our true life in Him.

The peace we have sought as Anabaptists through our seclusion is a false peace. It is not the "preparation of the gospel of peace" that Paul tells us to put on our feet (Ephesians 6:15). That peace is a ready peace, prepared to share the good news everywhere God leads. It is time to re-dig the wells of this *true peace* of the gospel from which our early forefathers drank. We need the same Living Water that washed their feet and refreshed their souls. We need the Prince of peace to cleanse us from the inside out, so we are always ready and eager to shout from the rooftops what He has whispered to us in the secret place of our lives with Him (Matthew 10:27).

Come now and pray, to find rest and to grow strong (Isaiah 30;15)! Remember to pray aloud to God, to build your faith.

Lord Jesus, what can I say about my heart and my devotion to You? Only You know me completely. Come, and help me to pray.

I want You to be my First Love. Soften my heart by Your Spirit of truth. You have said we love others because You first loved us.[1] Let me know Your deep love. Change me from the inside out, to love You more than anything else in my life.

With Your love, show me how to relate to people in the world. Forgive me for the times I have avoided them because I was afraid of their sin. And forgive me when I have insisted that they become like me, rather than becoming as they are in order to win their lives for You.[2] Help me to lay down my life for the lost, as You did. Give me Your Spirit of power, love, and self-discipline.[3]

Father, give me understanding about how to live in this world, yet not be of the world.[4] Where my family or I or my church fellowship have separated ourselves from those in the world in a way that is not pleasing to You, show us what is pleasing to You, and help us to change where we have erred. Give us wisdom from above, as You have promised.[5] Show us how to walk by Your Spirit in these matters, and not by our flesh.[6]

Turning away from silence:

Lord, wherever there has been any agreement or vow of silence in the heritage of my family line or of my congregation regarding our witness, I repent with all of my heart. I repent for myself, for my "fathers" and for my family.[7] Forgive us. Wherever we have disowned You by not acknowledging You before men, forgive us.[8] Forgive us for being silent when You have prompted us to

*say a word of testimony. And if there are any times we
have been ashamed of You, please forgive us—forgive me,
Jesus.*[9] *Cleanse us and heal us, that we may become like
You in this world.*

*In the name of Jesus, my Savior, I now renounce and
reject every vow or agreement of silence in the heritage
of my family line. I break all their power over our lives
and declare them null and void, through what Christ
accomplished at the cross on our behalf.*[10]

Prayer for restoration:

*Cleanse my family and me from any effects of heredi-
tary silence. Like you touched the tongue of the deaf and
dumb man, touch our tongues and heal us completely.*[11]
Open our mouths to fearlessly share the gospel.[12] *Restore
to us the passionate and fiery evangelism that was in my
early Anabaptist ancestors. You have promised the gifts
and call are irrevocable, so I ask You, return this gift back
to me and to my family and to my people.*[13] *Lord Jesus,
fill us that the world may come to know You!*

*Thank You for hearing me and for answering. I will
wait for You, my strength and my defense.*[14] *Cover me with
Your wings, that I may find refuge in You.*[15] *Thank You
for all that You have done for me.*

In Your Name, Lord Jesus, Amen.

---

[1] I John 4:19; [2] I Corinthians 9:22; [3] II Timothy 1:7; [4] John 17:14-16; [5] James
1:5; [6] Romans 8; [7] Psalm 79:8; [8] Matthew 10:32-33; [9] Mark 8:38; [10] Romans
6:6; [11] Mark 7:32-35 and Psalm 71:15; [12] Ephesians 6:19; [13] Romans 11:29;
[14] Psalm 59:9; [15] Psalm 91:4.

Promises for you, from Isaiah 61:3,4,6:

Thank You for praying. You have just begun to help re-build the "ancient ruins," as Isaiah has written. God says you are strong in righteousness, like an oak tree is tall and strong. He promises *you* gladness, and a heart that is full of praise. He will display His glory in your life. Be glad, because you have just ministered to Him!

FALSE PEACE:

SILENCE TOWARDS ONE ANOTHER

I have lived outside of Anabaptist-influenced communities for several years in California, Florida, and the country of
Italy. In each of these living experiences I discovered something
often lacking from Anabaptist communities as a whole: the freedom to *speak the truth in love,* to *confront each other* as necessary, and to *disagree and simply say what we think* without fear
of causing offense or being rejected. In church fellowships of
these non-Anabaptist regions, I watched as brothers and sisters
readily talked through problems and disagreements.

It was difficult to process their natural openness and
honesty, since I had learned to be *silent* when offended, or when
my opinion was unpopular. In my experience, there were two
typical responses to disagreement and offense: internalizing my
feelings and saying nothing, or talking *about* the person with
someone else rather than going directly to them and working it
out together. Speaking the truth was far too intimidating when
doing so meant the possibility of creating friction with another
believer.

Speaking The Truth To Each Other

It is through the fear of man and fearing man's rejection,
that many of us Anabaptists have struggled to share openly and
truthfully with others (more on these two topics in later chapters). These fears first settled into the lives of our ancestors

when they learned to "keep the peace" through withholding their thoughts and words. Rather than risking rejection or harm by speaking the truth in love, they held their tongues. Since fear cannot be compartmentalized in the heart, it impacted not only their witness but also their ability to speak to one another freely.

We have inherited these unhealthy patterns of communication. In fear, many Anabaptists want to avoid confrontation, which is why we internalize things rather than speaking our concerns. But when we consistently hold our feelings inside, like a wound that is not cleaned out properly, they "fester" and corrupt our hearts. Jesus instructs us to be reconciled to each other because He knows if we keep our frustration within us, we will move into judgment or anger. For our own sake and for the sake of another who may be offended, we must learn to speak the truth in love:

> . . . Let each one of you *speak truth* with his neighbor, for we are members of one another. *Be angry, and do not sin: do not let the sun go down on your wrath, nor give place to the devil.* (Ephesians 4:25-27 *NKJV*)

These verses are next to each other for a reason and though often used separately, in context they should be interpreted together. If we are angry, we may need to go and speak the truth to our "neighbor" so sin does not get a foothold, thereby opening up a place for the enemy to work in our lives.

Another scripture which speaks of our need to quickly "clear the air" with our brothers is found in the Sermon on the Mount:

> But I say to you that whoever is angry with his brother without a cause shall be in danger of the judgment. And whoever says to his brother, 'Raca!' shall be in danger of the council. But whoever says, 'You fool!' shall be in danger of hell fire. *Therefore* if you bring your gift to the altar, *and there remember that your brother has **something against you**, leave your gift there before the altar, and go your way. **First be reconciled** to your brother, and then come and offer your gift.* (Matthew 5:22-24)

Our attitudes towards each other are as important to God as our worship. If we have offended our brother, we shouldn't even complete our offerings before we go and make things right. God knows if we reconcile quickly, our brother or sister's anger will be cleansed from their heart, and bitterness and judgment will have no place to take root and defile many (Hebrews 12:15). And to keep our own hearts cleansed, we are *also* instructed to go to those who have offended *us* and speak to them lovingly:

> If your brother sins against you, go and show him his fault, just between the two of you. If he listens to you, you have won your brother over. . . (Matthew 18:15)

True Peace

Anabaptists are concerned about "keeping the peace" with others. Yet, the type of peace which comes through avoiding confrontation is actually a false peace that has developed in our lives the unbiblical pattern of not discussing or working through problems and disagreements. Recently, a clarification of two similar phrases was tossed back and forth among some of our friends: being a "peacemaker," or being a "peacekeeper." Peace-*maker* is the term used in the Bible.

A peacemaker not only makes peace by his cooperative spirit, but also by his willingness to work through issues—even if it requires pressing through awkward differences—to come to a place of true peace and unity, with no underlying tension or falsehood. On the other hand, the peace*keeper* wants to keep a façade of peace at all costs, avoiding confrontation or anything which will cause a disruption. The "peace" which remains is not really peace, but quietness. Underneath the quietness remains a hidden tension or resentment or unforgiveness. When the Scriptures urge us to live in peace, they are referring to the kind of peace which is found through true peace*making*:

> Now the fruit of righteousness is sown in peace by those who *make* peace. (James 3:18 *NKJV*)

In a healthy marriage or family, working through disagreement with honest, open discussion eventually yields peace and unity, as we forgive and reconcile. It is no different in the family of God. When we are willing to be open, to discuss differences and work through disagreements to the point of forgiveness if necessary, the unity of our spiritual family will be maintained and everyone will continue bearing the fruit of righteous hearts.

For My Brother's Sake

In our peace*keeping* ways, we have been taught to "mind our own business," even as the Scriptures indicate in I Thessalonians 4:11. Yet, this verse does not apply to a silence in witnessing, nor does it refer to holding our tongue when the Lord asks us to exhort a fellow believer. Clearly, there *is* Biblical precedence for loving confrontation, as Jesus teaches in Luke 17:3: "If your brother sins, rebuke him and if he repents, forgive him." In our silence, rebukes have gone unspoken which *should have happened* so that another person can be edified.

I have learned this lesson the hard way. Many times I have held my tongue even though I sensed an inner nudging from God to exhort another brother or sister. In one situation, a close spiritual brother had been deceived by false teaching. In my fear of confrontation, I said nothing and only prayed that God would somehow intervene. I thought showing him God's love by my actions would be enough. In time, our friend walked away from the Lord and has not returned. Now I understand that *I* was one whom God wanted to use to intervene, but my fear of rejection and the fear of man had overpowered my ability to hear God's voice. Had I obeyed God's quiet inner urging, perhaps my spiritual brother would have been snatched out of the fire (Jude 1:23) and remained in the faith.

Lives have been harmed and people wounded because we have not been willing to risk rejection for the sake of another's growth. It is *true love* to be willing to *lay down our lives* in this way, for a brother or sister's spiritual health, even knowing they may not immediately receive our love or admonition.

Speaking The Truth Without Love

From our struggle with fear, several other phenomena can occur if we do manage to finally speak. First, our words can be *void of love*. If we fear rejection we can build up an assumption that we won't be received, and before we say a single word we're already defensive. Subconsciously we "stew" and create preconceived ideas of what the other person must be thinking and feeling. Then, when we speak, rather than the Father's restful and confident love, our words are tainted with defensiveness or anger or shame. As a result, our emotional cloudiness often confuses rather than clarifies the situation at hand.

A second phenomenon can also happen if we speak up fearfully. In order to please the hearer, we can *compromise our words* and rephrase things in order to be more agreeable. We may avoid confrontation by speaking words we think they will accept, but in doing so we have just lied to ourselves and to others. This deeply engrained habit lays aside our own "inner truth" in order to maintain a sense of false peace. But Paul tells us to put away lying, and speak the truth to each other:

> Therefore, *putting away lying*, 'Let each one of you *speak truth* with his neighbor,' for we are members of one another. (Ephesians 4:25, *NKJV*)

Speaking the truth in love is equated with growing in maturity:

> Instead, *speaking the truth in love*, we will in *all things grow up* into him who is the Head, that is, Christ. (Ephesians 4:15)

Maturity requires that we learn to be lovingly honest with our spiritual family members. By God's grace, we can learn to walk healthily in obeying both parts of the equation: *speaking the truth*, and doing it *in love*.

Finally, we all err and need correction, but if we went to each other every time someone "missed the mark," none of us would have time for sleep! There are many times when we are *not* called to say anything, but simply to commit the entire matter to God in prayer. He can enable us to forgive an offense, assuring us that He will take care of our brother or sister's sin and requiring nothing more of us than our heart's forgiveness or our prayers for them. We can then go on our way with a clean heart and a renewed peace about our brother's spiritual life. As we learn to listen to God's voice and to His wisdom, He will let us know when we need to speak up and when we need to be silent. Speaking the truth in love is always to be tempered by our listening and obedient heart to God.

Recovering What Was Lost

God is willing to restore all that was lost through fear and silence. He is the Redeemer who can buy back everything we have "sold" through generational strongholds. When we take this harder road of speaking the truth in love regardless of its cost to our personal reputation, we will find potholes of rejection, mistakes, and other difficulties. But, we will also find a *greater freedom* in our hearts than we ever experienced on the old road of deceiving ourselves and each other. Then our unity will become a *strong and real unity,* because it will be based on truth and love rather than on pretense or false peace. And our honest transparency will be visible to those in the world who are watching our fellowships. We'll look just like our Father and our Brother in heaven as they see healthy, open friendships which exude the love of God and people will say, "the Kingdom of heaven is near!"

My Father, I am grateful that You spoke the truth in love when You showed me my sin. Without Your gentle confrontation, I would not have found Your eternal life. Thank You for loving me so much, that you would not be silent.

Repenting, and changing your mind:

Thank You for giving us a spiritual family on earth and for teaching us how to relate to each other through the Scriptures. I want to learn to speak the truth in love. Wherever I have failed You by not speaking up, I ask Your forgiveness. Where I have harmed another brother or sister's spiritual walk by keeping silent, please forgive me.

If I have lied by not speaking truthfully from my heart, forgive me (You may want to take time to let God reveal specific incidences where cleansing is needed). I repent for all deception.[1] I ask You to show me when I am being tempted to hide my true feelings inside, if You are asking me to be open and honest. Give me Your mind and fill me with Your loving truth.[2]

*In Jesus' name, I break off every generational or habitual pattern of false peace**keeping** and ungodly silence which has affected my life or my family. Please take them to the cross where Jesus died to bring me freedom, and break their power over me through the power that raised Christ from the dead.*

Prayer for restoration:

*Loose my tongue to declare Your truths. Fill me with holy boldness to declare Your Word.[3] Make me a peace**maker** in Spirit, in truth and in love. Teach me how to* *identify when You are asking me to speak up to someone and give me the courage to obey. Show me how to begin walking on this pathway of loving honesty. Thank You, Father. You are my Teacher, my Counselor.[4] I trust You to lead me. I know You will change me, and make me like You, so I can rest in this process of growth, because You are inside me.*

Thank You for Your love. I entrust myself to You completely, for You are my Father, and I am Your child. Because I have set my love upon You, You deliver me and set me on high.[5]

In the Name of Jesus, Amen

---

[1] Psalm 32:2; [2] I Corinthians 2:16 and Psalm 19:14; [3] Acts 4:29; [4] John 14:26 and John 14:16 (*NIV*); [5] Psalm 91:14.

Promises for you, from Luke 8:8,15:

You have just been heard in heaven, and you are *promised* a large yield—according to Jesus, it'll be one hundred times bigger than your prayers! And because you are pressing through (persevering) in prayer, you *will* bear spiritual fruit. He is pleased, and calls your heart noble and good!

~ 14 ~

FALSE PEACE:

GIVING UP THE SPIRITUAL FIGHT

Our early Anabaptist ancestors never denied that Christians are to be armed with weapons for battle. They understood we *must* be armed against our enemy in the spiritual realm. In the Schleitheim Confession of Faith, article number six, we are exhorted to bear *spiritual* weapons, to be used in *spiritual* battle against "the fortification of the devil":

> . . . but the weapons of Christians are *spiritual*, against the *fortification of the devil*. The worldly are armed with steel and iron, but *Christians are armed with the armor of God*, with truth, righteousness, peace, faith, salvation, and with the Word of God.

As they wrote, they were drawing references from at least two scriptures where Paul discusses the spiritual fight of believers. The first scripture is one we have already discussed in chapter six, and is taken from II Corinthians. The second is from Paul's letter to the Ephesians:

> For though we walk in the flesh, we do not *war according to the flesh*. For the *weapons of our warfare are not carnal but mighty in God* for pulling down strongholds, casting down arguments and every high thing that exalts itself against the knowledge of God, bringing every thought into captivity to the obedience of Christ . . . (II Corinthians 10:3-5)

> Finally, my brethren, be *strong in the Lord* and in the *power of His might*. Put on *the whole armor of God*, that you may be able to *stand against the wiles of the devil*. For we do not *wrestle* against *flesh and blood*, but against *principalities*,

against *powers,* against the *rulers of the darkness* of this age, against *spiritual hosts of wickedness in the heavenly places.* Therefore *take up the whole armor* of God, that you may be able to withstand in the evil day, and having done all, to stand. *Stand* therefore, having *girded your waist* with *truth,* having put on the *breastplate of righteousness,* and having *shod your feet* with the preparation of the *gospel of peace*; above all, taking the *shield of faith* with which you will be able to *quench all the fiery darts of the wicked one.* And take the *helmet of salvation,* and the *sword of the Spirit,* which is the *word of God* . . . (Ephesians 6:10-18)

In this passage in Ephesians, our foe is described in four ways: principalities, powers, rulers of darkness, and spiritual hosts of wickedness. These spiritual beings fight in the "heavenly places," meaning the spiritual realm, which also includes the realm of earth since their commander-in-chief, the devil, was given authority over the earth. He is called the "god of this age" (II Corinthians 4:4), the "ruler of this world" (John 12,14,16), the one who has the power of death (Hebrews 2:14), a dragon, a serpent, and the deceiver of the world (Revelation 12:9).

The reason we are instructed to put on armor is to protect ourselves against this spiritual foe. Every piece of armor we have been given is for the purpose of defense except for one weapon of offense we are instructed to carry: that is the sword of the Spirit, which is the Word of God.

Victory In The Battle

Some of us would rather not think about the devil. We don't want to talk about spiritual weapons or arming ourselves with armor. We don't like all this aggressive talk of "warfare," and we're a bit afraid of the possibility of demons and spiritual foes. Other people aren't convinced the devil is even a *real* entity, let alone someone to worry about. If you question the activity of demons and other seemingly mystical spiritual concepts, I encourage you to read on. By the end of this chapter, we will have walked through an examination of Scriptures which reveal the devil as both *real* and *active*. We'll understand why, as believers, we *must* take up our spiritual weapons and put on our spiritual armor for this "warfare."

The good news is, we win! As Menno Simons writes, we *triumph gloriously!* Though Menno describes visible and invisible enemies who want to steal our spiritual kingdom, our *faith* conquers all:

> You *triumph gloriously* by the conquering power of your faith both *in life and in death, over all your foes, visible and invisible, who would fain deprive you, yes, steal from you the promised kingdom through the counsel of the serpent and his seed* . . . [1]

Menno also wrote that our forefathers *ruled* and *reigned* "by Christ" over hell, fear, the devil, and much more:

> . . . over gold, silver, cities, countries, lords, princes, flesh, blood, apprehensions, banishments, sword, stake, water, fire, hunger, thirst, nakedness, *hell, sin, the law, fear, death, and the devil.* [2]

We *are* the victors, through Christ. As we look at Jesus' earthly ministry, He will reveal the complete and total authority that we have *in Him*, over all evil. His own dealings with the devil show not fear, but faith, not loss, but gain. As we'll see later, we are to gain *plunder* from this "enemy." There are many rewards for our "warfare" in this spiritual battle.

As Jesus walked on earth, He was always running up against the demonic. Here are just a few of the many Scriptures that reveal His heavenly confrontations:

> On a Sabbath Jesus was teaching in one of the synagogues, and a woman was there who had been *crippled by a spirit* for eighteen years . . . (Jesus) put his hands on her, and immediately she straightened up and praised God. Indignant, . . . the synagogue ruler said to the people, "There are six days for work. So come and be healed (then), not on the Sabbath." The Lord answered..."You hypocrites! . . . should not this woman, a *daughter of Abraham, whom Satan has kept bound*

for eighteen long years, be set free on the Sabbath day from what bound her?" (Luke 13:10-16)

Then one was brought to Him who was *demon-possessed*, blind and mute; and He healed him. . . . (Matthew 12:22)

. . . there met Him out of the tombs a man with an *unclean spirit* . . . Then they came to Jesus, and saw the one who had been *demon-possessed* and had the legion, sitting and clothed and in his right mind. And they were afraid. (Mark 5:2,15)

(Jesus spoke) . . . You belong to *your father, the devil*, and you want to carry out your father's desire. He was a murderer from the beginning, not holding to the truth, for *there is no truth in him*. When he lies, he speaks his native language, for *he is a liar and the father of lies*. (John 8:44)

Take a moment and read through a few other scriptures in the Bible which refer to demonic activity:

What am I saying then? That an idol is anything, or what is offered to idols is anything? Rather, that the things which the Gentiles sacrifice *they sacrifice to demons* and not to God, and *I do not want you to have fellowship with demons*. (I Corinthians 10:19-20, *NKJV*)

(Israel) made him jealous with their foreign gods and an-gered him with their *detestable idols*. They *sacrificed to de-mons*, which are not God—*gods they had not known, gods that recently appeared*, gods your fathers did not fear. (Deuteronomy 32:16-17)

Now the Spirit expressly says that in latter times some will depart from the faith, giving heed to *deceiving spirits and doctrines of demons*, speaking lies in hypocrisy, having their own conscience seared with a hot iron . . . (I Timothy 4:1-2)

Therefore *submit to God. Resist the devil* and he will flee from you. (James 4:7)

Be sober, be vigilant; . . . Your *enemy the devil prowls around like a roaring lion* looking for someone to *devour. Resist him*, standing firm in the faith . . . (1 Peter 5:8-9, *NKJV/NIV*)

According to these passages, demons can have influence in causing *physical infirmity*, as in the woman who was "crippled by a spirit," and the blind mute; in causing forms of *emotional trauma*, as in the man in the tombs who cried out and "cut himself with stones" night and day (Mark 5:5); in causing men to believe *lies* and follow *deceiving spirits* and *false doctrines*; and demons can be attached or associated with *idols* (either physical idols *or* idols of the heart). The devil lies, accuses, deceives, devours, roars, and prowls, wants to be idolized, and even performs miraculous signs (Revelation 16:14).

To those who think he was only active in these ways during Jesus' day, consider this: demons are spiritual entities as are angels. Being spiritual in nature, they are also eternal, and will be punished at the end of the ages (Revelation 20:10). So, until they are judged, they will be around . . . and if they are around, where are they active? They are active on the earth:

> The great dragon was hurled down—that ancient serpent called the devil, or Satan, who leads the whole world astray. He was **hurled to the earth, and his angels with him**. (Revelation 12:9)

> We know that anyone born of God does not continue to sin; the one who was born of God keeps him safe, and the evil one cannot harm him. We know that we are children of God, and that **the whole world is under the control of the evil one**. (I John 5:18-19)

No Fear!

But as heirs of our heavenly Father, we do not need to fear the devil. Though we are in the world, as we walk in fellowship with God and submit to Him, we can resist the devil and he will flee from us! We have been *seated in the heavenly places* with Christ, and we have been given authority "over all the power of the enemy" because of who we are in Jesus:

> And (Jesus) said to them, "I saw Satan fall like lightning

from heaven. "Behold, *I give you the authority* to trample
on serpents and scorpions, and *over all the power of the
enemy*, and *nothing shall by any means hurt you*. (Luke 10:
18-19)

Jesus won for the woman in the synagogue, healing. He
won for the blind mute, his sight, and his speech. He won for the
Gadarene, mental wholeness and peace. He won for so many
others in the Bible forgiveness and cleansing, healing and grace,
through His willingness to resist the devil. As we are willing to
put on our armor and follow our Lord, we will also *win* for
ourselves, our families, our churches, and even for the lost in
the world, blessings and health and peace and *victory*. We will
bear good fruit as Jesus bore fruit.

But if we do nothing: if we do not *stand* or *resist*, the
devil will win because he is an aggressor. That is why the Scriptures clearly tell us to *resist,* and why the passage in Ephesians
says we will *wrestle* against the enemy. Whether we like it or
not, the devil will prowl and look for a fight. If we avoid the
reality of his aggression, our pretense does not make him go away
and hide. Rather, "the devourer" is then able to win the battle
without so much as a fight on our part. Without taking up our
shield of faith and sword of the Spirit, the "wicked one" will be
able to shoot his "fiery darts" directly into our souls: if we
choose not to put on our armor and stand, he will have access to
our minds and our hearts. Without our armor and our spiritual
weapons, the "roaring lion" will be able to strike easily with his
claws.

Not An Even Match

The devil is a created being, like the angels are created
beings. The battle of the heavenlies is not an equal battle. God
has already won the battle, but has allowed the enemy to remain
in the earthly realm until such a time as He will vanquish him
forever. God is Almighty. The devil is a fallen angel. He and his
demons do have spiritual power, but their power as created

beings in no way compares with the infinite, all-powerful Creator. God is *far above* all *principality*, all *power* and *might* and *dominion* both in this age of earthly governments, and also in the eternal age to come, which is the spiritual realm. All things are under God's feet:

> . . . that you may know...what is the exceeding greatness of **His power toward us who believe,** according to the working of His mighty power which He worked in Christ when He raised Him from the dead and *seated Him at His right hand in the heavenly places, far above all principality and power and might and dominion, and every name that is named, not only in this age but also in that which is to come.* And He put all things under His feet, and gave Him to be head over all things to (for) the church . . . (Ephesians 1:18-23, *NKJV*)

God's exceedingly great power is given *toward us who believe.* He has promised He will not allow us to be tempted above what we are able to bear (I Corinthians 10:13), and that He will fight the battle with us and for us (II Chronicles 20:15-17). He will protect His own (Deuteronomy 23:14). When Elisha's servant feared the enemy who had surrounded them, Elisha prayed that his eyes would be opened to see the spiritual reality of their situation:

> When the servant . . . got up and went out . . . an army with horses and chariots had surrounded the city. 'Oh, my lord, what shall we do?' the servant asked. 'Don't be afraid,' the prophet answered. *'Those who are with us are more than those who are with them.'* And Elisha prayed, "O Lord, open his eyes so that he may see." Then the Lord opened the servant's eyes, and *he looked and saw the hills full of horses and chariots of fire* all round Elisha. (II Kings 6:15-17)

As with Elisha and his servant, the Lord and his army are on our side, and they outnumber any foe in heaven or on earth! Jesus told Peter that He could call on His Father, and at once He would send more than twelve legions of angels. According to one Bible concordance, that's more than 81,000 angels![3]
    Our God is the "Commander of the army of the Lord" who appears to Joshua (Joshua 5, *NKJV*). He is also called a

Warrior, or man of war, who is mighty in battle (Exodus 15:3, Psalm 24:8, and Revelation 19:11, *NIV*). He has won, and as we stand with Him, we also win! We are the victors, through Christ (I Corinthians 15:57; I John 5:4).

Impacting The Heavenly Realms

Later, we'll talk about our Anabaptist attitudes towards our spiritual foe. But right now we need to understand that there are spiritual ramifications for our earthly actions. When we make decisions on earth, there are eternal and spiritual effects for those decisions. For example, that is why we are commanded to forgive, and not to judge others. If we don't forgive, we won't be forgiven by the Father (Matthew 6:15). If we judge, we will be spiritually judged (Matthew 7:2).

Our response to God's call to "stand" in the spiritual fight will also have a heavenly effect. If we choose to stand and overcome, we will receive eternal rewards for overcoming. But, we will *also* receive great benefits in this lifetime for standing and fighting while we are still here on earth. These great benefits are found hidden in the Ephesians passage.

There are some mornings when I sense the devil is harassing me, and I will actually mentally pray through putting on each of the pieces of armor listed in Ephesians 6, as we will do later at the end of this chapter. As I pray, I find myself being encouraged in my standing in Christ. A strength then arises in my heart, and I am able to quiet the enemy's voice because I have put on my spiritual armor through my prayers. God is a very practical Father and He is full of wisdom. The armor He gives is a practical armor, created for our benefit.

If we *gird our waist with truth*, we will be able to strengthen our spiritual resolve. Peter tells us to "gird up the loins of our mind" (I Peter 1:13). In the Bible, girding had to do with tightening the waist belt as if preparing yourself for taking a journey, or being ready to go at a moment's notice (Luke 12:35-36). The spiritual equivalent would be strengthening your will to move forward. By girding our spiritual waist with truth, we are taking hold of truth and purposefully setting it into our minds and hearts for our spiritual journey in the Lord.

The second piece of armor, the *breastplate of righteousness,* has been one of the most helpful pieces of spiritual armor in my own life. So many times, the devil has tried to accuse me of sins that I have *already* repented of and which have been cleansed by Jesus' blood. The very word, "devil" is translated "false accuser" or "slanderer," and for good reason.[4] He would like nothing more than to prevent our spiritual growth and blessing by causing us to agree with his condemning accusations of our own hearts. But, if we have put on the breastplate of our righteousness in Christ, our hearts will not be overcome by his accusations. Instead, we will be able to repel his attacks and agree with all the Scriptures God has written about our righteous standing.

Ephesians 6 continues with the third piece of armor, the shoes. We are to have *"shod (our) feet with the preparation of the gospel of peace."* Imagine, if wherever we went throughout our day, we were able to walk in peace regardless of our circumstances. How wonderfully joyful we would be! We are told to lace peace to our feet so that our spiritual walk will be filled with God's peace in the midst of every situation (John 16:33).

The next piece of our spiritual armor is extremely valuable. It is our *shield of faith* which extinguishes the *fiery darts of the evil one.* The darts of the enemy's lies, deceptions, accusations, and so forth, are ready to pierce our souls like a searing fire. But if we run to God in every temptation—fear, despair, unbelief, doubt, or any other distress—and put our trust (faith) in Him, the enemy's darts will not reach our hearts or our minds, and we'll be able to stand.

The *helmet of salvation* protects our minds. The mind is probably one of the greatest battlefields where the enemy attacks believers. As we have begun to understand throughout this book, the enemy establishes *strongholds, arguments,* and *"high things,"* or *pretensions (NIV)* in our thoughts, and we are to pull them down with the mighty weapons of God. We are to take captive every thought and make it obedient to Christ. One of the ways we will be able to pull them down is by growing in our understanding of everything Jesus has purchased for us through *salvation*. As our mind is able to grasp our amazing position in Christ through His cross and resurrection, we'll grow in our confidence as His royal co-heirs and the enemy's lies and accusations to our hearts will have less and less power.

The one offensive weapon we have been given to accompany our armor is the *sword of the Spirit*, which is the *Word of God*. Jesus used this weapon to overcome the devil when He was tempted in the wilderness. Every time the devil taunted Him, He answered, "It is written . . .," and spoke from Scriptures (Matthew 4). Many times, the devil has attempted to defeat me through my mind or heart. Through an accusation or a lie, he has attempted to plant fear or anxiety or pride or another area of sin into my mind. As I turn and call out to God, a Scripture will often come to mind, and as I speak out the Word, declaring the truth to myself and to the enemy, the internal wrestling of my soul is quieted and my heart and mind are once again able to be at peace. The Word truly has living power to defeat the wiles of the devil.

Anabaptist False Peace

How does any of this talk of warfare or the devil apply to our ancestors, or to our family heritage? It all goes back to the days of our oppression. The *false peace* which caused us to lose our strength to witness, and affected our ability to speak the truth in love to each other (chapters 12 and 13), also cost us in our ability to resist the devil. There was a spiritual, heavenly ramification when we gave into our fear of harm and agreed to silence. In the natural, earthly realm we felt if we *spoke up, we would harmed*. The effect in the spiritual realm was that we have also felt, *if we speak up against our enemy, we will be harmed*. As we gave into our fears and withdrew, the spiritual enemy of our souls stole something very essential to living an effectual

Christian life: our ability to "be strong in the Lord and in the power of His might," through spiritually resisting him (Ephesians 6:10). The result has been a timidity of heart and soul towards our spiritual enemy, and an inability to effectively stand against his attacks because of establishing a *false peace* of silence.

Neglecting our exhortation to bear arms spiritually has cost us dearly in terms of walking as a victorious, free people. In laying down our call to stand and resist, we have allowed the enemy to plunder our own lives, our families, our churches, and our communities (John 10:10). Today, spiritual warfare is not a very common topic of study or discussion in many Anabaptist circles. Our awareness of our spiritual foe has been growing, but we have a distance to go, to "catch up" to many sectors of the present day worldwide church. We need help in renewing our minds in this area of our spiritual lives. There are many fathers and mothers in the faith who have been walking in these truths for years and can offer us their insight, if we are willing to avail ourselves of their help. Their wisdom and practical "know-how" training can help us in learning to resist the devil and discern evil.

Many books have been written on this subject (see Recommended Reading section for a few) and my purpose in this chapter is not to do an in-depth study. If I can bring about an awareness of the necessity to stand, to resist, and fight as God directs, as well as give insight on how to begin, I will have succeeded in accomplishing my goals. I have mentioned previously that Jesus said it is the strong, forceful, or violent people who will apprehend the Kingdom of God (Matthew 11:12). This is the kind of intentional attitude required in order to arise and fulfill our calling in the Kingdom of God. The enemy will protest our advances, but we have authority in Christ's name over all the power of the enemy. It is time to arise!

At the same time, we are not to spend the majority of our time and energy as Christians focusing on spiritual warfare. Jesus, though joyful that His followers had come to understand their authority over demons, admonished them not to rejoice that the spirits submitted to them, but to rejoice that their names are written in heaven (Luke 10:17-21). Our focus is to be *on God*, and our energies directed to seeing His Kingdom come on earth. But because as Anabaptists we have erred heavily on the side of "peace" and timidity, some adjustments are required to bring us back to a proper balance of bold faith that resists and stands in the Spirit.

Aspects of Warfare

The following topics are various aspects of spiritual warfare which will enable you to gain a picture of what it means to resist, or to stand. Each description is brief and by no means explains adequately the entire subject.

Enemy Strongholds

We have already discussed these fortifications of the mind in chapter six, and now want to consider how the enemy has used them to his advantage. The devil assaults the mind as the "father of lies." He instigates "doctrines of demons" to teach people error. He sends "deceiving spirits" to mislead (see earlier passages of Scripture). Strongholds are places in the mind where his lies, doctrines, and deceptions have become established: where he has been able to build a "strong-hold" or fortress from which he can maintain his deceiving influence (II Corinthians 10:4-5). He uses these strongholds as one basis for operating in people's lives.

We can stop the devil's influence over a stronghold by *binding* the *deceiving spirit* that has instigated the "doctrines of demons." We take captive every thought in our mind, which is part of our soul, but we *also* bind the activity of the deceiving spirits who are sent to whisper lies from within the strongholds of our established ways of thinking.

The word "bind" is used in several places in the Scriptures as an example of forbidding the enemy's activity in the life of a human being. One example is found when some scribes accused Jesus of casting out demons by the prince of demons, Beelzebub. Jesus' response explains His actions by the use of a parable:

> And the scribes who came down from Jerusalem said . . . 'By the ruler of the demons He casts out demons.' So He called them to Himself and said to them in parables: '*How can Satan cast out Satan?* . . . if Satan has risen up against himself, and is divided, he cannot stand, but has an end. *No one can enter a strong man's house and plunder his goods*, **unless he first binds the strong man**. And then he will **plunder his house**.' (Mark 3:22-27, *NKJV*)

Jesus corrects the scribes by explaining that if a person wants to enter the "house" of a *strong man*—meaning the devil—to take his "goods" he must first **bind** the strong man, and then he can take his "plunder."

Let's apply this to our discussion of strongholds which have been established in the mind. We have to *bind* the deceiving spirits, and then we will be able to effectively cast down the thoughts and lies which are established in our minds. After the deceiving spirits are tied up, we will be able to "plunder their goods" by taking away and pulling down what has been planted in our minds.

The second illustration of *binding* is found in Matthew. Jesus is speaking to Peter and to the other apostles about their authority in the earth, and its spiritual ramifications in heaven:

> Simon Peter answered . . ., 'You are the Christ, the Son of the living God.' Jesus . . . said to him, 'Blessed are you, Simon . . . for flesh and blood has not revealed this to you, but My Father who is in heaven. And . . . you are Peter (a piece of rock[5]), and on this rock (a mass of rock[6]) I will build My church, and the **gates of Hades (hell) shall not prevail** against it. And I will give **you** the *keys of the kingdom of heaven, and whatever you **bind on earth** will be bound in heaven, and whatever you **loose on earth** will be loosed in heaven.* (Matthew 16:16-19, *NKJV*)

The word "you" which is in bold is *plural* in the Greek, which means Jesus, is speaking to *all* His disciples when He promises to give the keys of the kingdom. With the kingdom keys, we can *bind on earth* and *loose on earth*, locking and unlocking spiritual gates or doors. Our authority to *bind* and *loose* affects the spiritual realm, as whatever we bind or loose here, is bound or loosed in heaven. Jesus has given the church His authority, and the gates of hell cannot prevail against it!

I have personally applied this quieting of individual strongholds of the mind binding their demonic influences, in my own life and in the lives of others for whom God has called me to pray. Through almost daily persistence, I have seen strongholds weaken and over time, be brought down by resisting the devil in this way. Binding the *deceiving spirits* and taking every thought captive to Christ enabled *truth* to come to the forefront of people's minds, since deception could no longer operate. And when truth comes, it sets people free, just as Jesus has promised (John 8:32)!

Corporate strongholds (where everyone has come to think the same way concerning error) require more concerted prayer efforts. They have been built up over time and are quite well established in the "heavenlies." We should never attempt to bring down corporate strongholds by ourselves, or before God's perfect timing directs. Seeking God and seeking counsel from God's servants who have become wise in these kinds of "weapons of warfare" are the best initial steps regarding the dismantling of corporate strongholds.

Deliverance

At the beginning of this study, we read of several examples of deliverance at the hand of our mighty Savior, Jesus. There was the Jewish woman whom satan had bound for eighteen years and the Gadarene who wrestled emotionally. Nothing has changed today, except our own negative mindsets about questioning the reality of deliverance. Some of our infirmities (not all) and some of our emotional struggles (not all) can *still* be demonically induced. Even believers can be affected, just as the Jewish woman whom Jesus called "a daughter of Abraham," was afflicted.

We have made deliverance such an anomaly that we discount it or dismiss it as fanatical. Yet, I have personally seen people set free from demonic bondage through effective deliverance and will attest that it is very real and very necessary. Just as Jesus delivered a woman in the synagogue, deliverance is needed even in our churches. It is not something to hide from or to fear. Deliverance is part of walking as Jesus walked, and of doing the "greater things" than He did in His ministry (John 14:12).

Idolization

As we saw in the scriptures in I Corinthians and Deuteronomy, idol worship is tied to the demonic. Just as demons live with humans, they can also "attach" to physical objects like idols. Even in our hearts we can give undue attention to money, material things, to a career or occupation, or even to religion, and open a door to the demonic. Anything we "worship" with our hearts can become a false god or idol. God commands us to have no other god before Him, and for good reason. Therefore, part of our resisting the devil will automatically include allowing God to rid our hearts and homes of anything which takes precedence over Him or which is tied to the demonic.

Other Spiritual Weapons

In addition to the armor of God listed in Ephesians, there are other "weapons of our warfare" which are revealed to us in the Scriptures. Praise and "hiding" prayers are two of these valuable protections against our foe. Praise to our God is a weapon that routs the enemy! When we praise God, He will act on our behalf to do battle for us.

Though the "enemy" in these verses is the physical enemy of God's people, the principles of warfare in the natural can be applied to the spiritual realm. In the same way that the earthly tabernacle of Moses was a copy of the heavenly tabernacle, the physical can and often does, represent the spiritual (Hebrews 8:5).

> As they began to *sing and praise,* the Lord *set ambushes* against the men of Ammon and Moab and Mount Seir who were invading Judah, and they were defeated. (II Chronicles 20:22)

> May the *praise of God be in their mouths* and a *double-edged sword in their hands* . . . (Psalm 149:6)

> Every stroke the Lord lays on them with his punishing rod will be to the *music of tambourines and harps,* as he fights them in battle with the blows of his arm. (Isaiah 30:32)

The Holy Spirit teaches us about spiritual warfare through the lessons of the Bible, just as David writes:

> Praise be to the Lord my Rock, who *trains my hands for war, my fingers for battle.* He is my loving God and my *fortress,* my *stronghold* and my *deliverer,* my *shield,* in whom I take refuge. . . . (Psalm 144:1)

Hiding prayers are another valuable gift from God.[7] When we step out in active warfare, it is wise to then ask the Lord to hide us from the enemy's eyes, with scriptures like these:

> . . . *Hide me under the shadow of Your wings,* from the wicked who oppress me, from my deadly enemies who surround me. (Psalm 17:8-9)

> He who dwells in the *secret place* of the Most High Shall abide *under the shadow of the Almighty.* I will say of the Lord, "*He is my refuge and my fortress*; My God, in Him I will trust." (Psalm 91:1-2)

Being hidden by the Lord will keep us from attack, just as in the natural, being hidden from a real enemy of earthly warfare keeps a soldier from drawing fire in the middle of battle. As a practical demonstration of hiding prayers, many of the prayers in this book end with scriptures to "cover" our souls.

Other weapons to overcome, resist, and stand, include the blood of Jesus, as we "overcome by the blood of the Lamb." The Name of Jesus is also a powerful weapon in the mouths of the saints:

> The *name of the Lord* is a *strong tower*; the righteous *run to it and are safe.* (Proverbs 18:10)

> The seventy-two returned with joy and said, 'Lord, *even the demons submit to us in your name*.' (Luke 10:17)

This survey of our some of our weapons of warfare, both offensive and defensive, has been brief. Hopefully, it has been enough "food for thought" to encourage you to seek God for more understanding and discernment regarding our place as those who follow wholeheartedly our "Commander of the army of the Lord."

Closing Thoughts

As we learn to stand and resist, we will find not less peace, but *more* peace. Our peace will be in the midst of activity, since resisting requires energy, as does standing. It will not be a false peace of hiding in timidity, but a true peace of being hidden by the Lord.

We will find *rewards* for our efforts. As we learn to walk in our God-given authority we will be able to take home the "plunder" of the enemy (see earlier scripture). In many scriptures, plunder means the spoils of war. In Jesus' example, it was the plunder of the "strong man." Either way, we gain something for our efforts! We gain freedom and a growing sense of victory as we walk on this earth as Jesus walked, and do the works that He did.

If we are willing to submit ourselves to God and resist the devil, we will find ourselves in an exciting adventure of watching God's presence in our lives increase and expand. He will protect us by His great power and might as we are learning to stand. He will keep us safe from "all the power of the enemy," because He is MUCH bigger than the enemy, and He is on our side (Luke 10:19 and Jeremiah 10:11-12)!

Lord Jesus, I admit, this concept of spiritual warfare is one that my flesh may not like, yet I want to walk in all *Your truth.*[1] *Lead me out of error in every place where I have believed error and still my anxious heart, and guide me by Your Word.*

Father, wherever my family or I, or even my people have failed to stand against the enemy, I repent. In every place we have not resisted the devil as You have commanded us, forgive us. Forgive us for being afraid. Deliver us from all our fears, and make us bold and stouthearted.[2]

Putting on your armor:

I now choose to put on the belt of truth.[3] *Help me to walk in truth in every area of my life. I put on the* breastplate of Your righteousness *over my heart. Thank You that I have been made right in Your sight through the exchange that happened on the cross. I put on my feet* the preparation of the gospel of peace. *Fill me with Your peace, and take all my worries and anxieties on Your shoulders as I give them to You now: (give any worries to God that come to mind)* ____. *I take up the* shield of faith, *with which* I can extinguish all the fiery darts of the evil one. *Father, I know there are areas where I do not fully trust, but I give them to You and I believe You will preserve me, as You develop trust within my heart.*[4] *Thank You that You will complete what You have started in my life.*[5] *I put on the* helmet of salvation *over my mind. Thank You that through salvation You have delivered me from the power of darkness and have brought me*

into the inheritance of the saints in Your light. You have trans-
lated me into the kingdom of Your Son and I belong to You.[6] *I am*
precious in Your sight.[7] *Now, I take up the* sword of the Spirit,
which is the Word of God. *Teach me to use the Word as a sword,*
by Your Spirit. Show me Scriptures that will answer the ques-
tions of my mind and heart, and then show me how to use them,
as You guide me.

Bringing down strongholds:

If there are any generational strongholds in my life
concerning the fear of resisting the enemy, or the doubt of his
existence, I pull down these strongholds of the mind. I bind
every demonic attachment to these strongholds and by the
authority of the Name of Jesus, I forbid your operation in any
way: be silent and be still.

Jesus, take to the cross now, and put to death all
ancestrally inherited fear and deception. Teach me to stand and
to resist the devil so that I will able to walk in true peace. Show
me Your power over the enemy, and show me my authority in
You. Show me how to use Your keys of the Kingdom. Give me
great courage and wisdom, to fight by Your Spirit and not in my
own strength.[8] *Lead me to wise counselors who can teach me*
and train me.

Thank You for hearing me and for answering my prayers.
Thank You for loving me and for giving Yourself to me.[9] *Give*
Your angels charge over me and hide me now under the shadow
of Your wing, for I trust in You.[10]

In the Name of Jesus, Amen.

---

[1] John 16:13; [2] Psalm 138:3 and Psalm 34:4; [3] Ephesians 6:10-18; [4] II Timothy
4:18; [5] Philippians 1:6; [6] Colossians 1:12-13 and I Corinthians 6:20; [7] Isaiah
43:4; [8] Proverbs 21:31; [9] John 3:16; [10] Psalm 91:4,11.

Promises for you from I John 4:4 and John 10:29:

You are a dear and precious child to God. He is *in* you, as He has promised, and He is bigger and stronger than anybody or anything, anywhere in heaven or in earth. That is why He says *you* have already won over every spiritual foe, because He is inside you. He's also holding on to you, and absolutely *no one* can steal you away from Him. Relax in His care, and receive His firm and sure promise of protection over your life.

~ 15 ~

WORLDLY SORROW
AND UNBELIEF

Our Mennonite fellowship often sang a song called the "day of the week" song. As we sang through all the verses, "It was on a Monday, somebody touched me . . .," "It was on a Tuesday . . .," then "It was on a Wednesday . . .," and so on, each person in the congregation was to stand on the day of the week that they had received Christ as Savior. Everyone loved to sing this song because of the joy we experienced when we saw the whole fellowship gradually standing, verse after verse, happily acknowledging God's salvation in our lives.

One particular Sunday towards the end of the song, a man walked quickly up the aisle towards the pulpit and cried out to our pastor, "I don't have a day! I don't have a day!" Pat, the man who had no day of salvation, met Jesus right then and there in front of the whole church, and we all sang the song once more so we could celebrate with him. As he repented for his sins and received Christ, his joy overflowed and for the rest of his life, Pat was one of the most bubbly, positive people I have known.

Pat's salvation experience was one of godly sorrow for his sins. He had lived in the world and by the world, and had confessed his sinfulness. But when he repented and met Jesus, he received his new inheritance and his sonship as God's child. His repentance brought *joy*.

As we continue on through this chapter, remember that the outcome of our journey is also joy. God is a God of joy, and He brings us joy through our obedience (John 15:11). We will walk through our heritage and acknowledge that we have missed

the mark—we will tackle weighty thoughts - but we will return
to joy as our final destination.

Godly Sorrow

We turn now, to the subject of sorrow and to our long
Anabaptist heritage of suffering and persecution. The Bible talks
about two types of sorrow: godly sorrow and worldly sorrow.
One brings death, but the other leaves no regret or grief. Be-
cause of the sins done against us in the years of persecution,
Anabaptists have experienced both of these types of sorrow:

> *Godly sorrow* brings repentance that leads to salvation and
> **leaves no regret,** but *worldly sorrow* brings **death.**
> (II Corinthians 7:10)

> For the *sorrow which God gives* is the cause of salvation
> through a change of heart, in which there is **no reason for
> grief**: but the sorrow of the world is a **cause of death.** (*BBE*
> translation).

In order to be able to identify these two kinds of sorrow
in our ancestry, it is essential that we understand their biblical
meanings. So before we think about our own historical sorrows,
we'll take time to look at a few biblical examples.

Paul writes that the sorrow of the Corinthian church was
a godly sorrow. He mentions their responses to the sin of sexual
immorality which had been found in their brotherhood:
(I Corinthians 5:1-2)

> See what this godly sorrow has produced in you: what
> *earnestness,* what *eagerness* to clear yourselves, what *indig-
> nation*, what *alarm*, what *longing*, what *concern,* what
> *readiness* to see justice done. At every point you have proved
> yourselves to be innocent in this matter. (II Corinthians 7:11)

Both godly sorrow and worldly sorrow can create all of
these reactions. People may be indignant and alarmed and eager
to clear themselves whether they are sorrowing in a godly way

or in a worldly way. But only *one* sorrow leads to "salvation" and leaves no regret. The other leads to death. As we will discover, the difference between the two is in heart attitude, or focus.

Jesus sorrowed over sin in a godly way. The Bible calls Him a "man of sorrows and familiar with grief" (Isaiah 53:3). Obviously He never sinned, so He wasn't sorrowing for His own personal sins. But as He walked on earth, Jesus grieved over the sins of those around Him. He actually wept over the hardness of heart which kept the people of Jerusalem from receiving God's blessing:

> As (Jesus) approached Jerusalem and saw the city, he wept over it and said, 'If you, even you, had only known on this day *what would bring you peace*—but now it is hidden from your eyes. The days will come upon you when your enemies will build an embankment against you and encircle you and hem you in on every side. . . . They will not leave one stone on another, *because you did not recognize the time of God's coming to you.*' (Luke 19:41-44)

> O Jerusalem, Jerusalem, you who kill the prophets and stone those sent to you, how often I have *longed to gather your children together,* as a hen gathers her chicks under her wings, *but you were not willing.* (Matthew 23:37)

Jesus wept because the Jews did not want *relationship* with God. God *came* to them, but they missed His arrival. God *longed* to bring them to Himself tenderly as children, and softly as a hen hides her chicks, but they did not want Him. God *wanted* to bring them peace, but they couldn't see. Jesus cried because the Jews weren't interested in knowing God.

Godly sorrow is grief over how sin has affected *relationship with God.* Just as Jesus grieved because the Jews couldn't receive Him, godly sorrow for sin recognizes that God wants to come to us and care for us, but that sin has hindered fellowship with Him.

When the prophet Nathan came to King David and confronted him about his adulterous relationship with Bathsheba, David's immediate response was, "I have sinned against the Lord"

(II Samuel 12:13). Godly sorrow quickly caused an understanding in his heart of how his sin had affected God. In Psalm 51, where he repents of this grave sin, he says,

> **Against you, you only, have I sinned** and done what is evil in your sight, so that you are proved right when you speak and justified when you judge . . . Cleanse me with hyssop, and I shall be clean; wash me, and I shall be whiter than snow . . . **Do not cast me from your presence or take your Holy Spirit from me.** Restore to me the **joy of your salvation** and grant me a willing spirit, to sustain me. (Psalm 51:4-12)

David tells God, "You are the *only One* I have sinned against." He knew he had also sinned against Bathsheba, Uriah her husband, and others. But his main concern was how he had offended God. He did not want to be separated from Him, either by being cast out of His presence or by God's Spirit leaving Him.

Since Godly sorrow understands God's love, it causes us to repent *quickly* in order to be reconciled. When we see our sin, we will take immediate action so that our relationship with Him can be fully restored. We do not want anything to hinder our prayers as we talk with our heavenly Father (I Peter 3:7).

Restored to Joy

At the end of David's prayer was his cry for a restoration to joy. Because David knew God's character, he knew there was forgiveness. He knew God's ability to cleanse him, and he knew God's ability to restore him to the joy of salvation. Like David, when we repent, God will always cleanse us from sin and return us to relationship with the Father. Through Jesus' exchange at the cross, peace and joy come once again, because we know we are forgiven, just as David knew joy would return through being washed as white as snow.

That is why godly sorrow leaves *no regret*, but instead, brings joy. A wonderful example of this is found in the book of Nehemiah. Recently returned from Babylonian captivity, the people of Jerusalem gathered together as Ezra and the Levites read and explained the meaning of the book of the Law. Throughout the morning, the people wept and grieved as they listened:

> Then Nehemiah . . . Ezra . . . and the Levites . . . said to them all, 'This day is sacred to the Lord your God. *Do not mourn or weep.*' For all the people had been *weeping* as they listened to the words of the Law. Nehemiah said, 'Go and enjoy choice food and sweet drinks, and send some to those who have nothing prepared. This day is sacred to our Lord. *Do not grieve*, for the *joy of the Lord* is your strength.' The Levites calmed all the people, saying, 'Be still, for this is a sacred day. *Do not grieve.*' Then all the people went away to eat and drink, to send portions of food and to **celebrate with great joy**, because they now understood the words that had been made known to them. (Nehemiah 8:9-12)

Though the Scriptures do not actually say their grieving was over sin, the context of the passage indicates that this remnant who had been brought back to their homeland after seventy years of captivity, was grieving over their failure to fully obey the Law. They were weeping in response to its commands because they were *sorry*, as the King James translates the word *grieve*.

Seventy years prior, their ancestors had been removed from the land and transported to Babylon because they had broken covenant with God (Jeremiah 50:7). But now they had returned, as the Scriptures proclaimed and sought the Lord in tears:

> In those days, at that time,' declares the Lord, 'the people of Israel and the people of Judah together will **go in tears to seek the Lord** their God. They will **ask the way to Zion** and **turn their faces towards it**. They will come and bind themselves to the Lord in an everlasting covenant that will not be forgotten. (Jeremiah 50:4-5)

Nehemiah understood the Israelites' godly grief over their long separation from God. He recognized their sorrow was genuine and shared with them God's response to their grieving:

God called the day holy, because it was the day His people returned to Him with all their hearts.

After weeping for sin, came *joy*! Released from their sin through godly sorrow and repentance, the people were filled with *great joy* and *celebration*. Truly, the joy of the Lord was their strength because they had returned into God's presence! They had turned their faces towards God and bound themselves to Him, and went away to enjoy "choice foods and sweet drinks." As with the Israelites, godly sorrow will always restore us to relationship with our heavenly Father, and bring us into rejoicing.

Worldly Sorrow

Godly sorrow looks *Godward* in its emphasis. Its focus is on God's heart and on being restored to God. On the other hand, the focus of *worldly sorrow* is on **ourselves**. Worldly sorrow is *afraid of being harmed by sin*. When we sorrow in a worldly way, restoration of relationship with God is not our primary concern. Instead, we want to be relieved of the pain that sin causes.

Looking back on my own salvation experience at the age of twelve, I realize now that I experienced worldly sorrow for my sin. I had just heard a sermon about the horrors of hell and I was afraid of spending eternity in the lake of fire. As I "repented" of my sin, I was overwhelmingly concerned about my own safety from eternal *harm*. Although it is important to understand the reality of hell, I completely missed seeing the power of the cross. Instead of grasping God's love and restoration through Jesus' death, I only feared God's wrath. Rather than being grieved because my sin separated me from God, I asked Jesus into my heart because I *had to,* in order to avoid hell. There was a subtle, yet crucial twist to the attitude of my heart as I sorrowed with worldly sorrow about my sin, fearing my own harm rather than really returning to God.

After I was married I continued to walk in worldly sorrow, this time as it related to fearing someone else's harm.

Because we are human, when two people are married, each partner brings to the union areas of blessing and areas of imperfection. Soon after our wedding, I started judging my husband when I felt he was falling short of the mark (Romans 3:23). I began to try to "fix" him because I was *afraid of being hurt.* Though I didn't realize it, even my prayers for him were from fear rather than love. When fixing him didn't work or my prayers went unanswered, I stewed in resentment over having to be affected by the weaknesses I feared, all the while giving little thought to how my own weaknesses and sins were hurting him. My worldly sorrow could only focus on my own harm, rather than on how our sins affected our relationships with God.

Biblical Examples

There are many examples of this kind of worldly sorrow in the Bible. One is found in Cain's response to God after he murders Abel. When God confronts him about the murder, he lies. And when God tells him the consequences of his sin, rather than confessing or repenting, Cain is focused on his punishment:

> Cain said to the Lord, *'My punishment is more than I can bear.* Today you are driving me from the land, and I will be hidden from your presence; I will be a restless wanderer on the earth, and whoever finds me will kill me.' (Genesis 4:9-14)

Cain was worried about the effects of his sin on his own life. He was afraid of being killed by others, though he never repented of murdering Abel.

My *King James Bible* also references Judas as an example of one who sorrowed in a worldly way. After Jesus was condemned to death, Judas went to the chief priests and tried to undo his sin of betrayal. He was sorrowful and remorseful, but his sorrow did not lead him to cry out to God for cleansing. Rather, it caused such a hopeless, self-grieving about his sin that he went out and took his own life (Matthew 27:3-5, *KJV*). As the II Corinthian passage confirms, his worldly sorrow brought death.

For a more thorough study of worldly sorrow, here are some other Biblical examples: Amnon in II Samuel 13:2; Ahithophel in II Samuel 17:23; Rachel in Genesis 30:1; Esau in Hebrews 12:17; David's fighting men in I Samuel 30:6; and Jonah in Jonah 4:9.

The Sorrows Of A People Group

Worldly sorrow can be a stronghold which affects an entire people group, as it was for the Israelites who were delivered from four hundred years of cruel bondage in Egypt. As they neared the edge of the Promised Land, their sorrowful focus of fearing harm prevented them from being able to enter the "land flowing with milk and honey." They camped near Canaan and sent twelve men to spy out the land and bring back a report. When they returned, ten of the spies spread a bad rumor about the "giants" who lived there, declaring it would be impossible to fight them and win.

The Israelites quickly decided God was going to let them be destroyed:

> "... They raised their voices and *wept aloud.* All the Israelites *grumbled* against Moses and Aaron, and the whole assembly said to them, '*If only we had died* in Egypt! Or in this desert! Why is the Lord bringing us to this land *only to let us fall by the sword? Our wives and children will be taken as plunder.* Wouldn't it be *better for us to go back to Egypt?*' And they said to each other, 'We should choose a leader and go back to Egypt.'" (Numbers 14:1-4)

They wept aloud and grumbled, wishing they had died in Egypt or in the desert! Though God had promised to give them Canaan, they could not trust Him because they were so focused on their fears of the sinful inhabitants living in the Promised Land.

Worldly Sorrow And Unbelief

Worldly sorrow always partners with *unbelief,* which is one of the reasons it leads to death. You might say it is a *faithless sorrow,*[1] because it doesn't believe God is a good, rewarding God. Look at this verse which defines two important parts of our trust in God:

> And without faith it is impossible to please God, because anyone who comes to him must believe that he *exists* and that he *rewards* those who earnestly seek him. (Hebrews 11:6)

Believing that God *exists* **and** believing He is a *Rewarder* are both an essential part of faith. The Israelites knew God existed, but they didn't believe in the goodness of His character. When they cried out to return to slavery rather than face the giants, they were in essence saying to God, "We would rather be oppressed and enslaved (where we knew what to expect), than believe that you will help us overcome." In worldly sorrow, they accused God of bringing them to the land, only to be destroyed by their enemy's sword.

Trust In God's Character

If we do not really understand God's character as One who is *for us* and not against us, we will be unable to believe He is willing to help us in our time of need (Romans 8:31). God has promised that for those who love Him, He will work things out for *our* good:

> ...in **all things** God *works for the good of those who love him,* who have been called according to his purpose. (Romans 8:28)

He is able to take everything in our lives—even when others sin against us—and cause it to be for our benefit. He can take absolutely every sinful action of mankind that has been done against us and work out good in our lives.

Joseph was betrayed by his own brothers, sold as a slave, and spent years in prison after being wrongfully accused. But when the Lord used him mightily to save the land from a great famine, he explained that God had used his brothers' evil for good:

> But as for you, you **meant evil** against me; but **God meant it for good,** in order to bring it about as it is this day, to save many people alive. (Genesis 50:20, *NKJV*)

In the New Testament, Jesus declared that a man's blindness had been allowed in order to reveal God's works (John 9). He had been blind for his whole life, but one day God demonstrated His glory and healed him. The man testified fearlessly to the Pharisees who promptly threw him out of the synagogue, and when he saw Jesus, he worshipped.

God is able to use everything for our good. He used Joseph's prison years to build his character so he would walk in humility and forgiveness toward his brothers, and lead all of Egypt righteously. He used blindness in the life of the man born blind, so that when he was healed he did not fear man, but instead worshipped God. In our own heritage, God has used our forefathers' martyrdom as a great testimony both in their day and throughout history. They received a wonderful "welcome home" celebration, even as the true church of the Anabaptists helped to restore to Christendom part of what had been lost during the Dark Ages.

Our Own Heritage of Sorrow

As we have already read in chapter two of this book, our early forefathers walked in godly sorrow as they died bravely and loved fervently. They communed with God's Spirit and overcame every trial with joy. Soon-to-be-martyred husbands bid farewell to their wives. Mothers prepared for earthly separation from their children, lovingly admonishing them through prison letters to serve God all the days of their lives.[2] These loved their Savior more than mother or father, spouse, or children.

Our early forefathers knew God existed *and* that He was their *Rewarder.* Their trust in the goodness of God's character never wavered, though they suffered tremendously. Like Jesus, their godly sorrow *held fast* to His love. And just as Jesus endured because He saw the "joy set before Him," our early ancestors were able to endure triumphantly because they saw the joy of their eternal home with God (Hebrews 12:2). They died believing that what man meant for evil, God would use for good.

But gradually, the godly sorrow of the Anabaptists began to change to worldly sorrow. Our passion waned as we wearied of suffering. Our vision of the "joy set before us" became blurred by the pain we experienced. And when oppression continued through decade after decade, our relationship with our Heavenly Rewarder became less and less intimate, as we focused on survival here on earth, instead of on our eternal rewards.

What are the evidences of worldly sorrow in the lives of our own ancestors? In the hearts of the Israelites, it was evidenced by their grumbling and weeping; by their desire to run back to slavery; by their threats of stoning their leaders (verse 10); by their fears and their unbelief (verse 9). Just as the outward actions and words of the Israelites demonstrated their inward hearts, we need to look at the outward actions and words of our ancestors to see their inward heart responses as the persecution years unfolded.

The primary evidence of our worldly sorrow—*a sorrow which is focused on ourselves as we are harmed by sin*—is our change from being passionate about witnessing, to choosing separation and withdrawal from society. If we had been able to continue seeing the sin of others through godly sorrow—*a sorrow that is concerned about relationship with God*—we would have remained steadfast in our witness. Though we suffered, our focus would have stayed on the *lost* and on their need to hear the good news about our Savior's love. Our witness about our Father would have continued *even* to the point of death, because of our anticipation of being in heaven with our Rewarder. But we chose silence because in our weariness, we had begun to lose sight of God's heart.

Fearing Sin's Harm

Our focus then turned inward toward ourselves, and our sorrow turned worldly. We started being concerned about protection from the harm of others' sins: not only our persecutors' sins from the *outside*, but also the effects of sin from the *inside*. As we began to separate and seclude ourselves and focus on our own needs, we became preoccupied with the sins of the brethren.

From the very start as Anabaptists, there was a strong emphasis on holiness in the brotherhood (more on this in a later chapter). In light of the incredible apostasy which existed in the State Churches, our early forefathers' concerns of having a pure church were justified. Being a *pure* church as the *true church* was essential. That is why *discipleship* automatically followed a new convert's baptism.

New believers were welcomed into the fellowship and taught the ways of Christianity. They were loved, cared for, and corrected as needed. Clear lines of right and wrong were established concerning things like drunkenness, laziness, honesty, morality, and other issues which had virtually been ignored in the State Churches. The goal of the early Anabaptists was to have a holy church where God could dwell by His presence,

> . . . a covenant community whose apprehension was one of embodying **God's presence** and **demonstrating His grace** in everyday life . . .[3]

But in our worldly sorrow, our motivations for addressing sin in our midst changed from its effect on *relationship*, to how it might *cause harm* and defile us. We began setting up guidelines to protect our communities from sin's corruption, but without the proper perspective on relationship, our attempts to differentiate between what was acceptable and what was not acceptable led to all kinds of trouble.

In many regions, divisions occurred. Others experienced a falling away of their members or adaptations of strict doctrines.[4] In France, church discipline expanded from matters of moral purity to include shunning people based on how they dressed or wore their hair.[5] In the Netherlands, divisions occurred in the East Friesland congregations over minor differences such as whether to pray silently or audibly.[6] Splits happened in other congregations over disagreements on how strictly to apply the ban and shunning.[7]

Peter Hoover writes that as their focus shifted, the rules of the Dutch Anabaptists increased:

> As the Anabaptists of the Netherlands turned their energies to *enforcing their authority and the rules they had made upon one another*, those who had persecuted them relaxed . . . instead of warning people against them (the Anabaptists) *they joined in making fun of their many divisions and small-minded rules. . . .* It was true. **As their focus shifted from following Christ to submitting to brotherhood authority**, the rules of the Dutch Anabaptists multiplied. Every area of life *from the kind of tools and trades* one used in making a living to the *exact style of clothing, shoes, hats, and haircuts* became important.[8]

Returning to Godly Sorrow

In our churches today, we *are* to be concerned about sin. Paul writes that godly sorrow worked into the hearts of the Corinthians a diligence to deal with sin, an eagerness to become clean, and a holy indignation. But, if we approach sin—including the sins of others—from any place other than how it affects relationship with God—we are walking in worldly sorrow. If we focus on how sin will harm our church or ourselves, our worldly sorrow and unbelief will cause regret, and our fellowships will lack the peace and joy of God (see earlier scriptures).

We do have directives in the Scriptures about dealing with sin. But, if we take those directives and enforce them with worldly sorrow, we will only *cause* harm, rather than preventing harm.

By responding fearfully without sensing God's heart toward the sin and the sinner, we will do much more damage than perhaps even the sin itself does in our midst. Though "tough" measures may sometimes be necessary if someone is not willing to obey God, godly sorrow will always do what is best for the relationships that are involved.

With the unrepentant and arrogant Pharisees, Jesus was firm. He called them a "brood of vipers" and warned them of their spiritual peril. But with many sinners, His "mercy triumphed over judgment" (James 2:12-13). An adulterous woman who should have been stoned was forgiven and released from punishment (John 8). Jesus healed a paralytic by forgiving his sins (Matthew 9). And He ate with Zacchaeus, the tax collector, who then repented and made amends for his sins. We see demonstrated through Jesus' life, a response to sin as the Father directed Him in each situation, according to the needs of the people who were involved.

Jesus chose two commandments which were to be set above all the other commandments in the Bible. The first commandment is to *love God with all our heart, soul and mind* (Matthew 22:35-40). The second is to love others just as we love ourselves. He chose the love of God as most important, and the love for others as second, because above all, God cherishes *relationship.*

Today's Joy

A Mennonite pastor friend of ours pointed out that in many of today's more conservative Anabaptist churches, there is a prayer uttered most Sundays which includes something along these lines:

> "Dear Lord, we thank you that we can gather today in freedom, unmolested, and undisturbed by the authorities."

Why are we still thinking about being harmed by "the authorities?" It has been several hundred years since the time of persecution, yet we regularly offer thankful prayers that we are no longer being pursued. We pray these kinds of prayers, because our worldly sorrow has caused us to focus on fearing sin's harm, as we doubt God's character.

One morning in my time with God few years ago, I heard God saying that the covering of the glory of the Lord had been lifted off the Anabaptist people. The covering He was speaking of was *joy*. He continued to impress on my heart that He longed to restore joy, so that we may once again experience the Lord's *delight* in us, as Zephaniah prophesied:

> The Lord thy God in the midst of thee is mighty; he will save, he will *rejoice over thee with joy*; he will rest in his love, he will *joy over thee with singing*. (Zephaniah 3:17, *KJV*)

When we turn honestly and humbly to God with our sin, His pleasure in us as sons and daughters stays strong. He knows we have set our hearts and minds to love Him, and He responds with joyful passion! He sings over us! As we learn to walk in *godly* sorrow when sin occurs, we'll return to joy, because GOD is in our midst!

> On that day *you will not be put to shame for all the wrongs you have done to me*, because I will remove from this city those who rejoice in their pride . . . I will leave within you the *meek and humble, who trust in the name of the Lord*. The remnant of Israel will do no wrong; they will speak no lies, nor will deceit be found in their mouths. They will eat and lie down and *no one will make them afraid*." *Sing*, O Daughter of Zion; *shout aloud*, O Israel! *Be glad and rejoice with all your heart*, O Daughter of Jerusalem! The Lord has *taken away your punishment, he has turned back your enemy*. The Lord, the King of Israel, is with you; *never again will you fear any harm*. (Zephaniah 3:11-15)

The humble trust in God, and *no one makes them afraid*. God has taken away our punishment and turned back our enemy. He is with us, so we don't need to *fear any harm*. We are *glad* and we *rejoice with all our hearts* because we are His children and He is our God!

Thank you, Father, that You are my Rewarder.[1] *You are good and You are delighted with me, even as I turn back to You in every place where I've missed the mark and sinned.*

Wherever my family and I have doubted Your good character, please forgive us. I repent for every time we have not believed You are our Rewarder. I am sorry, Lord. Please forgive us and establish our faith in You.

I also repent for any worldly sorrow my family or I have entered into, either because of our heritage or because of the hardships in our lives. Show us how to come to You with godly sorrow. Help us to pour out our hearts so we can receive Your comfort.[2] *Take away from my family and me all self pity and replace it with trust.*

If our family has inherited a stronghold of worldly sorrow or a stronghold of unbelief to cause us to doubt Your character, I tear down those strongholds of my mind now. In Jesus' name, I bind all spirits of worldly sorrow and unbelief which have become attached to me or my family through our heritage, and I forbid your operation in our lives.

Father, You know me completely. You know where my trust is lacking. I give You these places in my soul and ask You, restore my spiritual eyesight and build faith in me to see you as my Heavenly Father. Quiet me with Your love and restore to me great joy![3] *Thank You that You sing over me. Thank You that I bring You joy! I rejoice too, that I'm Yours. I'm glad that You are mine!*[4]

Give my family and me joy.[5] *Cleanse us completely, washing us with Your blood, and restoring to us what has been lost through the years.*[6] *Turn back our enemy, and*

help us to know You are with us, so we never again fear
any harm.⁷ Thank You, God, that You are our hiding place
and You are mighty to save.⁸
In the Name of Jesus, Amen.

---

¹ Hebrews 11:6; ² II Corinthians 1:4; ³ Zephaniah 3:17; ⁴ Song of Solomon
2:16; ⁵ Nehemiah 8:10 and Hebrews 12:2; ⁶ Joel 2:25; ⁷ Zephaniah 3:15; ⁸ Psalm
32:7 and Zephaniah 3:17.

For another example of how worldly sorrow has affected a people group in
the Americas, read the article, "Unveiling the Queen of Heaven's Oppression
of First Nations People," by Jim Chosa. It was printed in *Global Prayer News*
(Vol. 2, #2, April-June 2001), a newsletter from Global Harvest Ministries,
P.O. Box 63060 Colorado Springs, CO 80962-3060.

Promises for you from Psalm 149 *(KJV)*:

God enjoys you! He finds so much pleasure in knowing
you. He is delighted with you! When He saved you, He gave you
a crown of beauty. He wants you to sing for joy because He has
honored you! Praise God, and be glad! Rejoice!

EMBITTERMENT
AND COMFORT

God is a Comforter. He loves to meet us as our heavenly Father when we run to Him with our needs, our frustrations, or our hurting hearts. In all our troubles, He calls us to His side:

> Praise be to the God and Father of our Lord Jesus Christ, the *Father of compassion* and the **God of all comfort**, who **comforts us in all our troubles**, so that we can comfort those in any trouble with the comfort we ourselves have received from God. For just as the sufferings of Christ flow over into our lives, so also **through Christ our comfort overflows.** (II Corinthians 1:3-5)

The word "comfort" is translated, *"a calling near"* or a *"summons,"* or to *"call to one's side."*[1] Our compassionate Father draws us near to Himself in the midst of every situation of life. He scoops us up into His arms and holds us close, and we suddenly find all the strength we need for the circumstances we're facing. He is the God of *all* comfort, who calls out to us!

Embitterment or Comfort

One of the opposites of answering God's call to come near and receive His loving comfort, is *embitterment*. In this passage, the Israelites would not respond to God's call to come near. Instead, they hardened their hearts and turned away from Him out of their embitterment:

> So, as the Holy Spirit says: 'Today, if you **hear his voice**, do not **harden your hearts** as you did in the **rebellion**, (embitterment) during the time of testing in the desert. . . . See to it, brothers, that none of you has a **sinful, unbelieving heart that turns away from the living God.** But encourage one another daily, as long as it is called Today, so that none of you may be **hardened by sin's deceitfulness.** We have come to share in Christ if we hold firmly till the end the confidence we had at first. As has just been said: 'Today, if you *hear his voice,* **do not harden your hearts as you did in the rebellion.**' (embitterment) (Hebrews 3:7-15)

The word *rebellion* in this passage is translated from the Greek as, *"embitterment."*[2] Embitterment is defined even more completely as *irritation, exasperation or provocation.*[3] Because of four hundred years of hard toil, suffering and pain, the Israelites had become irritated at God. They were exasperated that He had allowed them to be enslaved. They were provoked at Him because of the whippings, cruelty and the hatred of the Egyptians. They were *bitter* towards their Maker for all they had suffered, and they had hardened their hearts to His voice.

In a sense, the words comfort and embitterment are biblical opposites. An embittered person *turns away* from God in irritation, but the one who receives His comfort *turns to* Him and answers His summons to come near. The Israelites turned away from God in the midst of their suffering (verse 12), but if they had turned to Him and poured out their grief, they would have received all the comfort they needed to go through their trials. Their eyes would have joyfully remained on their Rewarder and their comfort would have *overflowed*—spilled over to excess—through God (II Corinthians 1:5) .

No matter how difficult our circumstances, if we will turn *towards* God, He will bring us through in victory even if we are tested severely. Perhaps the most profound scriptural example is Jesus' supplication in the garden of Gethsemane, just before His crucifixion. The Bible tells us He was overwhelmed with sorrow, even to the point of death:

> He took Peter, James and John along with him, and he began to be deeply distressed and troubled. 'My soul is *overwhelmed with sorrow to the point of death*,' he said to them. 'Stay here and keep watch.' Going a little farther, he fell to the ground and prayed that if possible the hour might pass from him. (Mark 14:33-35)

Yet, even as He faced the most excruciating suffering a man could possibly face, Jesus was made able by pouring out His heart to the Father:

> In the days of his flesh, Jesus offered up *prayers and supplications*, with *loud cries and tears*, to him who was able to save him from death, and *he was heard* for his godly fear. (Hebrews 5:7, *RSV*)

He shared all of the sorrow in His heart through prayers of "loud cries and tears," and God answered Him. Jesus turned *towards* the Father and poured out His heart, and the Father sent an angel to give Him strength. Through the strength He received, Jesus kept His eyes on the "joy set before Him," rather than giving into fear (Hebrews 12:2). And as He kept His focus, He "scorned the shame" of the cross and came through in complete and total victory.

Seeking Protection

Several years ago, as I was taking a walk in the fields near our house, God spoke to my heart and lovingly rebuked me for being my own protector. I had turned *away* from God, erecting a guard between myself and the Lord. I felt unsafe with Him, because I had not understood His purposes for some of the things He had allowed in my life. I had also erected a guard over and around my heart to keep people at a safe distance, because the things God had allowed, had occurred through the hands and actions of human beings.

The guard God was speaking to me about came from suspicion concerning His trustworthiness and the trustworthiness of people. God showed me I was not to be my own protector, but that *He* was to be my Protector. I repented, and asked Him to teach me how to begin opening up my heart to Him and to others, purposing from that point on, I would trust Him to be the One who would keep me safe.

The Scriptures speak of the difference between protecting ourselves rather than relying on God to protect us:

> Who among you fears the Lord and obeys the word of his servant? *Let him who walks in the dark, who has no light, trust in the name of the Lord and rely on his God.* But now, all you who *light fires and provide yourselves with flaming torches*, go, walk in the light of your fires and of the torches *you* have set ablaze. This is what you shall receive from my hand: *You will lie down in torment.* (Isaiah 50:10-11)

> Thus says the Lord: "*Cursed* is the man who *trusts in man* and makes *flesh his strength,* whose heart departs from the Lord. For he shall be like a shrub in the desert, and shall not see when good comes, but *shall inhabit the parched places in the wilderness*, in a salt land which is not inhabited. (Jeremiah 17:5-6, *NKJV*)

Isaiah writes that even when we walk in the darkness, we are still to trust in God. When we have no light of understanding and cannot see the path for our lives, God still asks us to rely on Him, rather than on ourselves. If we try to create our own answers through our own abilities, we will only end up in torment and wander around in a spiritual wilderness. Trusting in our own strength and our own light will bring about a curse instead of blessing.

Anabaptist Protection

It was as our Anabaptist forefathers chose to separate from society in order to be spared from persecution, that they were making the choice to "light their own torches" of safety and protection. Using *seclusion* as a security measure, we experienced a gradual, overall withdrawal into closed communities that functioned mainly apart from society. No longer reaching out to others around us, we began relying only on ourselves.

These changes almost seem normal to us as we look back at our heritage. After all, doesn't it stand to reason that a persecuted people *would* withdraw? Yet, for the early Anabaptists, that was not the case. They continued to trust that God would see them through even in the midst of great suffering. Their hearts felt safe and protected by the Lord whether He allowed them to experience physical pain or physical blessing.

Our self-protection as a people revealed that our trust in God's protection had been strained and even broken. By the time our ancestors pulled away from fulfilling the witness of the Great Commission, they had already *pulled away* from God in their hearts. On the inside, our ancestors judged God to be unsafe. On the outside they protected themselves from the very people they were called to love and evangelize.

The Scriptures say that it is out of the overflow of the heart that the mouth *speaks* (Matthew 12:34). As we turned away from God, our attitudes changed from trust to questioning, from peace to anxiety, and from joy to worldly sorrow. We stopped speaking about God to others, because the "overflow" of our spiritual passion had begun to change to an "ethnic religion" (chapter 12). Our brotherly love slowly turned to division and infighting (chapters 15 and 20). In our embitterment, we responded to others with attitudes which were already residing in our hearts towards God.

Turning away from God internally, these men and women still served Him, just as the Israelites still served God in their embitterment. But there was a subtle change of attitude which gradually caused inner passion and the inner "flame" for God to wane.

Comfort And The Heart

If we have turned away from God and become embittered, we will not be able to hear or respond to Him when He calls us near. Though He is the Father of compassion and the God of all comfort, His mercy will be unable to reach our hearts because we have rejected the *Mercy-Giver* Himself. Unable to receive comfort, our faith will become less alive and our heart will grow less supple. Without comfort, our hearts can actually become hardened, as this Scripture indicates:

> But **encourage** one another daily, as long as it is called Today, so that none of you may be **hardened by sin's deceit-fulness**. . . .Today, if you hear his voice, **do not harden your hearts** as you did in the rebellion (embitterment) (Hebrews 3:13,15)

The English word *encourage* is the same root word for *comfort* used in the earlier passage from II Corinthians.[4] God tells us to comfort or call each other near on a daily basis, so our hearts don't grow hard and become open to deception through sin. Receiving comfort from both God and man helps to keep our hearts softened and firmly planted in the truth.

There are so many ramifications to the embitterment that set into the hearts of parents, children, and grandchildren during the years of persecution, as we will discover in the remainder of this book. Because we retreated from God's comfort in the midst of our suffering, the circumstances of life became unbearable. Worldly sorrow set in as we grieved over our misfortunes and oppressions, apart from the God of all comfort.

But the most devastating effect of embitterment is that eventually, it prevented our hearts from being able to receive deeply of God's love. Geri Keller, a retired Reformed State Church pastor who has been reaching out to Anabaptists with reconciling love, writes that love only reaches hearts which have remained vulnerable, just as God has been vulnerable with us:

> Love can only be real if it is willing to be vulnerable. *Whoever chooses to be **self-protective**, in order to avoid being hurt, **cannot receive love** and cannot give love himself.* God is vulnerable; He made Himself vulnerable by entering into a covenant with the Hebrew people . . . an eternal, irre-vocable covenant. God made Himself vulnerable in the

person of Jesus of Nazareth, . . . delivering Himself into the
hands of man. . . . God made Himself utterly vulnerable by
pouring out His Holy Spirit into our hearts . . . willing to
dwell in us, amidst everything that is still in rebellion against
Him . . . and . . . that is hurting and revolting.[5]

It is not simply because of our "Germanic" roots that many
Anabaptists are a "stoic" people. There is a deeper reason why
we do not easily share our true inner feelings. There is a reason
why we are so reserved in relating to God and to other people.
There is a reason why our worship does not explode with the
joy of the Lord and the praise of our Father. We have protected
ourselves and become invulnerable. We need to let God soften
our hearts.

Over time, through strongholds of thought and through
our corporate embitterment, our hearts hardened. One Mennonite bishop has commented that among certain groups of
Anabaptists, he has repeatedly heard this unsettling question:
"Has God forgotten us?" The answer is a resounding "No"! He
has not forgotten us: it is we who have turned away. God has
longed to be our Comforter and to give us His great affection,
and we have grieved Him because we have not been able to
receive the fullness of His love in our cold, dulled hearts.

He Will Give Us A New Heart

Yet God promises, if we will turn back to Him wherever
we have turned away in mistrust or in embitterment, He will be
there to meet us. In His great love, He will give us a new heart
that is restored to the same passion for Him that our forefathers
felt and lived:

> I will give you a *new heart* and put a *new spirit* within you;
> I will take the *heart of stone* out of your flesh and give
> you a *heart of flesh*. I will put *My Spirit within you*
> and cause you to walk in My statutes, and you will
> keep My judgments and do them. (Ezekiel 36:26,27,
> *NKJV*)

God is revealed in the Scriptures as One whose softened heart *feels much passion* towards us. As His children, we're made in His image to also feel passionately. As we return to Him, He will give us a heart that is able to express fervent emotion: a softened heart that laughs loudly, shouts freely, grieves fully, weeps openly, rejoices greatly, is angry righteously, and is boldly courageous: Psalm 149:5; Hosea 11:3-10; Psalm 100:1; Isaiah 35:4; John 11:33-37; Zephaniah 3:14; John 2:14-17; and many, many Psalms. Where we have had a heart like a stone, He will give us a heart of flesh; a heart that is pliable. He will put *Himself* in us, and love us fervently, until we are able to love as He has loved.

Heavenly Father, You are my Comforter. Thank You for calling me near. Thank You that I can tell You every-thing.[1] Help me to learn to run to You every time I feel sorrow or pain and to pour out all that's within my heart.

Forgive me when I have protected myself rather than relying on You to be my Protector. I repent for the times I have said in my heart or aloud, that I would only trust myself. I now reject those words and break their hold in my life, through Jesus' Name. Bring them to no effect through Your death and through Your blood.

From now on, be my only Protector. Help me to trust in You and to learn to trust people around me. Cause me to know I am safe in You in all circumstances. Show me when I need to be vulnerable, and help me to open my heart to You and to others, as You give me wisdom.

I confess every time when I have turned away from You because I have been embittered. I also confess the embitterment of my fathers and of my family. Heavenly Father, forgive us where we have rejected Your love and

Your comfort. Forgive us for hurting You by turning away. Heal our hearts, that we may once again hear Your calls to come and be with You.

Soften every part of my heart that is like stone, and give me a new heart that feels deeply, as You feel deeply. Show me how to express my feelings to You and to others, and put a new spirit within me.[2]

Forgive my sins and the sins of my fathers. Cleanse us of our hard hearts and replace them with hearts that are soft and pliable. Wash my heritage by Your blood, and wash the heritage of our people by Your clean water.[3]

Father, draw me near to Yourself.[4] Show me how to come to You each day to receive Your comfort. Give me ears to hear You calling me near. Thank You for hearing my prayer and for answering me. Thank You for Your love. I love You, my Deliverer and my Safe Dwelling.[5]

[1] Psalm 62:8; [2] Ezekiel 36:26; [3] Ezekiel 36:25-27; [4] Hebrews 10:22; [5] Psalm 4:8.

Promises to you from your Father—(Psalm 86:5-7,15)

Because you call to God, He overflows with love for you. His love to you abounds, and is plentiful and abundant! He hears you, especially when you cry for mercy. Because you call out to Him when you are in trouble, He always answers you. He feels compassion toward you, and He is faithfully devoted to you. He loves you!

BITTERNESS
TOWARDS AUTHORITY

In a small gathering of ancient times, Christian brotherhood blossomed like a rose in the desert of the State Church systems. Spiritual life flourished among this enthusiastic group of young Bible students who had a growing hunger for spiritual truth.

Reformer Ulrich Zwingli was a spiritual father to at least two of the students—Conrad Grebel and Felix Manz—whom he had led into relationship with Christ.[1] For a period of time, these were Ulrich's "close" and "most intimate fellow fighters" in the cause of bringing biblical reform to the State Church.[2] Conrad was:

> ... proud to stand at Zwingli's side in his great reform work,
> and grateful to God for the mighty strides which Zwingli
> was leading the governmental authorities to take.[3]

Ulrich Zwingli returned their admiration. He was proud of his spiritual sons and was especially close to Conrad, holding him in high esteem and great respect.[4] Counting them as men of integrity, he had planned to eventually give both Conrad and Felix teaching positions at the great Grossmünster church in Zurich.[5]

But, within a little over a year, their discussions over Church doctrine and Scripture became heated. Disagreements soon turned tense as they began to draw lines of defense in the sand, and the blossom of brotherhood began to die for lack of nurture. Discussions to resolve their differences failed, as

Zwingli accused them of "resorting to abuse already at the second conference," and Felix Manz complained that Zwingli and his colleagues wouldn't hear them or let them speak, but "choked one's speech in his throat."[6]

Ulrich Zwingli asked Grebel to focus on the places where they all agreed rather than emphasizing the issues of dissent:

> . . . Zwingli called out to Grebel that in the things essential to salvation (justification, Christ, faith) they agreed. Why then still wrangle over incidentals? . . . In conclusion, Zwingli begs Grebel and his associates to work on themselves and get rid of their spiritual pride, but to leave the difficult office of teaching and reproof to the pastors.[7]

Unable to reconcile, the spiritual father and his sons gradually grew apart over opinions on the way reforms were to occur, as well as over doctrinal differences. Grebel and Manz believed Zwingli was compromising biblically, and Zwingli "felt disappointed and hurt by what seemed like arrogance . . ." in his sons.[8] Grebel, who took a stronger, narrower interpretation of the Scriptures than Zwingli,[9] wrote bitterly to his brother-in-law, Vadian, that:

> . . . the leading theologians of Zurich had set the Word of God 'on its head, trampled it under foot, and put it into slavery,' . . .[10]

Author Fritz Blanke, agreeing with Harold Bender's assessment of Grebel, writes that Conrad tended towards legalism in his interpretation of Scriptures. He adds that Zwingli said Grebel's urgency came from a place of being "anxious."[11]

Zwingli and Grebel *both* wanted a reform of abuses which had been passed down through the rule of the State Catholic Church. But Conrad wanted an immediate and complete change, whereas Zwingli believed change would be better accomplished gradually, as the people were instructed in the Word of God.[12] The father believed the sons were being impatient and the sons felt the father was not going all the way in his calls for reform.

Things between them turned sour as the division widened. Blanke writes that:

> Grebel complained that . . . they, the 'renewers' (Grebel and the others) had been decried from the pulpits as *knaves and devils* who had disguised themselves as angels. But on the other hand, we also find in Grebel's letter *very harsh judgments* on Zwingli and the other personalities in the Reformation. They are accused of arrogating to themselves virtually papal power over the evangelical Christians. In one place they are even referred to as corrupters of the Scriptures.[13]

Stalls in private discussions led to public debates before the town council of Zurich. The council sided with Ulrich Zwingli and effectively sealed the family division between the Reforming father and his Anabaptist children for the next four hundred and seventy-five years.[14]

Less than a year after the third and final debate, Felix Manz was drowned for his faith in the Limmat River in Zurich. How had their unity turned so quickly to anger and impatience on both sides, and finally to persecution by the Reformers? We may never know all the answers to this difficult question until eternity overtakes time, but we may be certain the effects of this division and others like it between the spiritual "fathers and their sons" have been consequentially long term.

Concerning the heart responses of the spiritual sons, one historian quotes our forefathers:

> The Anabaptists . . . *nourished the most bitter resentment* toward those who had refused to go the whole way on the New Testament pattern and now purposed to persecute those who did. They called Zwingli '*more false than the Old Pope,*'[15] . . . and 'the *Zurich popular preachers the true anti-Christs.*'[16]

Zwingli's attitude changed as well. "Sorely troubled by his former associates," he responded by writing "bitterly" against them, calling them "opponents on the left."[17] In writings and in sermons, he accused the Anabaptists of all sorts of immorality and licentiousness, writing unfounded reports based on hearsay.[18]

A Spiritual Division

Not every Anabaptist is descended from these young men who first admired their Reformer "father," or from the other Swiss Brethren who followed in their footsteps. However, we can safely say that most of our early forefathers were greatly influenced by Martin Luther, Zwingli, and even by John Calvin. We have already affirmed in previous chapters that in one sense, Luther and the Reformers were our spiritual fathers, since it was reading and pondering their revolutionary writings which inspired many of our first ancestors to search for biblical truths as they began to examine the doctrines of the State Catholic Church.

It follows then, as the first wave of persecution was meted out by these Reformers, that the Anabaptists felt betrayed. When our forefathers experienced suffering and torture from their hands, they must have felt like the Israelite woman who cried out to the Israelite army as it laid siege against her Israelite city:

> I am among the peaceable and faithful in Israel. You seek to destroy a city and a mother in Israel. *Why* would you *swallow up the inheritance of the Lord?* (II Samuel 20:19)

Harsh verdicts were handed down from both State Churches all over Europe. Catholics and Reformers who had once taught us and led us spiritually no longer considered us "family."[19] Instead, we were worse than outcasts, deemed unfit and unworthy of life. We were labeled as dangerous heretics who were to be snuffed out by execution. Some of the Reformers actually taught that torture and death should be more intense and cruel for heretics like the Anabaptists, than for other offenders such as thieves, murderers, and the like.[20]

Zwingli's eventual hard-line condemnation of his former followers typified the increased hatred of the Lutherans[21] as well as the Calvinists.[22] The lies, curses, and attitudes of Ulrich Zwingli, of Martin Luther, and of John Calvin, towards the Anabaptists were carnal and ungodly. Their judgments along with those of the State Catholic Church, were unjust and unrighteous. They treated our ancestors cruelly and abominably, and with today's hindsight we understand that the atrocities practiced against our ancestors by their generations were heinous.

Attitudes Of The Heart

There is, however, a particular deep issue of the heart which must be addressed as we look at *our sides* of the historic separations which occurred from the State Churches. As a people group, this heart issue has affected our ability to trust. It has also affected our relationship with present day spiritual and physical fathers on earth, and our relationship with our spiritual Father in heaven. It has played a role in the historic divisions and splits between Anabaptist denominations. It is the issue of *rebellion.*

None of us likes to hear that our heritage may have carried strains of rebellion. Nor do we want to consider that rebellion may be a factor in our history of divisiveness. But, if confession enables healing (James 5:16), perhaps it is a good idea to at least consider whether there are rebellious heart responses which have become a part of us, passed down as strongholds through the generations. It is with this goal of healing that we will consider our corporate attitudes of the heart.

We have all been disciplined by our earthly fathers. I remember times when I was being punished by my own father that I became very angry inside, thinking and muttering things which ought not to be entertained by a child, about her father. In some of those situations I took those feelings and held onto them in my heart as unforgiveness, in response to my father's discipline.

We have already looked at this scripture which reminds us that we cannot allow bitterness to be planted in our souls (chapter 11):

> See to it that no one misses the grace of God and that *no bitter root grows up* to cause trouble and defile many. (Hebrews 12:15)

It is this kind of unforgiveness that we tuck away into our hearts which creates "soil" where a root of bitterness can grow. The Greek meaning of the word *bitter* in this scripture has to do with a sharp, *pungent acridity,* and even *poison.*[23] If we physically eat a plant that is poisonous, we may get very sick or even die. In the same way, ingesting unforgiveness into our souls sets into us a bitter heart attitude that "defiles" not only ourselves, but "many" around us.

Our heart responses to being disciplined by a father figure can be especially negative if we feel our discipline is unjust or unrighteous. For example, if there were times when we were punished instead of the sibling or neighbor who really should have been punished—but Dad just wouldn't believe us when we tried to tell him the truth—the bitterness of our hearts can be established even more deeply, if we were unable to forgive our father's injustice.

Bitterness Towards Authority

If bitterness is set into our hearts through our unforgiveness, it can lead to rebellion. *When we hold bitterness against the authority figures in our lives, it is called* **rebellion.**

> For *rebellion* is as the sin of witchcraft . . . (1 Samuel 15:23a, *KJV*)

The context of this verse is King Saul's rebellion against God, our ultimate authority. The word *rebellion* in this verse is actually translated as *bitterness.* Rebellion is given as the figurative translation, but bitterness is the literal meaning.[24] Bitter rebellion against God and against our earthly leaders is such a serious thing to God that He equates it with practicing the worship of the demonic (witchcraft). When we are bitter towards authorities, we are opening ourselves up to all sorts of evil.

The cost for a bitter complaint and rebellion against authorities is great. In the Bible, Miriam was offended by her brother Moses' marriage to a foreigner and merely "complained" about his spiritual authority. The Lord considered it rebellion and chastised her with leprosy. She died about a month later (Numbers 12:1 and Numbers 20:1). Korah accused Moses, his spiritual leader, of exalting himself. He and his family were swallowed alive by the earth for their bitterly rebellious accusations (Numbers 16).

We are to obey and honor our fathers and mothers so that our lives may go well (Ephesians 6:1-3). We are also commanded to obey those in authority over us and to treat them with *respect* and *honor,* both in the church and in society in general (Hebrews 13:17; I Thessalonians 5:12-13):

> Submit yourselves *for the Lord's sake* to **every authority** *instituted among men:* whether to the king, as the supreme authority, or to governors . . . *Show proper respect to everyone:* Love the brotherhood of believers, fear God, **honor** the king. (I Peter 2:13-14,17)

> But **even if you should suffer for what is right**, you are blessed. . . . Always be prepared to give an answer to everyone who asks you to give the reason for the hope that you have. **But do this with gentleness and respect,** keeping a clear conscience. . . . (I Peter 3:14-17)

Even when we "suffer for what is right" we are to always demonstrate respect and to honor others, and especially those in authority over us, whether they are a righteous authority or an unrighteous authority.

We *are* given permission in Scriptures to "be angry and sin not," but in the very next sentence we are told not to let the sun go down on our anger (Ephesians 4:26). In other words, we are to release the anger we feel rather than hold onto it. God knows anger occurs at injustice. He does not count that anger as sin. But, when that when anger *remains*, it "gives the devil a foothold" as *bitterness* grows in our hearts (verse 27). A few verses later, Paul shows us how we should properly let go of our anger:

> Let all **bitterness**, and *wrath*, and *anger*, and *clamor*, and *evil speaking, be put away from you*, with all *malice*: And *be ye* **kind** one to another, **tenderhearted**, **forgiving** one another, even as God for Christ's sake hath forgiven you. Be ye therefore followers of God, as dear children; And **walk in love**, as Christ also hath loved us, and hath given himself for us an offering and a sacrifice to God for a sweetsmelling savor. (Ephesians 4:31-5:2, *KJV*)

Just as Jesus forgave us, we are to forgive those who have angered us. In love, Jesus offered Himself. In love, we are also to let the sins of others be forgiven by our lips and hearts as an offering and sacrifice. None of this is easy, but it is possible as we know and walk with God, softened by His love.

Honoring Our Spiritual Fathers

It is with this understanding that we return to our Anabaptist ancestors. We have already established the gross error of persecution by the Reformers and the Catholics. There is no disputing the injustice of their inhumane and ungodly treatment.

Yet, as we look at our ancestral heart responses to these men who were over us in both political and spiritual authority, we also erred. We did not honor and respect them at all times, even though they were wrong. We did not always walk in "gentleness and respect" as we spoke of them to others. We did not always humbly ask God to forgive them. And, we did not always love them without anger or bitterness in our hearts. We often spoke harshly, denouncing them because of their sinful words and actions.

Biblically, honoring and respecting those in authority does not mean we have to agree with them. It may even be necessary to part from them peaceably, if they are leading their congregations into error, for example. But even if we are called to leave, we are to maintain a clear spirit and a heart of forgiveness towards those who are in authority over us, regardless of their response.

Though some of our ancestors did honor and respect those who were in authority over them, we may surmise that the name-calling, the angry accusations, the "bitter resentments" and the "impatience" which are found in our ancestry, are evidence that hearts became *bitter* towards our spiritual fathers in both the State Catholic Church and the State Reformed Church. There were times when our forefathers held impatient anger in the heart towards these who were over them in political and spiritual authority. Because of the injustices, the lies, and the unrighteousness of those who were *supposed* to be leading with justice, their bitterness against their authorities became rebellion, as evidenced by their slander and "evil speaking."

As we'll examine more specifically in a later chapter, much of the general populace during the 1500s experienced frustration over heavy taxation and injustice (chapter 26). Peasant revolts and uprisings are the more obvious signs of tensions that existed between ruling lords and their subjects. The outrage in the city of Münster where thousands perished, and the seizing of the Old Cloister at Witmarsum by several hundred zealots, are two of the better known incidents.[25]

We can understand the exasperation of these peasants over their financial lot in life, especially when we also consider the demands required of them by the State Churches. But *bitterness* against authorities, even if it *seems* justified, is still called rebellion. There is always a reaping of this attitude of the heart. These more general societal attitudes added to heart issues which occurred within our own heritage, and "defiled many."

Changing Our Minds

For some of us who are Anabaptists today, our own poor attitudes as we relate to the authorities in our lives, have been fostered partially through a generational stronghold of bitterness towards authority. Some of us have had a pattern of disrespect and dishonor towards leaders, especially when our spirits confirm that their actions and words were unbiblical or unjust. This pattern can be traced all the way back to our initial separations from the State Catholic and the State Reformed Churches and even beyond that, to the very first dishonoring of authority in the garden of Eden.

For those of us who recognize this tendency in our lives, take courage! In Christ, we are never condemned for our rebellion. Instead, God calls us to turn from our wicked ways and to humble ourselves in repentance, *that we may healed* (II Chronicles 7:14; James 5:16). He is the One who gives us grace to forgive. He will enable us to trust His hand to work out His justice, even when we are wronged by those who are over us in authority. He is able, if we are willing!

As soon as we turn to change our minds, God begins to change our hearts. Ask Him to show you the "treasure" in the lives of those who have been your authorities. Extract the precious, and discard the worthless (chapter 11). Ask Him to give you *His* eyesight towards authority. Ask Him to build your trust. God is faithful to heal. He is the perfect and righteous authority, whose mercy always triumphs over judgment (James 2:13).

Sometimes the process of cleansing requires thorough prayer. Set aside a quiet time when you can concentrate and press through. As we confess and change our minds, God moves on our behalf to bless and to restore.

Thank You, Lord Jesus, that You love me. Thank You for forgiving all my rebellion against You, through Your death. Thank You that even when I hold unforgiveness in my heart, You bring me to repentance so I can be healed.[1]

Personal repentance:

 I come before You now. As I stand in the heavenly courts, examine my heart and show me any unforgiveness I am holding towards authorities in my life, both past and present (take time now to allow God to bring any names to mind). Please help me to forgive these authorities and to let go of any anger or bitterness I've been holding against them. I choose now, to forgive _____ *(the names that came to mind) for* _____ *(name the specific injustices, sins, or hurts). Jesus, I forgive them because You forgave me.*

 I repent of every ungodly, bitter judgment I have made against these I have named. Take the consequences of my judgments into your death on the cross.[2] I release each person to You and ask You to forgive them. Please don't hold this sin against them, but bless them with Your grace.[3]

 Lord, You know where I have been sinned against in an unjust way. I place every sin and injustice in Your hands, and ask You to repair my heart. Take the pain of each incident and cleanse it by Your cross. Remove it from me, because I want to be free. Wash me with the oil of Your Spirit. Pour in Your balm of Gilead where every ache has been.

 Where trust has been betrayed by those who were over me in authority, reestablish my trust. Help me to know I am safe in You.[4] Heal my soul: my mind, will and emotions. Show me scriptures for renewing my mind.[5]

Repentance for your spiritual fathers:

 By the instruction of Your Word, I confess the sins of my "fathers" through the generations, on behalf of my people, my family, and myself.[6] Forgive our ungodly attitudes towards the authorities You placed over us, both earthly authorities and spiritual authorities. Forgive our bitter rebellion and our unforgiveness against You and also against people.

 Forgive us especially for our bitter attitudes of rebellion against the Reformers and against the State Catholic Church. Though they were wrong, our angry resentments and bitter responses were also wrong. Forgive every bitter judgment we have made against these authorities. Thank You that through Your cross, our judgments are cleansed.

Pulling Down Strongholds

In every place where a stronghold of bitter rebellion towards authority has existed in my life and in my family, I tear it down now in the Name of Jesus. I bind every demonic attachment of rebellion and by the blood of Jesus, forbid its operation in my life, and in the life of my family members. I cut off every generational heritage of rebellion in the Name of Jesus, from my family line and from my own life.

Father, give us Your eyes to see our heart attitudes. Give us restful hearts as sons and daughters of the Most High.[7] Give me a heart that is able to drink deeply of Your love.[8] Thank You. I put my hope in You, the Author and Finisher of my faith.[9]

I pray all these things in Jesus' name, Amen.

---

[1] James 5:16; [2] Matthew 7:1 and Luke 6:37; [3] Acts 7:60; [4] Job 5:11; [5] Romans 12:2; [6] Leviticus 26:39-40; [7] Luke 6:35; [8] Ezekiel 11:19; [9] Hebrews 12:2)

Promises for you from Isaiah 44:21-22:

God could never forget you. He made you! Because you have turned to Him and agreed with Him about your sins, He has swept away all your offenses, like the wind blows away a cloud. He's made your sins disappear, like the sun evaporates the morning mist. He has redeemed you—bought you with His precious blood—and is so glad you have returned to Him. You belong to the Father!

FEAR OF GOD
AND
FEAR OF DEATH

I once misplaced a sum of cash in my home and spent a frantic time searching for its whereabouts. Mild panic set in as I thought about dropping it somewhere in transit or accidentally disposing of it in yesterday's trash. When I finally did unearth it, I breathed a deep sigh of relief and a prayer of thankfulness for having discovered its hiding place.

If you've ever lost anything of worth and looked for it everywhere, you know the value of searching diligently until it is found. This is the same type of diligent search which embodies faith. A man of faith seeks after God because he knows his search will be worth every effort. Not only is there the reward of knowing Him, but there are many other rewards God has promised for those who look for Him with all their heart. Faith *expects* to be rewarded for a diligent search.

Favored Children, No Longer Punished

Fear, on the other hand, is afraid of searching for God because fear is not convinced the search will be rewarded with good things. Fear avoids the search, or only makes a half-hearted attempt at seeking, because it has become afraid of God's character and of actually drawing near to Him.

There *is* a God-given "fear of the Lord" that Christians can experience, which is really reverential awe of His nature. This positive fear of the Lord is wise and honors, respects, and esteems God in all His glory (Psalm 111:10 and Proverbs 1:7). This kind of holy "fear of the Lord" does not avoid God.

It is the unhealthy fear of being afraid which causes people to shrink back from approaching Him. This fear occurs because our trust in God as a Rewarder has been broken. Without the expectation of reward, we become afraid of approaching a holy God, just as the Israelites became fearful of drawing near to Him. They assumed that if they drew near, they would die:

> The Israelites said to Moses, "We shall die! We are lost, we are all lost! Anyone who *even comes near* the tabernacle of the Lord will die. Are we all going to die?" (Numbers 17:12-13)

> When the people saw the thunder and lightning and heard the trumpet and saw the mountain in smoke, they *trembled with fear*. They stayed at a distance and said to Moses, "Speak to us yourself and we will listen. But *do not have God speak to us or we will die*." (Exodus 20:18-19)

The New Testament way of expressing this unhealthy fear of God is written by the apostle John:

> There is no fear in love. But perfect love drives out fear, because *fear has to do with punishment*. The one who fears is *not made perfect in love*. (I John 4:18)

For years, I saw God as a punisher. To my heart, He was a big ogre sitting up there in heaven with His arms folded, peering down at me with disdain. I just knew He was waiting to pounce on me in holy irritation whenever I sinned. As long as I was "good," I believed God was pleased with me. But when I sinned, I was sure I was disappointing or angering Him. I almost always felt like a "bad child" who warranted punishment.

This kind of punishment mentality for sin came from embitterment and unforgiveness in my heart. As I turned to God and agreed with Him about my bitterness, He slowly began to show me the truth about our Father-daughter relationship and to dispel my fears. It is true, at one time I *was* a child of wrath and disobedience. I did deserve punishment for my wrong-doings. But, because of the cross, God now saw me as one of His *favorite* children (Ephesians 1:5).

We are all His favorites, because someone has *already* been whipped for our sins. Every rebellious word, every bad attitude, every sinful action we've ever done or will do, has *already* been laid on the back of our Elder Brother, who willingly stood in and received our blows (Hebrews 2:11). My Brother took my beating for the charges against me and now, my Father simply does not call to mind my sins (Hebrews 10:17-18).

As a matter of fact, because of Jesus there has been a complete turn-about of our circumstances. God has taken children who were once "sons of disobedience," and sat us down beside Him in heaven and made us royalty (I Peter 2:9). Forevermore, God is on our side. Our Father is rooting *for us,* and not *against us:*

> And *you* He made alive, who *were* dead in trespasses and sins, in which you *once* walked...according to the prince of the power of the air, the spirit who now works in the *sons of disobedience,* among whom also we all *once* conducted ourselves . . . and were by nature *children of wrath. . . .* But God, who is rich in mercy, **because of His great love** with which He loved us . . . **made us alive together with Christ** . . . and **raised us up** together, and made us **sit together in the heavenly places in Christ Jesus.** . . . (Ephesians 2:1-7)

> But he was pierced for our transgressions, he was crushed for our iniquities; the **punishment that brought us peace was upon him,** and *by his wounds we are healed.* (Isaiah 53:5)

> What, then, shall we say in response to this? If **God is for us,** *who can be against us?* He who did not spare his own Son, but gave him up for us all—how will he not also, along with him, graciously give us all things? **Who will bring any charge against** those whom **God has chosen?** (Romans 8:31-33)

If we can grasp the reality that Jesus has received every wound of our punishment—that by His wounds we are made whole—we will be able to walk in deep peace, without being afraid of God. Then, we will be able to trust the *discipline* of God in our lives, understanding that He always acts in love (Hebrews 12:10). Our hearts will continue to be at rest, even when faced with hardships (Hebrews 12:7).

Feeling Abandoned

But if our embitterment towards Him has caused us to turn away from God's comfort, when trials and suffering come our way we will feel *abandoned,* rather than defended by Him. If we see God as one who punishes us by putting us in difficult circumstances, we'll think that instead of being on our side, He has left us on our own to fend for ourselves.

This was how our ancestors felt in the years of oppression. In embitterment, they were no longer able to receive His *perfect love* and began to fear God as one who punished. Reverence for His holiness was exchanged for fear of His hand: if He allowed such heinous torture, poverty and oppression, what *else* might this holy God allow to harm us?

Their disillusionment about God may have been fostered at least partially from erroneous teachings that Jesus' second coming was imminent. Melchior Hoffman, Thomas Müntzer, Hans Hut, and other preachers during the formative years of Anabaptism taught that Christ would soon come to set up His reign on earth.[1] Though Hoffman and Müntzer were loosely associated with our forefathers, their teaching was heard by many who would eventually become Anabaptists. Hans Hut's influence also left its mark, particularly in the region of South Germany. As a result of these and other end-time teachings, some of the early Anabaptists felt Christ's return would happen during their lifetime.

But when Christ did not come and set up His Kingdom, the thinking of these weary Anabaptists changed as they considered being persecuted over the "long haul" of their life spans. Second generation Anabaptists who had seen their parents martyred, grew into adulthood. Having already been orphaned and poverty-stricken as children, it was now their turn to be hunted and harassed and forced to flee from one hiding place to another. God hadn't returned for them like they had expected, and He wasn't lifting their burden of oppression. As they retreated from witnessing into closed communities, their hearts moved from being at rest in the midst of suffering, to questioning why God had abandoned them.

    The original dictionary meaning of "a – ban – don" is, *to put under (a) ban.*[2] Through the years, our Anabaptist denominations have been fraught with "putting each other under a ban," or abandoning each other, through much division and separation.[3] If there is any evidence that Anabaptists have felt abandoned by God, it is that we have *abandoned* each other. Remember, we reap what we sow (chapter 11). If we judge God as One who abandons, we will reap the same fruit of abandonment somewhere in our lives. In our heritage, we have reaped towards *each other* the seed we sowed in our hearts towards God: feeling abandoned, our natural response was to abandon each other.

    But Paul writes that even when we are persecuted, we are never abandoned:

> We are hard pressed on every side, but not crushed; perplexed, but not in despair; *persecuted, but not abandoned;* struck down, but not destroyed. We always carry around in our body the death of Jesus, so that the life of Jesus may also be revealed in our body. (II Corinthians 4:8-10)

God never abandoned the Anabaptists and He never used the persecution years to punish us as though we were "bad" children. We have never, ever been abandoned by the Lord. The writer of Hebrews puts it this way:

> Keep your lives free from the love of money and be content with what you have, because God has said, '*Never will I leave you; never will I forsake (abandon) you.*' So we say with confidence, '*The Lord is my helper; I will not be afraid. What can man do to me?*'(Hebrews 13:5,6 parenthesis mine)

The Greek translation of these verses actually uses two and three negative predicates, declaring God's commitment to us in the strongest possible wording. The words "leave," "forsake," and "helper," also carry deeper meanings. These verses could be translated more completely by saying,

> I will **never, never** *slacken my pace from walking beside you,* and I will **never, never, never** *abandon you* or *leave you behind.* So we say with confidence, *The Lord* is the *One who* **runs and shouts for help**, I will not be afraid or fearful. What can man do to me? (Greek linear translation and *Strong's Concordance*)[4]

Now, that is a wonderfully strong promise from our good Heavenly Father!

Overcoming or Overcome

Michael Sattler, one of the early founding fathers of Anabaptism, had his tongue cut out and his skin poked through seven times with red hot tongs just prior to being burned at the stake. He had promised to give a sign to the brethren who were watching his execution, to let them know whether the pain and suffering he was enduring was bearable. Just before his death, as the ropes around his hands finally burned away, he was able to lift his hand in assurance that indeed, it had all been bearable. He died with the overcoming faith of other martyrs who had gone before him.[5]

The Scriptures talk about such overcoming faith in the book of Revelation. There, the Bible lists three characteristics which enabled martyrs like Michael Sattler to walk in the strength of victory, even through torture and execution:

> . . . For the *accuser of our brothers*, who accuses them before our God day and night, has been hurled down. They *overcame him* by the **blood of the Lamb** and by the **word of their testimony**; they **did not love their lives so much as to shrink from death**. (Revelation 12:10-11)

The three characteristics are:
- The blood of the Lamb
- The word of their testimony
- Not loving their lives, even to the point of death

Michael Sattler and other early martyrs overcame, knowing that because of the *blood of the Lamb* their spirits were eternally alive, though their bodies would die. Secondly, through the *word of their testimony* they overcame by speaking with boldness and courage. But it was with the third element of this scripture that their victory was sealed: they did *not love their lives so much as to shrink from death.* They *overcame* through trusting God to the very end, as they yielded up the last breath in their physical bodies.

They knew that Jesus had destroyed "him who holds the power of death":

> Since the children have flesh and blood, he too shared in their humanity so that by his death he might **destroy him who holds the power of death**—that is, *the devil*—and **free those** who all their lives were **held in slavery** by their **fear of death**. (Hebrews 2:14-15)

The word *destroy* in this scripture is actually translated as, to *render idle or useless.*[6] The devil's power to cause us to fear death is rendered useless, because in Christ we have already passed into life. We'll never die spiritually, so when the time comes for our spirits to leave our bodies we will go from our physical temples, right into the presence of God! The sting of a physical death has been defeated, in that we have *already* been spiritually resurrected (I Corinthians 15:50-58).

Anabaptists and a Fear of Dying

Even so, many believers alive today—and many Anabaptists—fear the prospect of suffering and death. Fear of death has to do with more than a physical deathbed experience. It is also revealed when we are afraid of *dying to self*, as God calls us to surrender. Unforgiveness can reveal an unwillingness to follow Jesus to our own death to self. Being quiet about our faith can show we're afraid to risk our life for the sake of others. And being afraid to admit our sin can demonstrate a fear of letting God put to death in us what is unlike His Son.

Through time, all three elements of the overcoming faith listed in the book of Revelation, have been compromised within our Anabaptist heritage. When we turned away from God in embitterment, we lost a measure of trust in the power of the *blood of the Lamb*, because we lost faith in the Lamb Himself. Our lack of witness silenced the second overcoming element, the *word of our testimony*. And as we began to pull into communities to protect ourselves, we lost the third element of overcoming faith by *loving our lives and shrinking from death*. To the degree that we lost these aspects of overcoming faith, we also returned under a *slavery to the fear of death*, as the passage in Hebrews so aptly expresses.

Dying is not easy, including dying to self. It is a lifelong process. But dying is necessary if we want to be resurrected! When we take up our cross and follow Jesus to a death of our own ways, He will always resurrect us into spiritual *life*. And when God's life grows in us, our experiences on earth will make sense. We'll begin to see with a heavenly perspective. Though our circumstances may seem unbearable, through the eyes of our spirit we can actually walk in peace and joy, much like the apostle Paul and Silas sang praise in prison just after they had been beaten and shackled (Acts 16:23-25).

Returning to Our Father

God calls us to return to complete trust in Him as our Father, even trust to death. He asks us to run and receive His comfort as children, so we may learn to know His character. When we know Him as the "Spirit of adoption," will be free from a spirit of fear:

> For as many as are led by the Spirit of God, these are sons of God. For you did *not* receive the *spirit of bondage again to fear,* but you received the *Spirit of adoption* by whom we cry out, "Abba, Father." The Spirit Himself bears witness with our spirit that we are *children of God,* and if children, then heirs—*heirs of God* and joint heirs with Christ, if indeed we *suffer with Him,* that *we may also be glorified.* For I consider that the *sufferings of this present time* are not worthy to be compared with the *glory which shall be revealed* in us. (Romans 8:14-18, *NKJV*)

God is our Father. We are His adopted children. We *are* called to suffer along with our Elder Brother. But just as Jesus walked through suffering in an attitude of Sonship, we can also walk through our sufferings knowing our Abba, Father, and confident that He is always right inside us. Then, rather than giving into a spirit of fear, we can experience His glory along with our suffering.

In order to lay down our lives in this world, we first need to have a heart knowledge of who we are, or we'll always be striving to prove ourselves. Jesus, "being in the form of God, thought it not robbery to be equal with God," but laid Himself down: He *knew* He was the Son of God and in rest, laid down His position. The apostle Paul writes, "I want to know Christ and *the power of His resurrection* and the fellowship of sharing in His sufferings . . ." The order of these thoughts is intentional. We *first* know the power of the exchange that happened through the cross and resurrection: that God made us *sons and daughters,* seated alongside our Brother, Jesus. It is out of knowing we are God's children that we are *then* able to share in His sufferings and lay down our lives.

Jesus tells the church in Smyrna not to fear suffering or death, and promises them a crown of life for their faithfulness:

> *Do not be afraid* of what you are about to *suffer.* I tell you, the devil will put some of you in prison to test you, and you will suffer persecution for ten days. *Be faithful, even to the point of death,* and I will give you the *crown of life.* He who has an ear, let him hear what the Spirit says to the

churches. He who overcomes will **not be hurt at all by the
second death.** (Revelation 2:10-11)

May God return our hearts to this kind of boldness and
courage, where we truly do not fear death. He has promised that
nothing in this life can harm us when we are walking in His authority and care (Luke 10:18,19). And for our faithfulness as His
royal co-heirs, Jesus will give us a *crown of life,* when we meet
Him in eternity (Romans 8:17). What a glorious spiritual *life*
awaits us!

Personal cleansing:

*Almighty God, thank You that You are my good Father. I
run to You: come and touch the places of my heart where I am
afraid of You and where I fear death. Give me instead a heart of
confidence, boldness and courage.*[1] *You have said nothing is too
difficult for You.*[2] *Change my heart. I need to see You as You
really are: as my loving Father,*[3] *my fierce Protector,*[4] *my gentle
Shepherd,*[5] *and my faithful Friend.*[6] *Please open my spiritual
eyes to know Your character*[7] *deep within my being.*

*Lay a foundation into my heart of knowing I can trust
You. When I have perceived You as One who punishes harshly,
forgive me. I confess there have been times when I felt You abandoned me because I didn't understand my circumstances. Father,
forgive me and cleanse me . Pour Your comfort into the places of
my heart where I thought I was being punished by You, and where
I have felt abandoned. You are my Healer.*[8]

*I choose to believe that You are able to guard my life com-
pletely, until I arrive in eternity to be with You.*[9] *Forgive me for
every time I have loved my life more than I have loved You.
I repent for fearing death more than I revere You. Father, I
purpose to take up my cross as You enable me, each day. Help
me to trust You in life and in death, because You have promised
to work everything for my good.*[10]

Pulling down and rebuilding:

If there are strongholds in my family line concerning punishment or abandonment or the fear of harm and death, I take captive those strongholds in the mighty name of Jesus, and by His authority, I bind every demonic attachment to the fear of death, the fear of harm, the fear of abandonment, and the fear of punishment. I proclaim God's promise of rescue from every single one of these fears: that "I will be established in righteousness and shall be far from oppression, for I shall not fear; and from terror, for it shall not come near me."[11]

Father, thank You that I am not a slave to fear. Instead, I have Your Spirit of sonship.[12] I receive Your love and Your affection as a healing balm in my soul. Deliver me from all my fears, as You have promised.[13] Let Your angels guard my life, and protect me, according to Your Word.[14]

In the Name of Your Son, Amen.

---

[1] Deuteronomy 31:5-8; [2] Jeremiah 32:17; [3] Jeremiah 3:19; [4] II Thessalonians 3:3; [5] Psalm 23:1; [6] John 15:15; [7] Ephesians 1:17-18; [8] Psalm 147:3 and 103:3; [9] II Timothy 4:18; [10] Romans 8:28; [11] Isaiah 54:14; [12] Romans 8:15; [13] Psalm 34:4; [14] Psalm 91:11-16.

Promises for you from Isaiah 43:1-4:

Your heavenly Father formed you. He knows you so completely, He even calls you by name! When He looks at you, He loves you immensely. He honors you and counts you as very precious to Him. If you go through difficult times, He has given His word to be with you. Even though the fire may seem hot and the rushing torrent may seem too forceful, He will protect you so that you come through them safely. He does not want you to be afraid in any way, because He is strong enough for anything you will ever face. You belong to Him!

A gentle reminder that you may need to be persistent in pulling down strongholds of the mind which have been established like castles (see chapter six), and binding the demonic attachments to those strongholds (chapter 14). Our minds are renewed gradually: be encouraged—one day at a time!

~ 19 ~

REVERENCE FOR GOD

OR

REVERENCE FOR MAN

Did you know that God wants *you* to do great things? He wants you to do great things on the earth, just like Jesus did great miracles, healing, teachings, and all kinds of signs and wonders when He walked the earth. Actually, God wants you to do even *greater* things than Jesus:

> I tell you the truth, anyone who has faith in me will *do what I have been doing.* He will do even *greater things than these,* because I am going to the Father. . . . You may ask me for anything in my name, and I will do it. If you *love me, you will obey what I command.* (John 14:12-15)

God wants to give you great things to do because He loves collaborating with His children. He delights in doing the work of the Kingdom *together* with you. As His child, God has prepared specific works for you to accomplish. Every task He has given you to do fits your personality and completes who you are as His son or daughter, while it also builds His Kingdom. He made you, and knows you completely as His "workman-ship."

> For we are God's workmanship, created in Christ Jesus to do good works, which God prepared in advance for us to do. (Ephesians 2:10)

The key to being able to accomplish these great works which God has prepared for each of us, is *obedience*. Obedience is our love and trust in God, put into action. Doing things God's way indicates that we know His character as the Head of the family of God, and love and respect Him as our Father. And because God is our Perfect Parent—always consistent, always loving, always right—there is no reason to mistrust His will.

The more we obey, the more we'll know God's love. The more we obey, the more we'll see His presence in our lives, because God *feels at home* with children who demonstrate a heart of loving cooperation:

> Whoever has my commands and *obeys them*, he is the one who *loves me*. He who loves me will be *loved by my Father*, and I too will *love him* and *show myself to him*. . . . If any-one *loves me, he will obey* my teaching. My Father will *love him,* and we will *come to him* and *make our home with him* . . . (John 14:21-26)

Ideally, as His sons and daughters we will obey our Father in absolutely everything. That's what Jesus did as our example of a true Son: not once did He serve His own interests instead of His Father's interests. He never acted independently, but always did exactly as He was instructed:

> . . . but the world must learn that *I love the Father* and that I *do exactly what my Father has commanded me.* (John 14:31)

> So Jesus said, 'When you have lifted up the Son of Man, then you will know that I am the one I claim to be and that *I do nothing on my own but speak just what the Father has taught me.* The one who sent me is with me; he has not left me alone, for *I always do what pleases him.*' (John 8:28-29)

> For I did not speak of my own accord, but the Father who sent me *commanded me what to say and how to say it.* I know that his command leads to eternal life. So *whatever I say is just what the Father has told me to say.* (John 12:49)

By far, the greatest reward for our obedience is that God will come and *reveal Himself* to us. But obedience also releases God's *greater things* in and through our lives. In the first scripture we read, Jesus promised that we could ask Him for *anything*, and He would do it for us. But the next words He spoke were, "If you love me, you'll obey. . . ." Our trust and love for God are what move His hand to *do* great things through our lives. Just as a child who serves his earthly parent is entrusted with greater privileges, God will give us greater Kingdom work as we learn to lay down our own independence and yield to His Fatherly commands.

Fruits of Disobedience

Obedience holds great blessings for us as God's children. The opposite is also true: when we disobey, we will *lack* the blessings of God. For years, I felt as though a great spiritual cloud existed between God and myself, that seemed to block my prayers and prevent me from hearing clearly from heaven. It wasn't a cooling Summer cloud, but more like a thunderhead that brought with it a rain, or reign, of turmoil and confusion. Often when I prayed, the heavens felt like they were made of brass and God's love seemed miles away.

I would discover in time that one of the factors of my spiritual blockage was my own *stubbornness*. I'd grown up hearing the words "stubborn Dutchman" used in conversations, but never once attributed that characteristic to my own life. Referring to those of us from Pennsylvania Dutch Anabaptist heritage, the connotation of being inflexible was fully intended by those who used the phrase.

As I read my Bible, God showed me that my lack of understanding spiritual things was directly connected to my inability to cooperate with Him. I was His child, but because I usually insisted on going my *own* way, I could not understand *His* ways. With a strong independence, I was like a horse or mule and needed to be harnessed:

> I will **instruct you** and **teach you** in the way you should go;
> I will **guide you** with My eye. *Do not be like the horse or*
> *like the mule, which **have no understanding**,* which must be
> harnessed with bit and bridle, *else they will not come near*
> *you.* (Psalm 32:8-9, *NKJV*)

Since I was resisting God like a mule resists its owner,
I could not understand His guidance. Instruction could not come
near me, because I had pulled away from His presence.

Disobedience will always cause a distancing from God,
not by His choice, but because we have chosen to go our own
way. As a good Father, God will then allow discipline in order to
mold our character and to restore relationship.

Reverencing Man

As a loving Father, God never forces obedience. He
always gives us a choice. But if we choose to disobey, a shift
occurs in our ability to hear our Father's voice. That is when
earthly things become *more clear*, and God's paths becomes
less clear. As God's voice becomes muted by our disobedience,
our reverence for God diminishes, and our reverence for man
increases.

The Bible calls reverence for man the *fear of man.* This
fear causes us to give more weight to man's opinions, words, or
actions than we give to God's words, opinions or actions:

> Hear me, you who know what is right, you people who have
> my law in your hearts: *Do not **fear the reproach of men** or*
> *be **terrified** by their **insults**.* For the moth will eat them up
> like a garment; the worm will devour them like wool. *But my*
> *righteousness will last for ever, my salvation through all*
> *generations.* (Isaiah 51;7-8)

King Saul is a Biblical example of one who revered man
more than God. The Lord had commanded him to go to war with
the wicked Amalekites and to destroy every living thing in battle.

Yet Saul permitted the Israelites to keep their best animals as plunder. The people had pressed him to allow them to take home some spoils of war and Saul was afraid to deny their request, so instead, he denied the commandment of God to put everything to death.

The prophet Samuel arrived and told Saul that because he had rejected God's word, the Lord was rejecting him as king. Saul then admitted, *"I was afraid of the people and so I gave in to them"* (I Samuel 15:24). Fearing man instead of revering God affected the course of Saul's life, costing him his kingdom and the blessing of God. And for the rest of his days, Saul was tormented by an evil spirit (I Samuel 16:14). He had been "caught" by his fear of man in a spiritually deadly trap:

> *The fear of man brings a snare*, But whoever trusts in the Lord shall be safe. (Proverbs 29:25, *NKJV*)

Saul wanted to justify his actions by declaring the plunder of battle was for offering sacrifices to the Lord, but Samuel summed up the Lord's opinion about his disobedient compromise:

> And Samuel said, Hath the Lord as great delight in burnt offerings and sacrifices, as in **obeying the voice of the Lord**? Behold, **to obey is better than sacrifice**, and *to hearken* than the fat of rams. For *rebellion is as the sin of witchcraft,* and **stubbornness is as iniquity and idolatry.** (I Samuel 15:19-23, *KJV*)

Saul's bitter rebellion cost him dearly (chapter 17), but he also paid a price for being stubborn. The meaning for the word "stubbornness" in this scripture is to *press, push,* or *urge.* Saul pushed and pressed for his own set of rules because he feared man. Like Saul, God equates our pushy insistence at having our own way with wickedness and idolatry. Essentially, when we press for man's way we are worshiping an idol by giving *reverence* to someone other than God.

Reverencing God or Shrinking Back

Historically, many of our early ancestors clearly *revered God* more than man. They didn't shrink back from obedience, but were willing to declare spiritual truths even while they stood before town councils who had the power to put them to death. Historical court proceedings have recorded their bold and un-compromising testimonies, as they willingly endured all things for the sake of the gospel.[1]

The early Anabaptists stood their ground and actually expected to suffer for the sake of the gospel. Dirk Phillips, a contemporary of Menno Simons, listed *the acceptance of suffering and persecution* as one of the seven ordinances of the true church.[2] Because they revered God more than men, the Comforter met them intimately through all their sufferings, and they knew the deep love of their Savior.

Gradually, however, our reverent obedience to God lessened and our fear of man increased. As we were exposed to insult and persecution, we failed to persevere in doing the will of God and began to shrink back:

> You need to ***persevere*** *so that when you have **done the will of God**,* you will receive what he has promised. . . But my righteous one will live by faith. And if he ***shrinks back, I will not be pleased with him.*** But *we are **not of those** who* ***shrink back and are destroyed,*** but of those who ***believe*** and are saved. Now faith is being *sure of what we hope for* and *certain of what we do not see.* (Hebrews 10:36-11:1)

The words "shrink back" have to do with *drawing away in timidity to take cover.* They create the image of someone cowering in a hiding place.[3] When we operate under the fear of man we will draw away or retreat rather than persevering in obedience to "do the will of God."

Without any condemnation, we understand that is exactly what our ancestors did when they withdrew and ceased their bold witness. They found safety in agreeing to abide by the demands of lords and rulers who forbade proselytizing, and revered the orders of men rather than obeying God's call to preach to gospel. When they shrank back, persecution eased and they *seemed* to be more safe. But shrinking back will always cause destruction, as the Word declares. Though they experienced less physical harm, their trust and reverence for God was "destroyed," and they were overcome with fears.

Recognizing the Fear of Man

Today, many of the choices we make in our daily lives, in our type of worship and in our speech and actions are because we want to be accepted by our church community and by our family and our friends. Wanting to be accepted by others is not wrong in and of itself, but if being accepted is *more important* than obedience to the Lord, we are reverencing man more than we reverence our Father. Motives are key in discerning our heart of fear or faith.

I have created a list of a some main "identifiers" which may be helpful in understanding the impact of this fear more completely. Not all of these indicators will apply to every one of us, but the list as a whole can enable us to recognize where our souls may be influenced by this stronghold of our heritage. Several of these identifiers will be discussed in later chapters.

Fear of man indicators:
- Afraid of what people think about us
  (*ie*/that we're odd or old-fashioned)
- Afraid to speak up when our opinion is not popular
- Afraid of making mistakes
- Afraid to be honestly open about what we think and feel
- Afraid of sharing our faith
- Afraid of those in authority over us (pastors, bishops, leaders)
- Unable to risk expressing our uniqueness as a person
- Unable to risk trying new things

- A strong concern for following rules correctly
- A tendency to control things so we'll feel safe
- Inability to speak the truth in love to our brothers and sisters
- Fear of suffering for the sake of the gospel
- Do not readily take a stand for what is right if challenged
- A strong independence
- (or) Going along with the crowd when we know we shouldn't
- Agreeing to do things we really don't want to do
- Fear of foreign enemies

Like Paul, when I realized my own propensity to yield to this fear, I could only cry out, *"O wretched man that I am! who shall deliver me from the body of this death?"* And, my answer, like Paul's answer, is *"Thanks be to God—through Jesus Christ our Lord!"* (Romans 7:24, *KJV*) Jesus is the One who sets us free and leads us out of our wretched fear. He will accomplish all that concerns us (Psalm 138:8).

Choosing Obedience

Though we have all surrendered to the fear of man, our Father only calls us to acknowledge we've missed the mark, and to turn to Him in repentance. His mercy then begins to work in us to *will* and to *do* according to His good pleasure (Philippians 2:13). He begins to transform our hearts and minds to choose obedience to Him above all else.

Even Jesus had to *learn* obedience. He learned through suffering, so that He could identify with our own plight as humans:

Although he was a son, he **learned obedience** from what he suffered and, once made perfect, he became the source of eternal salvation for all who obey him (Hebrews 5:8-9).

This verse translates wonderfully. Its root meaning is, Jesus learned to *hearken diligently* through the *painful pressure* He experienced.[4] It is helpful to know that pressures in our lives can sometimes be God's way of teaching us to listen carefully as sons and daughters! When we don't understand why we are in the middle of a difficult situation, we can sit down and say to our Father, "I don't understand why I am experiencing this pressure. I will listen to You: help me to hear your voice!" God will always answer that kind of prayer, because He *wants* us to learn to listen to Him carefully, that we may experience His blessings and love.

God will help us turn away from being afraid of man, to reverencing Him by our obedience. It will take time, but if the Father sees we are trying, He will immediately add His strength to our efforts and we will grow and change.

Your Father is looking for sons and daughters who will trust Him and obey Him. Through your obedience, His voice will grow stronger and clearer, and you'll be able to hear Him telling you what to do, and where to go. That's when you'll find yourself accomplishing *great things* in the earth, as you collaborate together with God!

Father, You are my loving Shepherd. You have promised to lead me to green pastures and beside quiet waters, to places of peace and rest.[1] Thank You for loving me.

*You are my **Lord**. I give You full rule in my life. I surrender my will to You. As Your son (daughter), I know as I obey You I will experience more and more of Your friendship and love.[2] Please strengthen me in my inner being so that You can live in my heart through faith, that I may rise up and do Your will.[3]*

Personal Cleansing:

For every time that I have surrendered to the fear of man, forgive me. I turn away from being afraid of people instead of revering You. I change my mind about drawing away and retreating from obedience. Father, give me grace to say and do what You desire.[4]

Lord, You know what causes me to shrink back in fear. Show me where the fear of man exists in my heart and give me grace to care more about what You think or say, than I care about the opinions of people. Give me boldness. Change my life.

Our Fathers' Sins:

I agree with You, we have sinned as a people by fearing man more than we have honored and revered You. Forgive us. Forgive our fathers for their error, and cleanse us from all their sins of fear and timidity. Restore us to the true and proper fear of the Lord. Glorify Your name through our lives.

Dealing With Strongholds:

If there is a stronghold of the fear of man in my life or in my family line, I tear down that stronghold, and I bind every demonic attachment to that stronghold in Jesus' Name. I forbid fear of man from operating in my life or in my family.

God, bring to death through Your sacrifice on the cross, every generational tie of the fear of man in my life and in the lives of my family members and in my people.

You said You have raised me with Christ through Your resurrection.[5] I ask that in every place where the fear of man has been in my soul, please resurrect a healthy, reverent fear of the Lord. I choose to obey You. As You have promised, work in me to will and to act according to Your good pleasure.[6]

Thank You for all You have done for me. You always teach me what is best for me.[7] You raise up a standard against my enemy.[8] You are good! Thank You for hearing me and for answering my prayer.

In the Name of Jesus, My Redeemer, Amen.

---

[1] Psalm 23:2; [2] John 15:10,14; [3] Ephesians 3:16-17; [4] John 8:28-29; [5] Ephesians 2:6; [6] Philippians 2:13; [7] Isaiah 48:17; [8] Isaiah 59:19, *KJV*.

Promises for you from Jeremiah 32:39-41:

God has promised to *give* you reverence for Himself. He will *inspire* you to revere Him so you'll never turn away. He's made a covenant to never stop doing good things for you, and He is joyful when He is able to fulfill it! With all His heart and soul, He will give you your spiritual inheritance.

DIVISION OR UNITY

Take a quick survey of your body parts. Look at your neck, eyes, or elbows, and how they function. Think about how differently your thigh muscles work in comparison to the muscles in your forearms. Consider your heart, the main "pump" for your blood and how it differs from your liver and kidneys, the filtration systems for this wonderful human vessel that is you.

Every part of your body has been created to fulfill a special and unique purpose. But, what if you had been born differently? Suppose that instead of having a neck, eyes, and elbows, you had been given three additional mouths. That would mean you can't see a thing or move your head, and your arms are always straight. You would probably also eat a lot more than you should, and talk incessantly! It's a strange concept, isn't it?

During the historical Dark Ages, the rulers of the State Church essentially tried to make everyone the same spiritual "body part" as they forced all people to agree with and abide by their Church laws. They told them what to do and how to do it, and gave them no freedom to disobey. It was as if the masses were told, whether they agreed or not, "You are all toes." Much of Christendom now realizes how poorly the body of Christ functioned under those circumstances.

But the invention of the printing press changed things. Suddenly, people could express their own opinions to all of society, as thoughts and ideas were spread abroad which did not necessarily agree with the State Churches. And as copies of the Bible were printed, the people could finally compare what the Church taught with the Scriptures. It is no surprise then, that *dissension* from the State Churches increased as other voices were heard and as errors of Church doctrine and teaching became apparent to the hearts and spirits of men.

This dissension was sometimes violent but most often it was expressed as a murmur of discontent, since any outward form of disagreement was soundly punished. Some taught that "freedom in Christ" permitted indulgence, and lived wanton lives. Others preached mysticism or humanistic or gnostic philosophies.[1] The Reformation, on the other hand, was a like a volcano of dissension. And if Luther, Calvin, and Zwingli's followers were a volcanic explosion, Anabaptism was a second eruption which further changed the surface of whatever it touched. It was a time of turmoil, when schism and faction rumbled just beneath the surface and opinions sometimes ran hot like molten lava.

Within Anabaptism there were many differing interpretations of faith and doctrine. When its leaders decided to meet in the town of Schleitheim in February of 1527, they did not come together in unity, but in disparity. They met to write a statement of their beliefs in order to avoid erroneous doctrines.[2] These leaders assembled,

> ...in disagreement and confusion, testifying later that during the meeting the Holy Spirit had *led them to* **agreement** *and* **common convictions**.[3]

In spite of their differences of opinion and disagreements, the Holy Spirit brought these emerging leaders of Anabaptism to the unity of the Trinity. They later testified of God's sovereign work in enabling agreement by His presence among them:

> Dear brothers and sisters, we who have been assembled in the Lord at Schleitheim . . . as obedient children of God, sons and daughters, who have been . . . *uncontradicted by all the brothers*, completely at peace. Herein we have sensed *the unity of the Father and of our common Christ as present with us in their Spirit.* For the Lord is a Lord of *peace and not of quarreling*, as Paul indicates. (I Corinthians 14:33)[4]

Almost five hundred years later, the unity of the Father, Son, and Spirit, which was so evident at Schleitheim is no longer a delineating mark of the greater body of Anabaptists. The peace brought about by God's presence has waned, and dissension and disunity have flowed once again. A bishop in a single Mennonite conference recently typed up a paper which listed every division that has occurred throughout his conference. There have been more than thirty from the time of Zwingli to the present day. The reasons for division have been varied, including disagreements over whether to hold services in English or German, church discipline, patriotism, style of dress, women's cut hair, radio preaching, driving automobile versus buggy, allowing electricity and telephones, and much more.[5]

It is valuable to understand that the separation of one brotherhood from another is not necessarily wrong. Amicable family separations occur every time a man and a woman leave their own homes to begin a new life together in the covenant of marriage. Likewise, if a separation between two groups in the body of Christ occurs as a result of a peaceable agreement to take separate pathways, it can be blessed by God's Spirit. If those groups are able to continue to fellowship together and to bless and affirm each other even though they are headed in different directions in their callings, God can honor the separation.

But many of the separations which have happened throughout our history as Anabaptists have been unhealthy in nature, being in reality divisions rather than peaceable separations. Unable to "agree to disagree," we have divided because we have taken offense at one another:

> An *offended brother* is more *unyielding* than a *fortified city*, and *disputes* are like the *barred gates* of a citadel. (Proverbs 18:19)

Patterns of Rejecting and Dividing

Historically, through our experience with the State Churches, we have learned a *pattern of rejecting and dividing* from others when they do not agree with us. Several years ago, as a small group of intercessors waited in God's presence, He showed us an image of a large sword used against the Anabaptists by the State Churches and political rulers. The power of that sword was fierce and devastating. The next image we saw was a group of people who after being struck by this great sword of persecution, began fighting each other with smaller swords or daggers. Reaping from the unforgiving judgments they had sown, these Anabaptists responded to being violently rejected by turning to stab each other with smaller swords of *division* and *rejection*.

After God showed us the destructiveness of our infighting and rejection, He took our intercessory group to the Scriptures and revealed that we have often carried the attitude of Cain towards his brother Abel. We have been "murdering" each other, just as Jesus and John equate *heart attitudes* with *murder*:

> Whoever does not practice righteousness is not of God, **nor is he who does not love his brother**. For this is the message that you heard from the beginning, that we should **love one another, not as Cain** who was of the wicked one and **murdered his brother** . . . We know that we have passed from death to life, because we *love the brethren*. He who *does not love his brother abides in death*. **Whoever hates his brother is a murderer** . . . By this we know love, because He laid down His life for us. And we also ought to *lay down our lives for the brethren*. (I John 3:10-16)

> You have heard that it was said to the people long ago, 'Do not murder, and *anyone who murders* will be *subject to judgment.*' But I tell you that **anyone who is *angry* with his brother will be *subject to judgment*.** (Matthew 5:21-22)

By taking offense throughout our history of church splits and disagreements, we have become *unyielding* like the fortified city or the barred gates of Proverbs. Our disputes have caused tensions, strained communications, and lack of respect and love for the "other side." Feeling we are right and "they" are wrong, we have been slanderers, backbiters, and gossipers, who have "stabbed" and "murdered" each other with daggers of rejection. And when we disagree, many of us have learned to reject rather than to forgive.

Historically Rejected

For well over two hundred years, our ancestors were rejected by Church and State, and by society members who either despised them or feared reprisals for relating to Anabaptists. Except for those within their own communities and "truehearted" sympathizers, they were on their own.[6]

Almost from the start, those rejections were strengthened because of the uprising at Münster in 1534 and 1535. Our reputation was greatly tarnished when authorities erroneously associated this violent and cult-like peasant revolt with true Anabaptists:

> The unsavory series of events at Münster had *permanent consequences*. The orthodox (Catholics, Protestants) felt . . . more justified than ever in *identifying Anabaptism with revolution*, an interpretation which has *continued* among Lutheran, Reformed, and Catholic filial historians down to the twentieth century. The civil authorities *intensified their repression* of any person who failed to submit to the rules . . . where he resided.[7]

Anabaptists experienced other rejections through betrayals. Faced with torture and suffering, some friends and family members revealed to authorities the names of those within their churches, causing their subsequent arrests. And like Judas, informers were sent out to infiltrate Anabaptist gatherings, worshipping with them as though they were joining their community. Sometimes these informers betrayed entire Anabaptist fellowships into prison, torture, or death.

Though extreme oppression slackened from time to time, Anabaptists were still punished. In Zurich, Mennonite marriages were nullified and children of Mennonites were declared illegitimate.[8] In many places, restrictions prohibited not only the preaching of the gospel but also the building of meetinghouses, the purchasing of land, freedom to marry, and even to bury their dead. There were financial fines for being Anabaptist, and for many, confiscation of property and expulsion from their country.[9]

Eventually, because of such long term harassment, we began to assume that being an Anabaptist *automatically* meant being rejected. Our reactions to centuries of persecution have caused a "persecution complex" to trickle down to our attitudes in the present. Today, whether from the brethren in our fellowships, family members, the people in the world, or other church denominations, many Anabaptists carry a *fearful expectation of rejection* in relationships. From one generation to the next, we have passed on the mindset of guarding ourselves from the rejections of others. We have barred the "walls" and the "gates" of our hearts and fortified ourselves through our offenses. We need God's help to forgive, and forgive, and forgive, until forgiveness has softened our defenses, and made our hearts pliable once again.

A Call To Unity In Diversity

In Christ, no matter how many times Christians divide or disagree, God still considers us *one* spiritual family. He has called us to a deep, abiding unity like the unity of the heavenly Father and Son, whose attitudes have always been to pour out favor and blessing upon each other. Every interaction in their "Family" has been with complete honor and respect. Three times in this prayer, Jesus stresses His unity with the Father and prays that *our* unity would be like *theirs*:

> I do not pray for these alone, but *also for those who will believe in Me through their word*; that they **all may be one, as You, Father, are in Me, and I in You**; that they also may *be one in Us*, that the world may believe that You sent Me. And the glory which You gave Me I have given them, *that*

they may be one just as We are one: I in them, and You in
Me; that they may be *made perfect in one,* and that the *world
may know* that *You have sent Me,* and have *loved them* as
You have *loved Me.* (John 17:20-23, *NKJV*)

There is one body and one Spirit, just as you were called in
one hope of your calling; one Lord, one faith, one baptism;
one God and Father of all, who is above all, and through all,
and in you all. (Ephesians 4:1-6)

It is because each "child" in our spiritual family looks
very different from all the others, that we sometimes think we
couldn't possibly be siblings who share the same Father. But in
earthly families, God has made each sibling very unique, so why
wouldn't He also do that in His heavenly family? It is *acceptable* and even *desirable* to be different, but we have assumed if
other spiritual siblings differ from us, they are "wrong."

In another analogy, Paul uses our original image of the
human body. Because we have been used to attitudes of
rejection and division, we have been unable to see that our
uniqueness as "body parts" is divinely intentional. In Jesus' body,
we all have a specific function and purpose to accomplish:

For as the *body is one* and has many members, but all the
members of that one body, being many, *are one body,* so also
is Christ. For *by one Spirit* we were all *baptized into one
body*—whether Jews or Greeks, whether slaves or free—and
have all been made to drink into *one Spirit. For in fact the
body is not one member but many.* If the foot should say,
"Because I am not a hand, I am not of the body," is it therefore not of the body? And if the ear should say, "Because I
am not an eye, I am not of the body," is it therefore not of the
body? *If the whole body were an eye, where would be the
hearing?* If the whole were hearing, where would be the
smelling? *But now God has set the members, each one of
them, in the body just as He pleased.* (I Corinthians 12:12-18,
NKJV)

We are not thirty or one hundred bodies in Christ, but
only *one,* and each denomination (and individual) is an essential
part. As a generalization, we might say the Amish have a

particular gift as a "leg" that is strong in the prophetic; Mennonites are gifted as an "arm" of helps; Brethren In Christ are a
"hand" of encouragement; Presbyterians are an "eye" of teaching; and the various independent churches an "ankle" of evangelism; Lutherans are an apostolic "ear"; and so on.

Just as the physical body suffers when a body part is
amputated, Christ's body suffers by cutting others away through
division. We have become an unhealthy body by rejecting the
gifts of other groups, or by not sharing our own strengths with
those who need our gifts:

> Instead, speaking the truth in love, we will in all things *grow
> up* into him who is *the Head*, that is, Christ. From him the
> *whole body, joined and held together* by *every supporting
> ligament*, grows and builds itself up in love, as *each part
> does its work*. (Ephesians 4:15-16)

Accepting the brotherhood of other groups is crucial to spiritual
health, so we can *grow* into the *mature* and complete body of
Jesus that we are meant to become.

Seeing With New Eyes

On earth, we think that if we divide from one another
and put space between us, we won't have to "deal" with each
other ever again. But we are mistaken, because we are all
already eternal beings (John 5:24). Though we have separated
humanly speaking, spiritually there is *no distance* between us.
Our Father, our Brother Jesus, and all the rest of us are already
an *eternal family* and our relationships as eternal siblings
have already started here on earth. All that is human and
mortal will be swallowed up, but *relationships* are eternal. That
is why we're told to view others from an eternal point of view.

We need new eyesight. If we are to learn how to reach out
to the other parts of the body of Christ who are very *un*like our
own churches or our own denominations, we will need to look
through new lenses. We need the **lens of the unseen:**

So we fix our eyes not on what is seen, but on *what is unseen*. For what is *seen is temporary,* but what is *unseen* is *eternal* . . . so that *what is mortal may be swallowed up by life.* Now it is God who has *made us for this very purpose* and has *given us the Spirit as a deposit,* guaranteeing what is to come. . . . *We live by faith, not by sight.* (II Corinthians 4:18-5:7)

From now on, therefore, *we regard no one from a human point of view*; even though we once knew Christ from a human point of view, we know him no longer in that way. So *if anyone is in Christ, there is a new creation*: *everything old has passed away; see, everything has become new!* (II Corinthians 5:16-18, *NRSV*)

By God's help we are not to see others through the eyes of our flesh, but through the lens of *eternal interaction which has already begun.* Relationships with others are not to be approached from "a worldly point of view" (*NIV*), but from the unseen and eternal place of being *new creations* in Christ.

Giving Grace and Fostering Unity

I have made pottery, taking it from raw clay all the way through to its finished product as a glazed ceramic pitcher or bowl. Before the firing processes, the clay is a dark brown, soft, and messy lump. After firing it is still the same piece of clay but now it is has a permanently defined shape which is much lighter in color. It has been hardened and beautifully glazed to seal its porous surface and to make it useful and attractive.

Like the clay's transformation, our Creator is making something of our earthly "clay" that looks entirely different in the spiritual realm. An imperfect piece of brown clay on a pottery wheel is basically "dirt", but a Master Potter's finished product is beautiful. If, by God's grace, we can begin to see each other as *eternal* creations, perhaps we will be able to stop examining the unfinished lump of clay on the wheel and taking offense at all that we think is incomplete and unattractive.

When we recognize earthly imperfections in others, we are still called to unity. Ephesians explains in practical terms *how* we can foster this true unity which allows for faults in others:

> I . . . beseech you to walk worthy of the calling with which you were called, with all *lowliness* and *gentleness,* with *longsuffering*, *bearing with* one another in love, endeavoring to keep the *unity of the Spirit* in the bond of *peace.* (Ephesians 4:1-3, *NKJV*)

We are exhorted to "walk worthy" of our calling, applying four attributes: *humility, gentleness, patience,* and *bearing with each other.* One meaning of the words "bearing with" is to *suffer.* There will be times when we suffer as we disagree with another believer or with another church because of our differences. For true unity, we may need to lay down our own preferences, our own styles of worship, our own theological backgrounds, our own lives. The word *longsuffering* (patience) is an additional clarification of the endurance required to keep unity: we may have to "suffer long", willing to permanently let go of causes and influences which have divided us in the past. By practicing this kind of yielding trust, we will be able to keep the unity of the Spirit in peace.

Recently, my husband and I attended a three-day conference where several different groups met for the purpose of developing heart "connections" together. Among the group which gathered were Reformed believers, Mennonites, Amish, Native Americans, Lutherans, those who attended non-denominational churches, and more.

The Amish hosted the meetings and led the worship times. In our church at home, my husband and I are very accustomed to a freer style of worship, using instruments. The Amish communities were much more comfortable with acappella singing, without instruments. For the first day and a half of the conference, I wrestled with fears and misunderstandings about the Amish-led worship times, because I could not "freely worship" during our singing. After pouring out my heart to God and with the encouragement of a more mature couple to give me insight, I received the wonderful revelation that to the Father, our *unity in light of our differences* was much more important to Him than the form of worship which was offered as we came together. With that understanding, I was able to focus on God as I sang a hymn beside my Amish friends, all fears and assumptions quelled by gaining His perspective on the matter.

Reconciliation

Good works of reconciliation have been occurring between the State Reformed church of Switzerland and Anabaptists (read the *Epilogue*) and will continue until, with God's help, they have been completed. There is much more reconciliation which needs to be accomplished, including reconciliation between our own Anabaptist denominations.

Jesus told the disciples, "Whoever is not *against* you is *for* you" (Luke 9:50). As Anabaptists who have experienced much rejection, we do need His healing touch to understand that those who are not against us are for us. Jesus has destroyed the dividing wall, not only between Jew and Gentile but between all believers:

> Here there is no Greek or Jew, circumcised or uncircumcised, barbarian, Scythian, slave or free, but Christ is all, and is in all. (Colossians 3:11)

> For he himself is *our peace*, who has made the *two one* and has *destroyed the barrier, the dividing wall of hostility*, by *abolishing in his flesh* the law with its commandments and regulations. His purpose was to create in himself *one new man* out of the two, thus making peace, and in this *one body* to *reconcile both of them to God through the cross, by which he put to death their hostility*. (Ephesians 2:14-16)

Thanks to God, through Christ, we can take action to walk away from our divisions and reach out in forgiveness, because

Christ has made peace through His death. He has created *one new man*, and that is *us*.

———————

Take time with this prayer. Don't rush through it, but let God speak to you specifically in order that healing may be full and thorough. It is a rather lengthy prayer, but each part is necessary and important.

Personal prayers of healing:
　　God, thank You for adopting me into Your family and for bringing others into Your family to be my brothers and sisters. Help me to pray, as I turn to You now.
　　You alone know how deeply I have personally been affected by a generational pattern of rejection. You are the only one who sees deep into my heart and can heal all the places where rejection has pierced like a sword. Please come and touch me: heal every place where rejection has existed. By Your Holy Spirit, apply your healing where rejection has affected my soul.[1]
　　Lord, You were rejected, that I might be received.[2] In Your presence, I now choose to forgive those family members whose names You bring to mind, for rejecting me: I forgive _____
_____ *(each name which comes to mind) for* _____. *(each offense which comes to mind). I forgive them, because I know You have forgiven me completely. I'm sorry I judged them. Carry every judgment I have made to the cross.*
　　Father, thank You for my church. I ask You now to bring to mind anyone in all my church experiences whom I need to forgive for their rejection. I forgive (each name) _____
_____ *for* _____ *(each offense).*

Cleansing For My Heritage:

You tell me to confess the sins of my fathers.[3] Forgive us for judging the Catholic churches and the Reformed churches for deeply rejecting Anabaptists. Father, forgive these churches and bless them with Your love and Your presence.

I confess that we have received rejections and carried them in our hearts through unforgiveness and embitterment. We have rejected others and judged and divided and "murdered" with our words and actions. Father, forgive us. Forgive those in my family heritage for rejecting and dividing from others. Forgive our bitterness and unforgiveness towards others in the body of Christ and others in the world.

Demolishing Strongholds:

Father, forgive us for being afraid of the rejection of others. If there are strongholds of rejection in my life or in my family line, I pull them down and bind every demonic attachment to these strongholds in Jesus' Name. I forbid rejection from operating in my life or in my family.

You say the Kingdom of God is advanced by those who forcefully lay hold of it.[4] So boldly, in the name of Jesus, I cut off all rejection and all division from my heart. I break their power in my life, in Christ's holy Name.

Prayers For Restoration:

Father, cleanse us and set us free. Heal us from the deep wounds of rejection we have experienced and cleanse us of all generational patterns of division. Fill with Your Spirit, every place where rejection and division have robbed us of the love of the Father and the love of Your family.[5]

Establish me in Your family and establish my earthly family and my people in their rightful and proper places in the body of Christ. Give us our spiritual inheritance.[6] Heal the divisions between our hearts and others, and bring us into Your true unity. Show us the pathway towards reconciliation and *make us ambassadors of reconciliation.*[7] *Give us Your grace to learn to walk in an attitude of forgiveness when offenses occur. Give us Your heavenly wisdom in these matters, that we may act in obedience and rest and not out of fear or anxiety.*[8]

Glorify Your name through my life. Thank You for all You are doing to make me like You. Thank You for hearing my prayer and for answering me.[9] *Keep me as Your precious one, hidden under Your wings.*[10]

In the name of my mighty Redeemer, Amen.

---

[1] Isaiah 61:1; [2] Isaiah 53:3-5;[3] Leviticus 26:40 and Nehemiah 9:2; [4] Matthew 11:12; [5] John 10:10; [6] Joel 2:25; [7] II Corinthians 5:18-20; [8] Isaiah 30:15 and James 3:17; [9] I John 5:14-15; [10] Isaiah 43:4 and Psalm 17:8.

Promises for you from John 17:20-26:

Your Father loves you *as much* as He loves Jesus. And Jesus *wants* you to be with Him, and He wants you to see God's glory. He promises to continue showing you the Father. By asking for unity and repenting for divisions, you have touched a deep place in God's heart, because His desire is that we would all be one. You have pleased God through your prayers. Be glad, and be encouraged in His love! Go, in His rest.

21

A RELIGIOUS APPROACH
TO GOD

How do we, as created beings, approach the Lord of the Universe, the Maker of all things, the all-powerful, almighty God who is self-existent? Certainly, we come into His presence with *reverence*. The Psalmist says, "God is *greatly to be feared in the assembly of the saints, and to be held in reverence* by all those around Him" (Psalm 89:7). We do not consider His holiness or His power carelessly as we approach His throne.

But assuming we have a reverent heart, we will find in the Scriptures many interesting descriptions of approaching God. According to David and the Psalmists, we may come with shouting, singing, blowing trumpets, playing a lute (guitar); with harp, timbrel (tambourine), or flutes; banging together loud and clashing cymbals, and even with vigorous dancing:

> Make a joyful *shout* to the Lord, all you lands! . . . *Come before His presence* with *singing*. (Psalm 100:1-4, *KJV*)

> Praise God *in His sanctuary* . . . Praise Him with the sound of the *trumpet*; Praise Him with the *lute and harp*! Praise Him with the *timbrel and dance*; Praise Him with *stringed instruments and flutes*! Praise Him with loud *cymbals*; Praise Him with *clashing cymbals*! (Psalm 150:1-5, *NKJV*)

> Then David *danced before the Lord with all his might*; . . . So David and all the house of Israel brought up the ark of the Lord with *shouting* and with the *sound of the trumpet* (II Samuel 6:14-15, *KJV*)

With all his might, David danced in God's presence, as all of Israel shouted and blew trumpets in celebration!

In the New Testament, we find another description of how to approach God's presence. We are told we may enter to stand right in front of the very throne of God:

> For we do not have a *High Priest* who cannot sympathize with our weaknesses, but (Jesus) was in *all points tempted as we are*, yet without sin. Let us *therefore* **come boldly** to the **throne of grace**, that we may obtain *mercy* and find *grace* to help in time of need. (Hebrews 4:15-16)

The word *boldly* is translated as, *all out-spokenness, frankness, bluntness.*[1] What an amazing thing that we may come before the throne of God and speak to Him frankly, bluntly, and with all out-spokenness! In another passage we are told *why* we can go to our God and "speak our minds" so openly:

> Having therefore, brethren, **boldness to enter** [2] into the holiest **by the blood of Jesus**, by a new and living way, which he hath *consecrated for us*, . . . Let us **draw near** *with a true heart in full assurance of faith*, having our *hearts sprinkled from an evil conscience*, and our bodies *washed with pure water*. (Hebrews 10:19-22, *KJV*)

It is because of the blood of Jesus that we *boldly* enter, summoned to draw near to our God with full confidence and assurance of faith. His exchange—His blood for our life—has purchased our permanent right-standing in God's sight (see chapter four). It is always in this light that we enter the throne room of heaven, with freedom to walk in boldly and confidently.

We never approach God's throne with the fear that Queen Esther felt as she prepared to enter the presence of King Ahasuerus. She was so afraid to come to his throne that she asked the Jews to fast for three days before she entered his courts. She knew she could die if he chose not to extend his golden scepter (Esther 4:11,16). Unlike Esther, we come to God as His child who has received full favor. We are the heirs of this King and He is *always* glad to see us.

The Corruption of Approaching God Freely

We know our hearts do not always allow us to approach God with this kind of bold freedom. Our minds agree with these truths, yet we feel hesitant to come so easily. We may have learned a different set of "rules" for approaching the throne. Many of these rules have come from being taught within a religious structure of faith. We've learned to worship in a certain way, to pray in a certain way and to live life according to certain religious perceptions about approaching God.

But the corruption of our free and childlike approach to God occurred long before man established structured religious practices (Matthew 18:3). It began all the way back in the garden of Eden at the tree of the knowledge of good and evil where the first sin occurred. It was there that humans began to *strive* in relating to God, and our approach to His presence changed.

Knowing Good and Evil

Let's look at the sin of Adam and Eve to understand how it affected man's approach to God. There were two voices that told Adam and Eve about the forbidden fruit of the tree of the knowledge of good and evil. One voice was the devil and the other was God. The devil (the serpent) told Eve her eyes would be opened, and she would know *good* and *evil* just like God, if she ate its fruit. The other voice, God, told Adam that the day he ate its fruit he would *die* (Genesis 2:17 and 3:5).

Adam and Eve did not physically die when they ate the fruit, but spiritually they died *immediately*. Suddenly, their "eyes were opened" and they became *afraid of God*. Before their sin, they were not afraid of God. It was only afterwards that they hid from His presence:

> Then the *eyes of both of them were opened*, and they realized that they were naked . . . Then the man and his wife heard

the sound of the Lord God as he was walking in the garden
in the cool of the day, and *they hid from the Lord God* among
the trees of the garden. But the Lord God called to the man,
"Where are you?" He answered, "I heard you in the garden,
and *I was afraid because I was naked; so I hid."* (Genesis
3:7-10)

The serpent was right: their eyes *were* opened. But he lied
about knowing good and evil exactly as *God* knows good and
evil. As a result of eating the fruit of the tree, they now knew
evil in the form of sin. And they also knew **good** *in the form of
sin.* Let me explain. Adam and Eve were created by God without
sin and were walking in *pure and holy goodness* **before** they ever
touched that piece of fruit from the tree of the knowledge of good
and evil. Now because of sin, they came to know an **impure**
good—a **sinful** good—not a righteous good. It was this "good"
and evil that caused their spirits to die.

We know well the *evil* of sin, but there are many aspects
of the seemingly *good* appearance of sin that we have not understood. For our purposes, we will only look at one: that is, our
attempt to be *good by our own efforts* rather than because God
has made us His righteousness. Ever since the fall, man has been
trying to be good enough to approach God. In the context of
church life, this "good" causes us to want to prove our worth
and our value through good works. When put into a religious
setting, Eden's fear of hiding from God's presence turns into a
seemingly "holy" *striving* to make ourselves acceptable to Him.
This kind of "good" is the **essence of religion:** *using God to
make ourselves look "good" either in man's eyes, or in God's
eyes.*

Righteousness By Our Efforts

Another way of saying it is that we religiously attempt to
be "right" by our own merit. We want to be *self*-righteous. For a
period of time, in order to show me the depth of my own self-
righteous attitudes, God allowed me to experience a series of

failures. The first failures were my impatience at others who were not doing things the "right" way. I was trying to study at a local library. All day long, in spite of an obvious sign at the entrance which read "Quiet, Please," there were various people —even library workers—who were talking out loud in conversations. I was agitated and judgmental, though I knew as a Christian I should have been able to give them a good dose of mercy.

I had already lost my temper on the way to the library when I'd driven behind no less than five different vehicles who were all traveling at least five miles per hour *under* the speed limit. By the time the fifth car pulled in front of my path, I grumbled angrily to God and yelled at the other driver. Convicted of my sin, I asked God to show me why I was so angry and immediately the words, "self-righteousness" came to mind. I had gotten angry because these slow-poke drivers weren't "following the rules," but were instead driving *under* the speed limit, and that was inconveniencing poor li'l-ole-me! At the library, I had gotten angry for the same reason: those who weren't following the rule to be quiet were affecting my studying time by their "disobedience."

Over the next several days, my trials increased. At my part-time job that weekend, I made several considerably large mistakes which required the help of my managers to set straight. For the rest of the work day, I felt like a failure and worked extra hard to *prove* to my bosses that I was dependable, even though they had both graciously forgiven my errors.

Still feeling condemned and discouraged the following day, my husband and I decided to drive to a nearby park and go for a walk. When we returned to our car we saw that it had been vandalized. I had stuffed my purse under a car seat, but apparently it had not been entirely hidden and the thieves had broken a window to get in. My purse was gone. I knew better than to leave it in the car. I'd felt a "nudge" in my heart to take it with me, but I hadn't wanted to be bothered by carrying it and disregarded the inner check.

I felt absolutely terrible. For the entire evening and into the next day, I chastised myself, upset at all the mistakes I had made. That was when I realized the issue of my heart was really self-righteousness, because I was condemning myself for all my errors and sin. A healthy spiritual response towards my mistakes and even my own sins would have been to repent, receive God's mercy and forgiveness, and rest in His favor. But in my heart, I felt "wrong" or "flawed" because I had made so many mistakes which revealed my lack of "rightness."

The Prodigal's Brother

Self-righteousness is an enemy of our souls because it prohibits us from receiving the depth of God's grace. When we are self-righteous, we're like the prodigal's *brother* in the story of the prodigal son (Luke 15). Though always around his father's house, he had never learned to know his father's love. All the years of his faithful service to his father were done through feeling duty as the "good" son. The older brother prided himself on being righteous. He had done the *right* thing by faithfully serving where the younger brother had so miserably failed. He expected to receive his inheritance because he'd *earned* it by his own hard work, but it was this very attitude that kept him from seeing his father's generosity:

> The older brother became angry and refused to go (into the house). So his father went out and pleaded with him. But he answered his father, 'Look! All these years I've been *slaving* for you and *never disobeyed your orders*. Yet you never gave me even a young goat so I could celebrate with my friends. But when this son of yours who has squandered your property with prostitutes comes home, you kill the fattened calf for him!' *'My son,' the father said, 'you are always with me, and everything I have is yours.* But we had to celebrate and be glad, because this brother of yours was dead and is alive again; he was lost and is found.'" (Luke 15:25-32, parentheses are mine)

The older brother felt like he was a slave (verse 29). His anger and resentment revealed that he didn't understand that the father's home was his home, and the father's provisions were his provisions. His perceptions of his father were more along the lines of a slave-owner and though "everything the father had was his," he could not perceive that the father's blessings also belonged to him. And because he did not know his father's generous heart, he continued to try to prove his goodness by earning his inheritance as a son.

The prodigal, on the other hand, knew his own righteousness was like a filthy rag (Isaiah 64:6). He had come to the end of himself and returned to his father, choosing not to hide his real, needy self. His only words as they met were an admission of his own inability to be right (Luke 15:21). When the father accepted him back fully as a son, the prodigal *received* his sonship, not based on his own merit, but because the father had graciously *given* him back his rights as a son.

The Pharisees

Jesus told His disciples that unless their righteousness *surpassed* the righteousness of the Pharisees, they would not enter the Kingdom of heaven (Matthew 5:20). The righteousness of the Pharisees was based on their pride in following every fine detail of the law correctly:

> (Jesus said to the Pharisees) . . . on the outside you *appear to people as righteous* but *on the inside* you are full of hypocrisy and wickedness. (Matthew 23:23-28)

The righteousness that Jesus provided is that which surpasses. It is free, *apart from striving* to do things right:

> But now a **righteousness from God, apart from law**, has been made known. . . . This righteousness from God *comes* **through faith** in Jesus Christ to all who believe. There is no difference, for *all have sinned and fall short of the glory of God, and are* **justified freely** by his grace through the redemp-

> tion that came by Christ Jesus. God presented him as a
> sacrifice of atonement, **through faith in his blood**.
> (Romans 3:21-27)

Our righteousness as children of God will always be because He
has loved us. It will never be based on law, because Jesus
fulfilled the law for us, meaning He did everything righteously,
and we only need to depend on Him in order to be counted *right*
before God:

> Do not think that I have come to abolish the Law or the
> Prophets; I have not come to abolish them but to *fulfill them*.
> (Matthew 5:17)

Jesus calls the religious leaders of his day hypocrites
(Mark 7:6). In the Greek, a hypocrite is described as someone
who is feigning an act or playing a part on stage.[3] The Pharisees
didn't recognize the motives of their own hearts and only
pretended to know God.

> Also (Jesus) spoke this parable to some who **trusted in them-
> selves that they were righteous,** and despised others: Two
> men went up to the temple to pray, *one a Pharisee and the
> other a tax collector.* The Pharisee stood and prayed thus
> with himself, 'God, I thank You that *I am not like other men*
> —extortioners, unjust, adulterers, or even as this tax collec-
> tor. *'I fast twice a week; I give tithes of all that I possess.'*
> And the tax collector, standing afar off, would not so much
> as raise his eyes to heaven, but beat his breast, saying, '*God,
> be merciful to me a sinner!'* I tell you, *this man went down to
> his house justified rather than the other. . . .* (Luke 18:9-14)

Tax collectors were despised because they often inflated
the amount of tax collected, for their own gain. But this man
openly admitted his need, and was counted as right. The Pharisee did all the right religious deeds, but remained impure
because he trusted in himself rather than in God. Instead of
knowing God's generous character as Provider of righteousness,
the Pharisee lost touch with God's heart and clung fast to a for-
mula of "rightness" long after God had removed His presence.

God hates this kind of false religion of our own making, because it prevents intimacy with Him and with others.

Religious Striving

God's love is already ours. We will never win it and we will never lose it. Religion is based on a subtle lie which says, "*I* know God and *I* do things for God," with the focus on "*I*". True understanding of God places the focus and the attention on God because we know Him as love and are at rest in his deep affection.

But if we do not understand how much God loves us and as a result, attempt to win His love by *doing* things for him, we are striving religiously. Years ago, as God was uncovering the reality of my own religious striving to please Him out of a heart of unworthiness, God whispered to me, "Don't DO, just BE." I was aware of the many Scriptures in James and other books of the Bible that tell us faith without works is dead (James 2:20), but I had gone so far overboard in doing works to *prove* my worth, that God was correcting my error of self-righteous living. He wanted me to be healed so I could enter the throne room anytime I desired, without feeling like I had to prove my right to be there. God was lovingly giving me freedom to do absolutely nothing for Him until I could know my true "rightness" by His grace alone.

It would be sad for an earthly father if every time His child came to him, she came with some proof of how good she had been that day. At first, it may appear she is a very obedient child, but soon her efforts of trying to be accepted would become clear, as the father began to see the true motive behind every gift she brought or every good deed she did. A loving father would immediately set about helping his little one to know his approval *without* her attempts to prove her worth or win his favor.

Hiding From God and Man

Our self-righteous approach to God comes mainly from a deep fear of rejection (chapters 13 and 20). Feeling like we could never be truly accepted with all our flaws, we bury the "rotten" person we *really* think we are, and put before God and men a cleaned up version of ourselves. Just as Adam and Eve hid from God because they were afraid of standing before him naked, we hide from God the real "naked" truth about ourselves. And like they hid their nakedness from each other by putting on fig leaves, we also cover up our real self and keep it hidden from others. From the garden until now, man has been creating ways to hide who he is in order to try and disguise how he really feels about his inner man.

One of the ways we hide is by using our religion as a mask. The religious person hides behind rules and regulations and "dos and don'ts." He thinks that following the rules will "fix" the problem of the unworthy and sinful man inside, so he pretends and tucks away his weaknesses and his inner life from other people and from God. But this hiding is no different than the feigned hypocrisy of the Pharisees.

Jesus calls us into the light of exposure where we admit truthfully that all the good we have done is purely because of God and not because of our own "rightness." As God's children, whatever we do is done "in God" and because of His grace.

> He who *believes in Him is not condemned;* but *he who does not believe is condemned* . . . And this is the condemnation, that the light has come into the world, and *men loved darkness rather than light,* **because their deeds were evil.** For everyone practicing evil hates the light and does not come to the light, **lest his deeds should be exposed.** But he who does the truth **comes to the light,** that his **deeds may be clearly seen, that they have been done in God.**" (John 3:18-21)

The only response we can have if we see that we are religious is to humble ourselves and come out of hiding from both God and man. In God's presence, we ask Him to show us the reality of His love and approval, and call out for help to lay down our pretense. Layer upon layer, He begins to soften our hearts of hiding and striving. We invite His Spirit to come and to lay a new foundation into our hearts; **a foun-**

dation of our *worth* and *value*, of His *favor* and *love*.

With fellow believers, we begin to share openly and honestly who we are—both strengths and weaknesses. Learning to be vulnerable with other believers who are also willing to be vulnerable, is one of the greatest spiritual "weapons" we have against religious hiding. Our humility of word and deed as we share our inner beings will enable us to come into the light where we will find love, mercy, and grace.

Anabaptists and Religion

If you are like me in any way, as you have been reading you have probably thought of your own examples of self-righteous and religious striving, either personally or in the lives of others. There are most likely situations you can think of which demonstrate the religion of being "good" or of hiding.

As an Anabaptist, I have asked myself why we are often religious as a people. There is no singular answer. *Many* influencing factors have contributed to our tendencies to be religious. From judging the State Churches for their extremely religious approach to God, to our embitterment and turning away from God in fear, to unbelief, worldly sorrow, and the fear of man or fear of death: all these things and more have caused us to attempt to prove our own righteousness, because as we lost touch with God, we "forgot" His great grace. And perhaps the greatest influence has been *receiving the rejections of our heritage* deep into our hearts (chapter 20) so that we began to feel a need to prove our worth and our "goodness".

Whatever the reasons for the establishment of religion in our forefathers' lives, we only need to recognize that we have all inherited in varying degrees, a measure of approaching God religiously. The "fruit" in our generation was born out of the "root" of an ancient tree planted in the garden of Eden, nurtured in the Dark Ages State Church, and carried through the Reformation, and into Anabaptism's historical pathway to the present day.

Elements of Religion

In the Bible, there are four aspects of religion, *three* of which I will call "false" religion:

• True religion. This healthy and true religion does good deeds, but *always* with the Father and always *because* of love (James 1:27).

• Pharisaical religion which places overemphasis on traditions and forms of how things are to be done,

• Idol worship. Giving undue attention/affection to something other than God, either a physical statue or icon, or by an attitude of the heart (*ie*/money, a job).

• Philosophies of men, like those Paul addressed in Athens (Acts 17:18-21),

In order to turn away from "false" religion, it is important to understand some of its causes, as well as its ingredients. We have already discussed some of these issues which can contribute to approaching God's throne room religiously, and we'll continue with the others after we present our list of topics here:

• Using God to make ourselves look good
    (*self*-righteousness)
• Hiding from God and each other
• Believing lies about God's character
• A critical spirit (judgment)
• Control
• Spiritual pride
    (Wanting to be like God apart from the work of the cross)
• Legalism
• Placing tradition above the Word of God

- Worldly Sorrow
- Fear Of God
- Fear Of Man

Lies Or Truth

A distorted view of God comes from believing lies about Him. These lies are not obvious to us, but are implanted subtly into our hearts and minds through our religious experiences or our life experiences (II Corinthians 11:3-4). That is why the Word tells us to renew our minds so we can know God's will. The lies we may have believed about God are harmful, coming from the "father of lies" and the "accuser," so it is essential to understand and turn away from the errors in our hearts and minds where our concepts of God are concerned (John 8:44).

One of the lies we have already uncovered in previous chapters involves our perception of God as one who punishes harshly, rather than seeing Him as a Father who lovingly corrects His children (I John 4:18). This single error is enough to create within our souls the need to prove ourselves and to approach God with fear and form, instead of freedom. Other lies which the enemy whispers to us about God's character also warp our ability to approach freely: for example, believing He is not trustworthy, believing He is authoritatively demanding, believing He sees us as "bad" people, or believing He has abandoned us. There are many other lies which corrupt our family relationships with the Father, with the Son and with our spiritual brothers and sisters. Each lie is an attempt by the enemy of our souls to accuse God to our hearts and twist His character (Job 1:11 and 2:5,9). By God's grace (and often with the help of other believers), we are to "cast down" these arguments and accusations, and bring our thoughts into obedience to the mind of Christ (2 Corinthians 10:5). As lies and error are uncovered and we begin replacing them with truth, we will find a greater trust in the One who summons us to "draw near" and a greater ability to *humbly* and *confidently* approach His holy throne.

A Critical Spirit or Love

One of my friends owned and boarded horses at her stables. "Sky" was the dominant male horse, quickly establishing himself as the head of the herd through sparring with the other horses. Once Sky established his preeminence, the other horses also sparred with each other to establish their own "rank" of dominance, from highest to lowest.

When we are religious, we often establish a sort of "pecking order" in our relationships because we feel unworthy. Carrying a critical spirit is one type of response towards people which masks our heart of unworthiness. We begin to *compare* in order to feel more "right" about ourselves, examining another's actions and making internal judgments regarding the correctness of those actions.

As religious people, our human pecking order will look different from those in the animal kingdom, but the principle is the same. When we meet others, we begin sizing up their "spirituality," their intelligence, their cleverness, their physical appearance or dress, and anything else that strikes our minds and hearts. We see them from that place of "rightness" or "wrongness," determining where they are "missing it" and where they are right according to the rules of our religious training or perceptions. Comparing ourselves to others, we place ourselves either above them or below them in the family structure of the Kingdom.

If a person seems to be very spiritual or clever or attractive, for example, we may place them above us in the pecking order in our hearts. In that case, we start to feel unworthy in their presence and we *strive* to impress them by our behavior or our words. We may feel awkward or uncomfortable when we are with them because we esteem them as "better" than us. Afraid that they will reject us if they discover our sinfulness or our lack, we relate to them without letting our true self be seen.

If we meet another brother or sister and determine through our critical eye that *we* are more spiritual, more attractive, or more gifted, we automatically place them below us in our religious pecking order. Relating to others who are "below" us will not make us feel uncomfortable, because we have a measure of personal confidence when we are around them. Often, however, if we have determined they are *far* below us in stature, we simply will not want to spend much time with them because by virtue of our description of religion, we want to *look good*, and they will not help us in achieving that goal. The persons we feel most comfortable with are those whom we consider close to our own level of accomplishment and value.

When we act out of a religious, critical spirit, we feel we need to compete for our place in the family. For many, the competition will drive us to be the best and to strive for approval in whatever we do in life. We will not truly be able to love others without discrimination because of our need to find approval through our "position" within the family.

But when we are aware of other's sins and error, we are not to enter into a condemning, critical attitude. Jesus had this to say about how we perceive the faults of our brothers in the Lord:

> And *why do you look at the speck in your brother's eye, but do not consider the plank in your own eye?* Or how can you say to your brother, 'Let me remove the speck from your eye'; and look, a plank is in your own eye? Hypocrite! *First remove the plank from your own eye,* and then you will see clearly to remove the speck from your brother's eye. (Matthew 7:1-5)

One of the greatest evidences of humility is recognizing that *we* are the person who needs God's mercy more than anyone else on the planet. As we allow God to touch the gross "plank" of our own sins, our compassion for others who are walking in sin and error will rise up, and we will be able to carefully address their comparatively small specks.

Years ago, one of my mature spiritual "fathers" in the faith shared with my husband and me a tremendously helpful insight on the difference between the voice of condemnation and the voice of the Holy Spirit's conviction of sin. When the enemy points out our sin, it is always with *condemnation* and *accusation*. But when the Holy Spirit points out our sin, His manner is always *positive* and *affirming* in its correction. Conviction of the Holy Spirit is always *absent* of any shame or condemnation.

Just as we learn to discern the difference between the voice of God and the enemy's voice concerning our own sin, we can also learn to discern whether the enemy is whispering condemnation about our brother or sister, or whether the Holy Spirit is speaking to us about their sin because He is calling us to prayer, or to forgive, or to speak His truthful love concerning a matter. There truly is *no condemnation* for those who are in Christ Jesus, first toward ourselves, and then toward others (Romans 8:1).

Knowing our Father's constant love is one key to silencing our critical spirit. If we understand His love for us as fully complete, whether we are perfect or whether we have just stumbled and fallen, we will be able to see that God also loves all of our siblings in this same manner. As we grasp this depth of His love for us though we are flawed, we will be able to give favor to others who are weak. We will also be able to enjoy God's favor poured out on those who seem to have a greater measure of wisdom, blessing or anointing than we do, because we are at rest in the Father's absolute affection for us. The grace of God towards ourselves (love your neighbor *as yourself)* and the grace and favor of God towards our brothers and sisters will go a long way in quieting the voice of the accuser of the brethren, as he whispers condemnations to our minds (Matthew 22:39).

Control or Service

Unhealthy control is another element of religion. The most obvious example in light of our history is the extreme control of the State Catholic Church over all who lived within their domain. The Pharisees were also controlling as they required strict obedience to their traditions. Jesus counseled the disciples not to follow their example of burdening the people with undue demands:

> The teachers of the law and the Pharisees sit in Moses' seat. So you must obey them and do everything they tell you. But *do not do what they do, for they do not practice what they preach.* They *tie up heavy loads* and *put them on men's shoulders, but they themselves are not willing to lift a finger to move them.* (Matthew 23:2-4)

We are called to be like Jesus and not like the Pharisees or like many of the historical State Catholic Church leaders. We are to serve one another out of love rather than dominate one another because of fear or selfish exaltation or ambition.

Since we will be addressing control more thoroughly in another chapter, we will only mention it as one of the elements of religion and move on to the next element.

Pride or Admitting Our Need

Pride is devastating to our churches, our families, and to our own lives. Religious pride comes from our self-righteous hiding from God and man, but is even *stronger* than self righteousness. You might say pride is self-righteousness that has hardened our hearts. The prophet Ezekiel exposes pride as one of the devil's original sins:

> Your *heart became proud* on account of your beauty, and you *corrupted your wisdom* because of your splendor. So I threw you to the earth; I made a spectacle of you before kings. By your many sins and dishonest trade you have desecrated your sanctuaries. (Ezekiel 28:17-18)

Like Lucifer, pride causes us to exalt our own gifts and our own desires above the gifts and desires of others. In essence, we want to be worshiped instead of giving God all worship and praise. And like the religious leaders of Jesus' day, we do things in order to be seen by men:

> And when you pray, you shall not be like the hypocrites. For they love to pray standing in the synagogues and on the corners of the streets, *that they may be seen by men.* Assuredly, I say to you, they have their reward. (Matthew 6:5)

Because pride exalts us before God and man, it keeps us from *admitting our mistakes.* It is motivated by hiding great insecurity, so we find it hard to repent when we miss the mark. Afraid of exposure, we are unwilling to allow God to uncover what is hidden and will not admit our need for healing. Instead, we deny failure and weakness and rather than admit fault, we take offense or blame others. Pride does not apologize and resists attempts to reconcile.

We will often separate ourselves from others through our prideful lack of vulnerability and openness. The Pharisees separated themselves from the common man because they did not want to be "corrupted" by sinfulness. They condemned Jesus as one who ". . . eats and drinks with tax collectors and sinners":

> When the teachers of the law who were Pharisees saw him eating with the 'sinners' and tax collectors, they asked his disciples: *"Why does he eat with tax collectors and 'sinners'?"* On hearing this, Jesus said to them, *"It is not the healthy who need a doctor, but the sick. **I have not come to call the righteous, but sinners.**"* (Mark 2:16-17)

Jesus responded to their prideful separation by telling them it is the repentant sinner who receives the *healing* of the Lord. Jesus came to heal the brokenhearted, the captive, the blind, and the oppressed (Isaiah 61). In reality, every single person on earth qualifies as brokenhearted, captive, blind and oppressed, simply because we are a fallen race. But, only those who are *willing to admit their need* will receive the healing of the Physician. God actually *esteems* those who admit their need and open up to both God and man. He responds to those who are willing to uncover everything to receive their loving Father's gentle work:

> Has not my hand made all these things, and so they came
> into being?" declares the Lord. *"This is the one I esteem*: he
> who is *humble* (poor, needy, afflicted)[4] and *contrite* (lame,
> stricken, smitten)[5] in spirit, and trembles at my word. (Isaiah
> 66:2, parentheses are mine)

But if we are proud and consistently unwilling to humble
ourselves, we will eventually become hardened by our sin:

> For this people's *heart has become calloused*; they *hardly*
> *hear with their ears*, and they have *closed their eyes*. Other-
> wise they might see with their eyes, hear with their ears,
> understand with their hearts, and *turn, and I would heal*
> *them*. (Acts 28:27; see also Isaiah 6: 9-10)

The prideful have closed their eyes to God, and their ears cannot
hear. With calloused hearts, they can no longer see that God is
waiting to heal, if they will only return to the Lord. It is the
humble who turn to Him who will find the healing hand of
God touching their lives.

False Humility or Worth

In our churches, there is a type of false humility which is
really just another form of pride. We might call it an "upside-
down pride." This pride is also based on the deep inner
unworthiness we feel. As a matter of fact, this false pride is
straightforward about feeling unworthy.

When we are honored or used by God, or when we are
given good things, false humility responds by saying, "I am so
unworthy," or "Who am I, that I should receive this, or that . . .?"
False humility is not able to receive our *position* in Christ. It
rejects the blessings and riches which the Father and Son have
given to us through the cross. It is only willing to apprehend a
part of the cross and resurrection in order to *appear* pious.

Unfortunately, this is an aspect of pride which has greatly
assailed Anabaptists in our present day. False humility is not able
to fully agree that God has made us righteous and holy. Rather

than embracing the fact that we *were* condemned sinners but in Christ we have *become* righteous children and saints, false humility stops short of apprehending our position as a new creation in Christ.

True humility is willing to receive what Jesus has done on the cross in *full measure*. True humility says, "Yes, I was condemned, but now I am God's precious child. I was a child of wrath, but now I am fully and completely pleasing to my Father. I was rebellious, but God is changing my heart to make me an obedient child. I am able to do exploits for Him because He has changed me from sinner to saint and from fetid to favored (Daniel 11:32). I am loved by God and I am worthy of His love because He has declared it to be so (I John 3:1)! I have a purpose; I have a destiny; and God has given me something important to accomplish on this earth (Acts 13:36; Jeremiah 29:11; Romans 8:28; Ephesians 2:10; Philippians 2:13)." These declarations are a part of *true* humility, but to our religious ears, they sound like pride.

The Jews in Antioch rejected the good news of the provisions of the cross and Paul and Barnabas boldly rebuked them:

> Then Paul and Barnabas grew *bold* and said, "It was necessary that the word of God should be spoken to you first; but since *you reject it,* and **judge yourselves unworthy of everlasting life**, behold, we turn to the Gentiles. (Acts 13:46)

Paul identified the crux of their sin: by rejecting God's Word, they *judged themselves unworthy* of the life God *wanted* to *give* them through Christ. They rejected God's free gift and held on to their own form of piety. In Christ, we have become righteous, holy, and redeemed; but we need to choose to agree with Him about our new position as His child and not reject or judge ourselves as unworthy (I Corinthians 1:30; II Corinthians 1:21-22).

We have believed we are not to embrace our righteousness or to agree that we are cleansed or holy, because to do so would *appear* to be prideful. Instead, we have thought that by debasing ourselves, we have arrived at humility. But our own pious acts or self degrading words and deeds which are done to *appear* humble, will burn up as wood, hay, and stubble, because they are built on the wrong foundation. The only true foundation is Jesus Christ and He has provided the way for us to say, "I have been made perfect and holy" (I Corinthians 3:11-12; Hebrews 10:10,14). Praise His Name!

Legalism and Tradition

We will study these final two elements of religion in the next chapter. These topics are so entwined into the practice of our faith as Anabaptists, that they require a more thorough discussion.

Coming Boldly As We Are

The hymn refrain, "Just As I Am," has been sung by thousands, if not millions of repentant people who have made their way to the altar. It is indeed appropriate to approach God freely and openly, "just as we are," then to understand we have been forgiven in Christ's blood. We have nothing to hide from the Father of our spirits (Hebrews 12:9), whether we are weak or strong, poor or rich, sinful or forgiven. We come boldly, made clean by His blood, with frankness and forthrightness. God sees all and never reproaches us as we stand and sing and dance and shout before His throne, with joy and exaltation for this complete and total Lover of our souls (II Thessalonians 2:13).

> Praise the Lord. *Sing* to the Lord a new song, his *praise in the assembly of the saints.* Let Israel *rejoice* in their Maker; let the people of Zion *be glad* in their King. Let them *praise* his name with *dancing* and *make music* to him with *tambourine and harp. For the Lord takes delight in his people; he crowns the humble with salvation.* Let the saints *rejoice in this honor* and *sing for joy* on their beds. (Psalm 149:1-5)

Heavenly Father, thank You that I can approach You confidently, speaking everything in my heart.[1] *Thank You that I can come with complete freedom into Your presence.*

Personal cleansing:

If there are parts of me I've tried to hide from Your all-seeing eyes, forgive me. I don't want to draw back from You in any way. Shine Your light on the places within me that need healing.[2] *I open all of my life to You.*

I confess the times I've used You, and used "serving You" in order to make myself look good. Father, I'm sorry, and I ask Your forgiveness. Tear down all the walls of religion in my life and replace them with a deeper relationship with You. I choose not to walk religiously in any way, as I interact with You and with others.

I know sometimes I've created my own righteousness instead of receiving Your righteousness.[3] *I confess my pride and arrogance. I receive my value, my righteousness and my position as Your child, as gifts from You to me.*[4]

And forgive the times I've acted with false humility. Help me to be open with others about my weaknesses and my strengths. Thank You for my gifts and talents.[5] *I accept them fully, along with every blessing and every good gift You want to give to me.*[6] *Teach me to be truthfully humble, yet bold. Give me wisdom as I relate honestly to people.*

Father, at times I have had a critical and judgmental attitude. I have also given undue adoration to others, if I thought they were much better than me. I repent for both these sins of unholy comparison. I invite You to convict me when I'm being critical. Wash away all my habits of judging others: take them to the cross and give me a new way of seeing people. I need to know Your favor so I can become a person who favors others and blesses them rather than cursing.[7] Heal the root causes for my critical attitude.

I choose now to forgive those who have taught me to be religious. (Take time to forgive specific names which God brings to mind). I forgive _____. I forgive them, because You forgave me. Carry my pain to Your cross. Take my past and use it for Your glory.[8]

Confessing the sins of our fathers:

As an Anabaptist, I confess our unforgiveness and our judgments against the leaders of the State Catholic Church and the State Reformed Church for teaching us religion, rather than relationship with You. Where we judged them, forgive us and cleanse us by the blood of Jesus.

I also confess the religious ways of our fathers. Forgive us for hiding ourselves from You and from people. We confess our self-righteousness and pride. Forgive us for all the times we used You to try and appear right by our own good deeds. Forgive us for our critical attitudes, and for our false humility. We repent.

Casting Down Generational Strongholds

I ask You now, place the blood of Jesus between me and the heritage of my family line, and bring to death all religion, self-righteousness and pride. If there are any strongholds of religion, self-righteousness or pride in my life or in my family—I now demolish those strongholds. I bind every demonic attachment to these strongholds and forbid their operation in my life or in my family in any way.

Abba, Father, You helped my early ancestors to walk away from the religion of the State Churches: glorify Your Name in our lives by helping us to walk in an even greater measure of freedom from religion. Fill us with power to walk worthy of our calling.[9]

Thank You that I can approach Your throne. Thank You that as Your son (daughter), I'm free to stand here and express exactly who I am. I love You with all my heart. Free me to rejoice before You, with all my might.[10] *Cover me under the shadow of Your hand and let every plan of the enemy for my life be brought to destruction.*[11]

In Jesus' Name, Amen.

---

[1] Hebrews 4:16; [2] John 3:19-21; [3] Romans 5:17; [4] Colossians 1:12; [5] I Corinthians 12:7; [6] Ephesians 1:3; [7] Romans 12:14; [8] Genesis 50:20; [9] Ephesians 4:1; [10] II Samuel 6:14; [11] Deuteronomy 33:27.

Promises for you from Ephesians 1:3-6:

Before the world was created, God chose you. He loved you so much, He determined way back then to call you His child. He blesses you. Be encouraged, God sees you as completely, one hundred percent righteous through the work of the cross!

22

RELIGIOUS LEGALISM

OR

WALKING IN RELATIONSHIP

Jim Newsom served as the pastor of a church in Florida and has ministered in prisons all over the east coast of America. Jim has a strong prison ministry which came out of his own experience as a former prisoner.[1] He met God just before being incarcerated for second degree murder. After serving eight years of a thirty year sentence, he was released to begin a new life of serving God on the "outside".

Years later God called him to continue his prison ministry in and around Lancaster County, Pennsylvania. He relocated and settled into a lovely home in our local region. Soon after his move, as was his usual custom, Jim opened his garage door on a Sunday afternoon and began to fire up his riding mower to mow his lawn. Jim absolutely *loves* to mow lawn. He considers it very relaxing and restful and, in accordance with God's command to rest on the Sabbath day, he often saved mowing for Sundays so he could unwind and refresh after a busy morning of preaching or teaching the Word in local churches or in local prisons (Exodus 31:15).

Needless to say, mowing his lawn on Sundays was not readily embraced by this "Bible-belt" community, especially since he was a *pastor*! So, in order to keep from offending those who believed it was a sin to mow lawn on the Sabbath, Jim changed his mowing day to a weekday and figured out another way to relax on his day of rest.

Prisoners of a Different Kind

To those of us who have grown up in religious settings, several aspects of Jim's story may surprise us. Mowing his lawn on a Sunday strikes at our sense of what is acceptable for Christians. And, serving a prison sentence for second degree murder does not seem like a prerequisite for eventually becoming a pastor! But as we will discover in this chapter, God's "law" of what is acceptable and our law of what is permissible may be very different.

Our own life experiences may have caused us to be held behind prison walls that are just as binding as Jim's former prison cell. As a matter of fact, the Scriptures declare that we have *all* been imprisoned at some time during our lives. Every one of us has been locked up and carefully guarded by two different captors:

> But the Scripture declares that the *whole world* is a ***prisoner of sin***, *so that* what was promised, being *given* through *faith in Jesus Christ,* might be *given* to those who *believe. Before* this *faith* came, we were held ***prisoners by the law***, locked up *until faith should be revealed.* So the law was put in charge to *lead us to Christ* that we might be *justified by faith.* ***Now that faith has come***, we are ***no longer under the supervision of the law***. You are all ***sons of God*** *through faith in Christ Jesus*, for all of you who were baptized into Christ have clothed yourselves with Christ. (Galatians 3:22-27)

Sin and the *law* have held us in captivity. The law in these verses refers to the Old Testament Law which gave very specific rules and regulations on how to obey and worship God, with exact methods of religious ceremony and ritual. It is this demanding law that we have all broken repeatedly, and which has taken us captive through our sinful disobedience.

Yet, God declares He has accomplished His divine purposes through the imprisonment of our souls. In His great and unfathomable wisdom, He allowed our bondage in order that we may be led to faith in Jesus, where we are given the *gift* of being made fully "right" in God's sight. The Scripture says we were "locked up" by the law only "until faith should be *revealed,*" or uncovered, in our understanding.

But many of us have been unable to turn and see our way of escape. Instead, we've stood within our prison walls, waiting and praying for freedom, when all along freedom has been inviting us to walk out the opened doors and to forever slam them behind us. Those of us who still feel imprisoned by sin and law will need a *revealing of faith* in order to be able to walk away from our captors.

A New Covenant

Through faith, our whole world has changed. Before, we had a prison supervisor named "law". But in faith, we've now become *children of God.* We went from being prisoners to being His children, through the cross:

> You are all **sons of God through faith in Christ Jesus** . . . (verse 27)

Now, we walk as sons and daughters in daily fellowship with our heavenly Father. The New Covenant is a **covenant of sonship.** Walking with God as *His child* has superceded obedience to a form of law. The Law was a supervisor or schoolmaster that was put in charge only until we were brought into family relationship with God. The former has given way to the latter.

Just like a supervisor or schoolmaster would write instructions on a chalkboard to give us our assignments, the Old Law was given as *external* guidelines (Hebrews 9:9-11). But through our New Covenant of *sonship,* the things we are taught are written into our heart, as a loving Father teaches and guides His child. This New Covenant is an *internal* covenant that has been placed into our souls:

> Whereof the **Holy Ghost also is a witness to us**: for after that he had said before, this is the **covenant** that I will make with them after those days, saith the Lord, I will **put my laws**

into their hearts, and *in their minds will I write them;* and their *sins and iniquities will I remember no more.* Now where remission of these is, there is *no more offering for sin.* (Hebrews 10:15-18, *KJV*)

This New Covenant keeps getting better and better. Now, as our Father, God does not bring to mind (remember) our sins: they have all been put behind Him. But the best is yet to come! He has even given us someone to help us obey. He has put His own Spirit *in* us and *moves us* to obey:

> . . . I will put my Spirit *in* you and *move you* to follow my decrees and be careful to keep my laws. (Ezekiel 36:27)

The New Covenant is radically different than the Old Covenant. In the first covenant, we were given a big set of regulations to follow, and we failed miserably and felt imprisoned by our sin. In the New Covenant, all our sins are forgiven, we are brought into the family as a child, and our Father Himself has decided to live in us to help us obey the things He has asked us to do. We are no longer prisoners, but *children!*

Walking As Jesus Walked

Though He physically walked under the Old Covenant while on the earth, Jesus demonstrated how to live in the *New* Covenant through His *Sonship*. He communed with the Father throughout His daily life by an internal "law" of cooperative and loving obedience as a Son with the Father (chapters 18 and 19).

This is the same internal covenant by which we live our faith today. The Scriptures reveal God *in* us as the Father, Son and Holy Spirit. It is a spiritual mystery that each member of the Trinity is present in our "temples":

> Know ye not that ye are the temple of God, and that the *Spirit of God dwelleth in you*? (I Corinthians 3:16, *KJV*).

> . . . For it is not ye that speak, but the *Spirit of your Father* which speaketh in you. (Matthew 10:20, *KJV*)

> And I will pray the Father, and he shall give you
> another Comforter, that he may *abide with you forever;* even
> the *Spirit of truth;* . . . I will not leave you comfortless:
> *I (Jesus) will come to you.* (John 14:16, *KJV,* parentheses
> are mine)

A New Relationship

In the New Covenant, instead of the former supervisor,
the Law, the Holy Spirit is now our Teacher, Guide and Counselor who shows us the ways of both the Father and the Son:

> But the Comforter, which is the *Holy Ghost,* whom the
> Father will send in my name, he shall **teach you** *all things,*
> and bring all things to your remembrance, whatsoever I have
> said unto you. (John 14:26, *KJV*)

> But when he, the *Spirit of truth,* comes, he will **guide you** into
> all truth. He will not speak on his own; he will speak only
> what he hears. . . . He will bring glory to me by taking from
> what is mine and making it known to you. (John 16:13-14)

> But I tell you the truth: It is *for your good that I am going
> away.* Unless I go away, the **Counselor** will not come to you;
> but if I go, I will send him to you. (John 16:7)

It is the Holy Spirit's presence in each of our individual
lives and in our churches which enables us to escape our prisons
of sin and of living by an *external form of law,* to walk instead
by the *Spirit of sonship*:

> For you did not receive a spirit that makes you a slave again
> to fear, but you received the **Spirit of sonship.** And by him
> we cry, "Abba, Father. *The* **Spirit himself testifies** *with our
> spirit that we are* **God's children.** (Romans 8:15-16)

The answer to the dilemma of imprisonment to our captors is to
realize that because of Christ's payment, we have been taken from
our horrid prisons and brought into a warm and loving family
where we have been offered the Father's own presence to live *in*

us for the rest of our lives. His mercy, compassion, and pity have officially sealed our adoption papers and the One who "testified" to the signing of the papers was the Holy Spirit (Romans 8:15-16).

Our History With the Spirit

But as Anabaptists, we have a historical problem with the Holy Spirit. Though many of our ancestors invited and treasured His presence in their lives, and though our founding fathers taught of His importance (chapter seven), *He* has been associated with error, heresy, and the violence of radicals. *His gifts* have seemingly caused the escalation of our persecution by the Lutherans, the Reformers, and the Catholics. And by being associated with those who have abused His gifts, we have experienced much harm.

Even before Anabaptism began, a group of men called the "Zwickau prophets" had turned Martin Luther firmly against any sort of emphasis on the "Inner Word". These "prophets" said the Scriptures were unreliable for teaching people: it was only the Spirit who could teach. They insisted on the "inner voice" being the true authority for a New Age and preached the end of the world was at hand, and claimed special angelic visitations.[2] Since they, like the Reformers, had "rebelled" from the State Catholic Church, their extremism hurt the Reformers' standing in the eyes of the political leaders and created all sorts of turmoil. The final effect was that Luther eventually turned against *all* dissension, including the Anabaptists who would soon follow these "prophets" in pulling away from the State Churches.[3]

The peasant revolts in 1524 and 1525 demanded social reform by using the Bible's teachings as a platform, and Anabaptists were blamed. Luther said their "excited prophetism" was the cause and once more, the reputation of the Holy Spirit and of His gifts were tarnished through error.[4]

Melchior Hoffman used errant spiritual dreams, visions, and revelations to gather his followers.[5] He believed he was

Elijah and that the end of all things was near, with Christ's return occurring in the city of Strasbourg.[6] Jan Matthijs took over leadership of Hoffman's followers and used false prophecy to change Christ's predicted return to the city of Münster.[7] His successor, Jan Van Leiden, was even more in error, proclaiming himself as a king and instituting polygamy.[8]

After the infamous Münster uprising (chapter 20), another false prophet, David Joris, continued with error concerning God's Spirit. Like the Zwickau prophets, he taught the inner Spirit was all that mattered to believers, to the *exclusion* of the Word of God.[9]

Among false prophetic messages in more recent history, there are the teachings of Conrad Beissel, the founder of the Ephrata Cloisters in America. Again, he is not considered a pure Anabaptist, but practiced some Anabaptist beliefs, and was associated with the Dunker Brethren churches and Radical Pietism.[10] Beissel, with his bent towards a mystical faith, taught grave errors which included the practice of a new, heavenly language (not tongues, but a mystical language), the marriage of Christians to Sophia, the "female side of God",[11] and the abhorring of the marital union of a man and a woman because of our intended marriage to Sophia before the fall of Adam and Eve.[12]

Hearing of these past spiritual abuses, we should not be surprised that many of our present day Anabaptist churches have become wary of the Holy Spirit. We have associated His presence with unhealthy and dangerous spiritual imbalance. Yet, we have a choice of living either as prisoners of sin and the law, or walking by this Spirit of sonship. We are forced to make a decision: we either *risk His presence* or *forfeit our sonship*.

> You, however, are controlled not by the sinful nature but by the Spirit, if the Spirit of God lives in you. And *if anyone does not have the Spirit of Christ, he does not belong to Christ*. (Romans 8:9)

If we do not have the Spirit, we do not belong to God. Alright, we decide: we'll welcome the Holy Spirit, but all things like prophecy and tongues, visions, dreams, these are not of God, but of the devil. They have to be, since they have created so many problems! But the Bible tell us we are not to turn away from these things:

> Therefore, my brothers, be **eager to prophesy,** and **do not forbid speaking in tongues.** But everything should be done in a fitting and orderly way. (I Corinthians 14:39-40)
>
> **Do not put out the Spirit's fire; do not treat prophecies with contempt.** Test everything. Hold on to the good. Avoid every kind of evil. (I Thessalonians 5:19-22)

Now, our hearts are torn. If we treat prophecies with contempt or forbid His gifts, we are putting out the Spirit's fire. But, we argue, some say these gifts ended when the New Testament came as "perfection":

> But where there are prophecies, *they will cease*; where there are tongues, *they will be stilled*; . . . For we know in part and we prophesy in part, but **when perfection comes, the imperfect disappears.** When I was a child, I talked like a child, I thought like a child, I reasoned like a child. When I became a man, I put childish ways behind me. *Now we see but a poor reflection as in a mirror; then we shall see face to face. Now I know in part; then I shall know fully, even as I am fully known.* And now these three remain: faith, hope and love. But the greatest of these is love. Follow the way of love and **eagerly desire spiritual gifts, especially the gift of prophecy.** (I Corinthians 13:9-14:1)

But what is the "perfect" referring to in this passage? The perfect is when we see "shall see face to face," and when we shall "know fully". The *perfect* is seeing God in heaven. If perfection referred to the New Testament, it wouldn't speak of seeing face to face or knowing fully, because we do neither of these as we read the Scriptures. We only "know in part" and see a "reflection in as in a mirror." And a few verses later, Paul adds, *"eagerly desire spiritual gifts, especially . . . prophecy."*

How then, are we to welcome the Spirit *and* His gifts, yet survive heresy, excess and abuses? We *test everything* and *hold onto the good* (I Thessalonians passage). We allow the gifts to operate, even eagerly, but examine them and keep what is of God. We'll never completely do away with imbalance, but we can learn to speak openly and lovingly as we train one other in discerning between good and evil (Hebrews 5:14). As one teacher shared, wherever the Spirit of God "manifests" His gifts, both the devil and the flesh will often rise up to imitate: the flesh, because people who are immature or not yet healed from life's hurts, try to copy the Holy Spirit in order to gain personal attention; the devil, because he will mimic the gifts of the Spirit, masquerading as an angel of light in order to try and deceive (II Corinthians 11:14, *NIV*).

But we do not need to fear. If we fear the presence of the Holy Spirit and His gifts, we are fearing GOD. The Spirit *is* God. His gifts are the tools He has given to the church, along with the Scriptures, for the common good and for the maturing of His body (I Corinthians 12 and Ephesians 4:11).

The Law or the Spirit in the True Church

Our early ancestors' great desire was to reestablish the True Church: the one founded by the apostles. But it was God, by His Spirit, who *really* founded the True Church on the day of Pentecost. After His ascension, Jesus told the disciples not to do anything until the Spirit had come. They were to wait for God:

> On one occasion, . . . he gave them this command: 'Do not leave Jerusalem, but *wait for the gift my Father promised*, which you have heard me speak about. For John baptized with water, but *in a few days you will be baptized with the Holy Spirit.*' (Acts 1:4-5)

When God came, this time not as Emmanuel (God with us), but as *God in us*, He turned the apostles' lives upside down and inside out. They had all grown up under the Old Covenant and had to do some major shifts in their thinking. Just as our forefathers had to sort through State Church laws to determine what was true and what was false, the apostles had to sort through how to handle the Law, a process of understanding which was gradual as well as supernatural.

At one point, the young New Covenant church was being faced with a critical issue. Some of the Pharisees who had become believers felt strongly that the Gentile believers should be required to obey the Law of Moses, just as the Jewish converts obeyed the law. The apostles and leaders began a lengthy discussion to discern God's will in this matter. After a time, they reached a decision and dispatched a letter to Gentile believers everywhere, which said:

> It seemed good *to the Holy Spirit and to us* *not to burden* *you with anything beyond* the following requirements: You are to abstain from food sacrificed to idols, from blood, from the meat of strangled animals and from sexual immorality. You will do well to avoid these things. Farewell. (Acts 15: 28-29)

Other than these few requirements, Gentile believers were free to walk *by the Spirit* rather than fulfilling the law of Moses. The Gentiles did not have to offer sacrifices or follow the Jewish rituals of fasting or festivals. They were free to walk by the New Covenant which was written in their hearts and minds, and were *released* from the law:

> But now, by dying to what once bound us, we have been *released from the law* so that we serve in the *new way of the Spirit*, and not in the *old way of the written code* (Romans 7:6)

Christians could now live by obedience to the Holy Spirit, and not in the old way of obeying rules and regulations. Thank God for the decision of the leaders in Acts. In wisdom, they limited their directives to things which they considered spiritually endangering. For example, sexual immorality, aside from its obvious sin, was often tied to idol worship and idol worship, as Paul wrote, was tied to demon worship (I Kings 15:12; Deuteronomy 23:17; I Corinthians 10:19-21). As for avoiding the eating of blood,—which the Old Covenant had repeatedly forbidden—the *life* of a creature is in its blood (Leviticus 17). Blood is the essence of our earthly life and the foundational element of our salvation through the shed blood of Jesus on our behalf. Therefore, the apostles felt clearly that eating blood should be avoided. But other than these few requirements, the Gentiles were free to walk in the "new way of the Spirit". It "seemed good to the Holy Spirit" and to the apostles that, "where the Spirit of the Lord is, there is freedom" (II Corinthians 3:17).

A Biblical Look at Legalism

Jesus obeyed the Law of Moses *from His heart,* and most of the religious leaders despised Him because their own beliefs had become merely an external religion. They were constantly offended by the things He said and did, because the *action* of their duty, rather than their *motives,* had become the important emphasis in their religion. That is why Jesus rebuked them. He understood their hearts had separated from true faith and were holding on to religious form:

(The Pharisees and all the Jews do not eat unless they give their hands a ceremonial washing, *holding to the tradition of the elders* . . . And they observe *many other traditions*, such as the washing of cups, pitchers and kettles.) So the Pharisees and teachers of the law asked Jesus, "Why don't your disciples live according to the *tradition of the elders* instead of eating their food with 'unclean' hands?" He replied, "Isaiah was right when he prophesied about you *hypocrites*; as it is written: 'These people *honor me with their lips, but their hearts are far from me. They worship me in vain; their teachings are but rules taught by men.'* You have let go of the commands of God and are holding on to the traditions of *men."* And he said to them: "You have a fine way of *setting aside the commands of God in order to observe your own traditions!"* (Mark 7:3-9)

Whenever we replace *relationship* with *traditions*, our *hearts* will be far from God. Jesus' rebuke could not have been more clear. The apostle Paul also warns us to avoid the captivity of *men's traditions*:

> See to it that no one *takes you captive* through *philosophy and empty deception*, according to the **tradition of men**, according to the elementary principles of the world, *rather than according to Christ.* (Colossians 2:8, *NASB*)

The traditions of men that have preempted Christ will always lead us astray into empty deception and away from fellowship with God. In Matthew, Jesus calls the Pharisees, "children of hell" and "blind guides". His description of their religiosity gives us further clues in our search to understand legalism:

> You blind guides! You **strain out a gnat but swallow a camel**. Woe to you, teachers of the law and Pharisees, you hypocrites! . . . You are like *whitewashed tombs*, which look beautiful *on the outside* but *on the inside* are full of *dead men's bones* and everything unclean. (Matthew 23:14-17)

If we are legalistic, we will be extremely zealous, but in our zeal we'll "major on the minors" by giving close attention and focus to the things which are not really important in the grander scope of our Christian life. By doing so, we'll completely miss the crux of what really matters, since we "strain out a gnat," yet swallow a deceptively worthless "camel" of religious practice.

Starting Well and Ending Well

The legalistic hearts of the Pharisees kept them from entering the Kingdom, which is the reason Jesus spoke so strongly against their pretense. He knew their *hearts* needed to be washed, so they could walk with God. All throughout the New Testament its writers, as concerned fathers of the faith, corrected the errors of young churches that had fallen into a legalistic adherence to rules and regulations. Practically the entire book of Galatians is a letter from Paul calling their church back into a walk of *faith*, rather than living by external laws.

Men had come to the Galatian church preaching that *works* were necessary in addition to faith in order to guarantee salvation. As a result of their teachings, the Galatians had returned to observing practices which were part of Judaism (Galatians 4:9-11). Three times in this passage of Paul's letter, he contrasts *walking in fellowship* with God's Spirit to a life lived through our human effort of *following a set of laws*:

> You foolish Galatians! Who has bewitched you? Before your very eyes Jesus Christ was clearly portrayed as crucified. I would like to learn just one thing from you: *Did you receive the Spirit by observing the law*, or by *believing* what you heard? Are you so foolish? *After **beginning with the Spirit**, are you now trying to attain your goal **by human effort?*** . . . Does God *give you his Spirit* and work miracles among you **because you observe the law**, or because you *believe* what you heard? (Galatians 3:1-5)

Paul actually calls the Galatians *bewitched* because they exchanged walking in God's Spirit with obeying the law. He warns them not to return to a *yoke of slavery* by submitting to the Old Testament practice of circumcision:

> It is for *freedom that Christ has set us free*. Stand firm, then, and *do not let yourselves be burdened again by a **yoke of slavery***. Mark my words! I, Paul, tell you that if you let yourselves be circumcised, *Christ will be of **no value** to you at all*. . . . You who are *trying to be **justified by law*** have been **alienated** *from Christ; you have **fallen** away from grace*. But *by faith* we eagerly await **through the Spirit** the *righteousness* for which we hope. (Galatians 5:1-5)

Freedom is why Jesus has set us free. It's such a simple statement, but we miss its impact. Living by obeying rules makes us *prisoners of law* and takes us back into striving to be right on our own merit. Trusting "through the Spirit" in *grace*, give us *freedom*. One denies Jesus' *value*, the other *welcomes His presence* through the Spirit. One *alienates* us from God, the other *invites Him* into our human temples.

Our Own Historic Legalism

As I share in this section of writing, I will be pointing out examples which demonstrate historic legalism, but not with the intent of condemning anyone. My goal is to only help us understand our heritage—even its error—always and only for the sake of our freedom in Christ.

Both the Reformers and the Anabaptists came out of a legalistic State church where dissenting views were simply not allowed, and where the Scriptures had been largely used to *control* rather than to bring the *Spirit's life*. So it is no real surprise that within fifty years of Anabaptism's beginnings, divisions and dissension over many issues had revealed our own pattern of legalistic religion. We had already created rules for living which were zealously sincere, but based on fear of man rather than on relationship. In many ways, our focus became *external* law, rather than the *law of the Spirit*, as we banned each other from fellowship over lesser issues of outward dress, style of worship, or even over "the ban" itself.[13]

Jakob Ammann, a leader in the Alsace region of France and founder of the Amish church, believed lying was a sin unto death. He demanded that anyone who told a lie should be expelled from the brotherhood without warning, and shunned by the brethren. He chastised the Swiss and Alsatian fellowships for not strictly shunning a woman who had admitted telling a lie.[14]

Clearly, lying *is* a sin, but if Christians were excommunicated for lying, there would be no one in the church: we would all be banned, because we all have been deceived and *believed* lies. We have all *spoken* lies. But as the Holy Spirit has convicted us (not condemned), we have confessed to God and have been forgiven.

As a result of Ammann's disagreements with the Swiss brethren, he excommunicated most of the Anabaptist leaders in the Emmental and called other leaders who disagreed with his stance "the devil's servants . . . who denied the doctrine of avoidance."[15] Later, Ammann's group reached out in humility to repent and make amends, but sadly, most of the Mennonist (Mennonite) leaders rejected Ammann's group and refused reconciliation.[16] God is grieved when we curse our brothers and He is grieved when we sow seeds of divisiveness and discord. The sins of both these "sides" are as grievous to God, if not more so, than the sin of the woman who lied and then confessed her sin (James 3:9-10; Titus 3:10-11).

Peter Hoover writes about other divisions among the Dutch Mennonites:

> Practically every group "delivered unto Satan" the group from which it came and got "delivered unto Satan" in return. Within thirty years of Menno Simon's death, most Dutch Anabaptists had gotten excommunicated three or four times by other Anabaptists who claimed to have authority over them.[17]

In light of the original decision of the New Testament leaders in Acts to *only burden the Gentiles with what was necessary to keep new believers from serious spiritual peril,* our own disagreements over issues of lifestyle and community living made us seem more like the Galatians church than like the "true church" in Acts that our ancestors wanted to emulate. Our "majoring on the minors" was evidence that we had lost our understanding of how to walk by God's Spirit.

As our confessions and agreements of faith were drawn up over the years through meetings at Schleitheim, Strasbourg, Emden, Dortrecht, Zofingen, and other towns of Europe, attempts were made to unify the many Anabaptist believers from different countries and social classes. But even as confessions of faith were created, differences of opinion about *how they were to be interpreted* soon erupted and we reacted as we had been taught to respond by our State Church experience, with intolerance towards those who disagreed.[18]

Legalism and the Scriptures

Recently, I was driving towards home and saw a sign which was posted for encouragement by a local church. The sign read, "Many books can inform, but only the Bible can *transform*." There is a measure of truth to this saying that we may apprehend, but the Bible cannot truly transform unless the Spirit interprets it to our spirits.

Our ancestors knew well the harm of interpreting the written Word without the Living Word, since the State Church systems carried out great manhunts and widespread persecution as a result of holding to incorrect interpretations of the Scriptures. Just days before George Blaurock poured out the ladle of water which baptized Conrad Grebel in 1525, Ulrich Zwingli erroneously equated infant baptism with Jewish circumcision in a disputation with our early forefathers.[19] Though Ulrich Zwingli had taught salvation by grace, his mind and heart were veiled concerning this particular Scriptural truth. In a very real sense, following the "letter of the law" without the Spirit's interpretation killed our ancestors:

> He has made us competent as ministers of a new covenant—
> not of the letter but *of the Spirit*; for **the letter kills**, but **the Spirit gives life**. (II Corinthians 3:6)

Like the Pharisees, Zwingli attempted to interpret the Scriptures without the presence of the Living Word. But is the *Living Word* who has given us the *written Word*. Jesus Christ is the Word who is "*living* and active" in our lives (Hebrews 4:12). Rick Joyner, of Morning Star Ministries, explains it this way:

> The primary way we have been given to know the Lord is His Holy Spirit, which He gave to us for that purpose. *Many would exalt the written Word over the Spirit, but the Lord Himself did not do that.* He did not say, "I must go away, but I am going to give you this Book to lead you into all truth..." No, He said when He left He would send *His Spirit* to lead us into all truth (see John 16:7). This is *not in any way to belittle* the place of the Scriptures, but *without the*

Holy Spirit, we cannot understand the Scriptures. There-
fore, our great ambition should be to know the Holy Spirit,
to obey Him, and to be the most hospitable temple for Him
that we can possibly be.[20]

Legalism and the Fear of Man

Legalism is tied to our fear of man. In Galatia, men
preached *circumcision* to *"avoid being persecuted for the cross*
of Christ" (Galatians 6:12), and Saul (Paul) persecuted Christians to gain man's approval:

> Am I now trying to win the approval of men, or of God?
> Or am I trying to *please men?* If I were **still trying to**
> **please men,** I would not be a servant of Christ. . . . For
> you have heard of my previous way . . . how intensely I
> persecuted the church of God...and was extremely *zeal-*
> *ous for the traditions of my fathers.* But when God, who
> set me apart from birth and *called me by his* **grace,** was
> pleased to *reveal his Son in* me. . . . (Galatians 1:10-16)

> If anyone else thinks he has reasons to put confidence in
> the flesh, I have more:...in regard to the law, (I was) a
> Pharisee; as for zeal, *persecuting the church*; **as for**
> **legalistic righteousness, faultless.** But whatever was to
> my profit *I now consider loss* for the sake of Christ. . . .
> I consider everything a loss compared to the **surpassing**
> **greatness of knowing Christ Jesus** my Lord. . . .
> (Philippians 3:5-8)

As a Pharisee, Paul had been zealously religious for the
traditions of his spiritual fathers, but his zeal was tied to
pleasing men rather than pleasing God. He had done all the
"right" things in man's eyes but then, God called him by **grace,**
and the Son was revealed *in* him. When Paul knew God's presence inside, suddenly everything else lost its value. Compared
to the thrill of *knowing* Christ Jesus, his legalistic righteousness
was worthless.

Like Paul, in our legalistic fear of man we may believe
we are so right, yet be completely wrong. We may even resort

to *persecuting others who are walking by the Spirit* as Paul persecuted them, because we are living our lives in order to please men. Several of us were praying together about our corporate Anabaptist tendencies to approach God religiously, when one sister saw that many of us have despised other churches and believers who have pursued the freedom of the Lord. We have judged them in the same way Michal, the wife of David, despised and judged David for dancing before the Lord with all his might:

> David, *wearing a linen ephod, danced before the Lord with all his might,* while he and the entire house of Israel brought up the ark of the Lord with shouts and the sound of trumpets . . . Michal . . . watched from a window. And when she saw King David *leaping and dancing before the Lord, she despised him in her heart.* . . . When David returned home to *bless his household,* Michal . . . came out to meet him and said, "How the king of Israel has *distinguished himself today, disrobing in the sight of the slave girls . . . as any vulgar fellow would."* David said to Michal, *"It was before the Lord*—I will celebrate before the Lord. *I will become even more undignified than this,* and *I will be humiliated in my own eyes.* But by these slave girls you spoke of, I will be held in honor." And Michal daughter of Saul *had no children* to the day of her death. (II Samuel 6:14-16,20-23)

David was so overjoyed to have the ark—the presence of God in that day—returned to Israel, that he broke out into a spontaneous and vigorous dance "before the Lord". When he returned home ready to joyfully bless everyone, he was met with Michal's legalistic anger. She had not seen David's dancing from God's perspective, but from a fear of man. She only cared that he had debased his position as king, failing to see his humility in God's presence. Michal cared more about what people would think of David's radical display of fervor than she did about his heart motive of love for God.

Though David had been among a throng of people, he had "danced before the Lord" and only for the Lord (verse 21). His dance was free, fervent, and full, because he simply could not contain the passion he felt for God at that moment. His motives were pure, and he answered Michal's bitter complaint by saying that he would be willing to be even *more* humiliated and *more* abased, in order to worship God.

When we are legalistic, we will respond to the spiritual freedom of others with judgment and condemnation. We'll perceive their actions of freedom through our own fear of man, and despise them. When others give fervent worship in order to please God, we'll condemn them because of our need for keeping up appearances. And though we maintain our reputation by our "legalistic righteousness," we miss the heart of the Father, who calls those like David, "men after his own heart" (Acts 13:22).

Just as Michal was barren for the rest of her life because she sinfully judged David's freedom, so we will be spiritually barren when we insist on condemning the spiritual freedom of others. Becky Jones, the intercessor who understood this comparison as we prayed together, actually saw entire congregations that have become bound with a spirit like the spirit of Michal, barren and spiritually empty as a result of their own judgments of other congregations and moves of God.

Legalism or Grace in Our Own Lives

If we are to begin once again to fulfill the mandate we have been given to reach out and share Jesus with the world, we will need to let go of our concerns of "fixing" everyone around us so that their lives are "right" in terms of our own traditions. But before we can grow in grace toward those in the world, we need to *first* start demonstrating freedom as we relate to others within the body of Christ. For example, let's look at the following Scripture and consider our *own traditional Anabaptist interpretations*. Then we'll compare it with African American traditions:

> (Wives), your beauty should not come from outward adorn-
> ment, such as braided hair and the wearing of gold jewelry
> and fine clothes. Instead, it should be that of your inner self,
> the unfading beauty of a gentle and quiet spirit, which is of
> great worth in God's sight. (I Peter 3:3,4 parenthesis mine)

Most of us will interpret this Scripture in terms of how
we have been raised. If we are more conservative Anabaptists,
we'll believe this Scripture means women should wear no
makeup or jewelry, and dresses should be plain or of simple,
printed fabrics without any added decorations.

Less conservative Anabaptist churches will interpret it to
mean we shouldn't give undue focus to things like jewelry or
hair styles, or spend a lot of time or money on clothing. But to
these Anabaptists, it is acceptable to dress moderately according
to individual choice, and to wear some jewelry and perhaps even
makeup.

Expanding our view beyond the fences of our own
cultural back yards, consider the believers in African American
churches in New York, for example, and their interpretation. They
understand this Scripture as meaning a woman's beauty should
not *only* come from external adornment, as several translations
indicate, ("And let not your adornment be *merely* external" *NASB*)
but *also* from the development of an inner friendship with God.

The believers in African American churches have laid into
the foundations of their church experience a perception that when
they go to church, they are entering the courts of their Royal
King Jesus. With this in mind, they believe they should dress
well, just as one would wear his or her best suit of clothes when
being brought into an earthly king's court. As a result, many
African American women use bright makeup, gold jewelry, and
dress in all kinds of current fashions with matching shoes and
hats, even wearing fingernail and toenail polish in full assurance that they are walking in obedience to God's "law" of the
Spirit. These same women are strong Christians who spend much
time in prayer, lead others to Christ, serve their churches faithfully, and love God with all their hearts.

Now, which church tradition is right? The key words in this question are, *tradition* and *right*. Each Anabaptist denomination has certain *traditional* interpretations that we believe are the *right* interpretations. But, so do the African American churches and so do other denominations.

If we ask the Holy Spirit to help us interpret this Scripture, we will find *His freedom* in our hearts as we relate to each other. But if we force the Scriptures to *fit into our traditions*, we will find legalism, and we'll use our differences of interpretation as a reason to separate ourselves from other fellowships or other people, because we have not understood that God gives us freedom to walk in grace.

Concerning this Scripture, all of the cultures can be *right* if the heart motive is to please God and not to please man. Walking *by the Spirit*, we can allow each church room to breathe regarding their interpretation of this Scripture portion. We can *accept* each other, because this is not a matter which determines anyone's eternal destiny. We can *love* our brother, knowing they are also loving God, though we disagree on lesser issues of faith.

Making Allowances

Paul encourages the Roman believers to make allowances for each other concernings *matters of personal conscience* when living out their Christian faith, because each man lives *for the Lord*, just as David danced only *for the Lord*:

> One man's faith *allows him to eat everything*, but *another man,* whose faith is weak, *eats only vegetables*. The man who eats everything **must not look down** on him who does not, and the man who does not eat everything **must not condemn** the man who does, for **God has accepted him. Who are you to judge someone else's servant? To his own master he stands or falls.** And he will stand, for the Lord is able to make him stand. One man *considers one day more sacred* than another; *another man* **considers every day alike**. Each one should be fully convinced in his own mind. *He who regards one day as special,* **does so to the Lord**. *He who eats*

*meat, **eats to the Lord**,* for he gives thanks to God; and he who abstains, ***does so to the Lord*** and gives thanks to God. *For none of us lives to himself alone and none of us dies to himself alone. If we live, **we live to the Lord**;* and if we die, we die to the Lord. So, whether we live or die, we belong to the Lord...*You, then, **why do you judge your brother?** Or why do you **look down on your brother?*** For we will all stand before God's judgment seat. (Romans 14:2-10)

The Scriptures clearly teach that we are to keep the Sabbath day holy, yet Paul gives room for one man to "consider every day alike," and still be fully accepted by another. Paul commands us not to judge our brother's lifestyle according to our own legalistic interpretation, because each one is *serving the Lord* in his heart and for that reason, each choice is acceptable to God. We are not even allowed to **look down** on another, let alone judge them for how they have chosen to live out their faith in these matters. We can now understand that Jim Newsom's preference of mowing his lawn on Sunday is entirely acceptable to God, though we may not feel the same personal freedom to mow our own lawn on the Sabbath!

The Face of Legalism Today

As we look at legalism within our Anabaptist churches and homes today, it appears with many faces. It cannot be identified by simply creating a list of right and wrong behaviors, and it cannot be corrected by "fixing" each one until the entire list is checked off. That kind of approach would be legalistic! We can, however, identify some of the indicators of legalism by recognizing actions and attitudes which are void of the Spirit's love. Two sayings come to mind which I've heard in many Anabaptist churches: "That's not the way we do things around here," or "That's the way we've always done it." Both sayings indicate an inflexible mindset which comes from legalism.

Our legalism has caused an overbearing discipline and a lack of affection in many of our families and churches. In our churches, it has caused *tradition* to become the primary factor in determining codes of dress, of transportation, of career choices, of the use of the arts and of the use of modern technology. Legalism has caused overly-busy lifestyles as we attempt to fulfill the mandates of Scriptures by our own strength and energies. It has fostered religious control in our churches and homes (more on this chapter 23). It has enabled worship services which are inflexible, redundant, and which lack the presence and power of God. Legalism has caused an unhealthy treatment of men and women, and it has caused much division and hatred. But most of all, legalism has hindered the work of God's Spirit in our churches, our homes, and our personal lives.

Spiritual Wariness or Spiritual Fullness

In the Kingdom of God today on earth, the Holy Spirit and His gifts are in operation all over the world, with "demonstrations of the Spirit's power" (I Corinthians 2:4). Miracles are occurring, the dead are being raised, gifts of healing abound, and manifestations of every single gift of the Holy Spirit exist throughout the earth.[21] Even as the darkness increases, so the Kingdom of God is advancing. The Holy Spirit is expanding the rule and reign of God on the earth to men, women and children of all nations.

God desires to come and live in us through His Spirit, but He will not come unless He is *welcomed*. One of the reasons we have not seen more of God's presence in our lives is that we have not truly welcomed Him because of our fears and misunderstandings about His nature. We have felt left behind by God, when in reality we are often the ones who have unknowingly hindered, by our resistance, His desires to come and be in our midst through His Spirit.

Someone has said the Holy Spirit is a gentleman. I can personally attest to that truth. Though He is a "consuming fire" in the earth, in God's dealings in my life I have never once found Him harsh, demanding, or forcefully insistent (Hebrews 12:29).

His voice and manner in relating to me have been more like the gentle whisper to Elijah, or the restful humility and gentleness of Christ (I Kings 19:12; Matthew 11:29).

God showed one small group of Anabaptist intercessors that we need to repent as a whole for being ashamed of the Holy Spirit and for rejecting Him. Both historically and in the present day, we have chosen to limit His presence among our people. In following the "letter of the law" we rejected the "Spirit of life," substituting instead our rules, traditions, and even our *intellectual knowledge* of God, all of which seemed more safe to our hearts than risking a relationship where we invited the Holy Spirit to rule completely.

The Holy Spirit is waiting for a full and open invitation. He is longing to come to us, to our families, to our churches, and to the greater Anabaptist body. He is waiting. We must not tell Him *how* He is to come, and we must not be afraid of His coming. When we invite Him, we must also trust that He will show us how to handle any excesses and abuses *by the Spirit.* He is able to lovingly teach and train us in the mistakes—and there will be mistakes because we are human—so we need not fear.

If we welcome His presence, we will be set free from our prisons of sin and law, and we will discover true and wonderful freedom. The Holy Spirit is a perfect gift from the Father and the Son, to us. God is waiting to give Himself to us!

> So I say to you: *Ask* and it will be given to you; *seek* and you will find; *knock* and the door will be opened to you. For everyone who asks *receives*; he who seeks *finds*; and to him who knocks, *the door will be opened*. Which of you fathers, if your son asks for a fish, will give him a snake instead? Or if he asks for an egg, will give him a scorpion? If you then, though you are evil, know how to give good gifts to your children, *how much more will your Father in heaven give the Holy Spirit to those who ask him*! (Luke 11:9-13)

> On the last and greatest day of the Feast, Jesus stood and said in a loud voice, "If anyone is *thirsty, let him come to me and drink*. Whoever *believes* in me, as the Scripture has said, *streams of living water* will flow from *within him*." *By this*

he meant the Spirit, whom those who believed in him were later to receive. (John 7:37-39)

John answered them all, "I baptize you with water. But one more powerful than I will come, the thongs of whose sandals I am not worthy to untie. **He will baptize you with the Holy Spirit** and with fire. (Luke 3:16)

Holy Spirit, thank You that You desire to be with me. I am awed by Your great love. Forgive me for any way I have been ashamed of You. Forgive me for the times I have chosen to honor the traditions of men more than I have honored You, or when I have honored the Bible more than You, Living Word. Holy Spirit, forgive me if I have arrogantly tried to interpret the Bible by my own human effort, without Your help.

I don't want to walk by an external form of religion, in any way. Please forgive me for when I have been legalistic and have harmed others through my legalism.

Forgiving Others

I repent for any judgments I have made against those who have taught me legalism by their words or their deeds. I choose to forgive each one by name: _____ (take time to forgive those whom God brings to your mind). I ask You, my Father, to fill up those places where I have lacked spiritually because of the ignorance and unbelief of those who have gone before me. You are able to restore all that was lost and to restore my soul.

Repentance for our fathers' sins:

As one who has Anabaptist roots, I confess the sins of our fathers as they judged, condemned and hated those who erred in spiritual mysticism, false prophecies and the abuse of Your gifts of the Spirit. Though these people were wrong, our attitudes towards their sins and errors were also wrong.

Forgive also our legalistic interpretations of the Bible and our legalistic practices. Forgive us for judging the State Reformed Church leaders and the State Catholic Church leaders for their legalistic practices and interpretations of the Bible. We change our minds and turn back to You, Father.

Holy Spirit, I repent for myself, my family and my church congregation, for judging others who have moved more freely in Your gifts. Forgive us for condemning those who have served you from their hearts. Forgive us for "persecuting others" out of legalism, and for any slander we have spoken. By Your grace, remove from us every curse of spiritual barrenness that has affected us because of our sins.

Holy Spirit, please heal me, my family and my people from both the legalistic errors and the radical spiritual errors of the past. Help our unbelief where we have not trusted You, and heal our hearts and minds. Teach us to walk by Your guidance and give us ears to hear Your voice, as God's children.

Taking captive every thought. Asking for fullness:

I speak now to every stronghold of legalism in my life and take you captive in Jesus' name. I bind every demonic attachment to that stronghold and forbid your activity in any way.

Holy Spirit, become a stream of water that is alive in me and that flows out to others. Come and fill me once again. Immerse me. I want all You have to give me, and not one drop less. I invite You, I welcome You, I eagerly desire You, for only You can quench my thirst. I also welcome any gifts You desire to give to me. From now on, I invite You to pour into me whatever You desire, knowing that I must learn to go with You, and not expect You to go with me.[1]

Show me how to respond when I make mistakes, or when

others misuse Your gifts: not in fear, but with love and truth. Show me how to respond when others walk in legalism, with forgiveness yet without compromising my walk with You.

Thank You, God, that You have given Yourself to me as a Father, as a Brother, and as the Spirit. Thank You that You are my very Breath. Breath of God, blow upon all my spiritual enemies and make them like tumbleweed that You drive along.[2] Guard me now, and deliver me from the hand of the wicked ones.[3] Thank You,

In Jesus' Name, Amen.

---

[1] John 3:8; [2] Psalm 83:13; [3] Psalm 97:10.

**Promises from your Father
(John 14:16-18,26; John 16:13-15):**

God is so excited to come and live in your life. He loves to be with you. He tells you all about Jesus, and He talks to you when you need advice. He answers your questions about your life's direction. He affirms that you belong in His family. He'll never, ever leave you. Since you have shared yourself with Him, He is utterly devoted to you. Enjoy His friendship and love!

~ 23 ~

RELIGIOUS CONTROL
OR
SPIRITUAL RELEASE

We were standing along the sidewalk at San Giovanni basilica in Rome, Italy, offering copies of the Bible to passersby. San Giovanni is one of four Catholic basilicas where our small groups of believers often went to distribute copies of the Bible to Catholic pilgrims who had come to Rome for the Catholic Year of Jubilee.

A young woman in her early twenties walked by and one of our team members held out a copy of the Scriptures, offering it to her as a free gift. The woman stopped and began to question why we were giving away Bibles to anyone and everyone who desired a copy. She had been taught that for anyone other than the priests, bishops, cardinals, and leaders of the Church, it was dangerous to read the Scriptures. She had come to believe if a lay person read the Bible they could go insane since in her mind, they were not meant to read God's sacred Word. She was convinced that priests had to interpret the Scriptures for the people.

We were incredulous. For years, through the tutelage of God's Spirit, the Bible had been for us a source of spiritual food, refreshment, strength, comfort, correction, and so much more. But through what she had been taught, this woman genuinely believed she would suffer mental illness if she personally tried to read and understand the Scriptures. And though not every Catholic believed as this woman, her line of thought was not uncommon. We had previously experienced outright anger from other pilgrims as we handed out copies of the Bible. Carlo, an

Italian friend with whom we worked closely, explained to us the reason for their beliefs.

It was in the year 1229 AD, at the State Catholic Church's Council of Toulouse, that the Bible was placed on the Index of Forbidden Books.[1] From that time forward in the history of the Catholic Church, it was illegal for the common people to own a copy of the Bible or to read the Bible. It was only as recently as 1961-1962, that the Second Vatican Council repealed this church ruling.[2] Although the Bible is now officially "legal" to read according to Catholic church law, many lay people with whom we spoke during our year in Rome still avoid reading the Word. Through deep, historical tradition their hearts believe its wisdom is "off limits" to all but their priests.

Though many people continued to hold to this tradition and responded in fear or anger to the free Bibles we were offering, there were others who thanked us gratefully, for they had never before read the Scriptures for themselves. For the entire year, as various teams of believers distributed almost 700,000 portions of the Scriptures, we watched God deeply move many people with their first personal taste of the Word of God.

An Anabaptist Perspective

Prohibiting lay people from reading the Bible is one example of the effect that religious control can wield over a people group. I had seen first-hand the results of this control over the lives of many people with whom we interacted during our year in Italy. They feared and avoided of the Word of God, doubting their own ability to discern and interpret God's Word. As a result, they remained in spiritual darkness and in a place of spiritual immaturity.

You can imagine then, my utter surprise when I discovered a similar attitude within Anabaptism concerning the interpretation of the Scriptures. There is a subtle and underlying perception in some of our own present day churches, that the

Scripture's interpretation must be filtered through local bishops or local pastors before it is passed on to the rest of the congregation. Take as an example, a sermon of one Mennonite bishop who taught that the way to keep sound Biblical doctrine is by presenting "all personal convictions" to the brotherhood: that the brotherhood is to be the interpreter of Scriptures, and to "bring the Bible to the people."[4]

But, our forefathers taught that neither the Church, nor a priest of the Church, nor any man, was to serve as the interpreter of the Bible for Christians. The early Anabaptists believed that the Living Word, the Holy Spirit, was our "mediator" between God and man. Peter Hoover writes that Menno Simons did not believe the Church was to mediate for its people:

> Menno Simons *rejected the belief that the church stands between God and man*, and stepped out of Roman Catholicism.

Menno instead directed the people to *Jesus* as their Mediator:

> We counsel and admonish *everyone* to take good heed to the Word of God. . . . We have *not directed you to men* nor to the teachings of men, *but to Jesus Christ alone and to his holy Word*, preached and taught by the apostles. . . .[5]

Nowhere in Scriptures does it indicate that the people of God are not to search out and study the Scriptures for their own edification and maturation. As we examine the original intent of the church of Acts, we will come to understand that "mediatorial" churches and "mediatorial" leaders make the flock powerless, greatly weakening the bride of Christ on the earth. The concept of mediatorial leaders is another corporate stronghold of our thinking which has permeated some of our churches to the point that it has caused lay people to remain immature, since in their hearts they believe they are unable to rise up and fully apprehend God's Word for themselves. One pastor recently described its effects as creating whole congregations of "passive spectators" in the Kingdom of God.

But, what do the Scriptures say? It is Jesus who has made each and every one of us *priests* of God. He has given us Himself to live *in* us so we can all have direct access to God. His Spirit *in* us guides us into all truth:

> To him who loves us and has freed us from our sins by his blood, and has made us to be a kingdom and *priests to serve his God and Father*—to him be glory. . . . (Revelation 1:5-6)

> But when he, the *Spirit of truth*, comes, *he will guide you into all truth*. He will not speak on his own...He will bring glory to me by taking from what is mine and *making it known to you*. (John 16:13-14)

The New Covenant, written on our hearts, means that each person knows the Lord because He has come to teach *each one* His ways. From the least of them to the greatest, God will speak:

> "This is the covenant that I will make with the house of Israel after that time . . . I will put my law in their minds and write it on their hearts. I will be their God, and they will be my people. *No longer will a man teach his neighbor, or a man his brother, saying, `Know the Lord,' because they will all know me, from the least of them to the greatest'* declares the Lord. (Jeremiah 31:33-34)

Back To The Beginning

In the days soon after Pentecost, though different apostles' names are mentioned in certain aspects of giving leadership, not one of them is ever singled out as a primary apostle who is above all the other apostles.[6] Rather, they led *together* through the Holy Spirit's guidance, as evidenced by their discussions regarding requirements for the Gentile converts (Acts 15).

Later on in the book of Acts, the churches established in different towns were led by *groups* of elders, as indicated when Paul appointed or called together these groups of elders (Acts 15:4, 20:17). Paul never uses the *singular* form of the word "elder" when *appointing the leadership of a church*, but only when denoting the qualifications of an elder or when giving instructions about a fellowship's relationship to an elder (I Timothy 5:19; Titus 1:6).

The word elder is also translated as *overseer* (in the King James Version, overseers is translated as "bishop") or as *shepherd*. These words all refer to the elders assigned to lead the flock, and each of these "titles" is able to be used interchangeably with the others.[7]

In all their writings, the New Testament authors never point to the establishment of *one* particular leader to govern the flock. As Charles P. Schmitt writes in *Floods Upon The Dry Ground,*

> The churches of the apostles . . . were originally headed up by a . . . (group) of presbyters, or elders. These were (also) the bishops, or overseers, of the church . . . official distinctions were not made between them as they later would be in the Church when bishops were distinguished from presbyters (elders).[8]

There are several reasons for the eventual separation of certain leaders out from the flock. The primary reason was the *waning of the presence of God's Spirit* in the midst of the church. As the flow of the Holy Spirit subsided, the confidence in His gifts operating through people also subsided.

In the early church, times of fellowship were loosely structured around the operation of the gifts of the Spirit, with each one being given a gift, as Christ apportioned them:

> When you come together, **everyone** has a *hymn*, or a *word of instruction*, a *revelation*, a *tongue* or an *interpretation*. All of these must be done for the strengthening of the church. . . . Two or three *prophets* should speak, and the others should weigh carefully what is said. (I Corinthians 14:26-29)

> But to *each one* of us grace has been given as Christ apportioned it. (Ephesians 4:7)

Schmitt explains more about the governmental framework of the church changing as the Spirit's presence lessened:

In the churches of the apostles *spontaneity is the rule of the day*. The church is an (living) organism, carried along by the buoyant life of the Holy Spirit. In the second century we notice a change. The church becomes less an organism and more an **organization. Structure begins to replace spontaneity**.[9]

Lars P. Qualben, in *A History Of The Christian Church*, writes about this change as well, explaining the gradual shift from the *practice of the gifts of the Spirit*, to the establishment of *offices of leadership* within the church. In describing the church of Acts, he writes:

The local churches had elders and deacons, who . . . directed the work of the congregation. . . . But the early church organization was not centered in *office* and in *law*, but in the *special gifts of the Spirit*. . . . An elder might also teach, preach, and administer the Sacraments, . . . *but (only) because he was known to have 'the gift'* . . .

Toward the close of the first Christian century a change took place. A general **lack of confidence in the special gifts of the Spirit**, a desire for *more specific order*, and a pressing demand for proper *safeguard against heresy* resulted in a *gradual transfer* of the preaching, the teaching, and the administration of the Sacraments **from the *'gifted men'*, to the *local elders*. . . .** The official functions were now performed by *elders only*. The ministry of the Word and the Sacraments became *official*, which marked the beginning of the **division of the Christians into 'clergy'** *(chosen ones)* **and 'laity'** *(the masses)*.[10]

Everyone Participates

The encouragement of the New Testament writers is that *all* are priests, and *all* are ministers of the gospel. Though some are given the responsibility of leadership within the flock, *all* are to have some part in ministering to others, according their spiritual gifts:

But ye are a chosen generation, a *royal priesthood*, an holy nation, a peculiar people . . . (I Peter 2:9, *KJV*)

And you will be called *priests of the Lord*, you will be named *ministers of our God*. (Isaiah 61:6a)

Another author, Jim W. Goll, explains it this way in *Father Forgive Us!*:

> The early Church made no distinction between "clergy" and "laity." Any individual believer's position or function was determined by the *spiritual gifts that were manifested in his or her life.* Since *every believer was a priest, every believer had direct access* to the throne of God, *could interpret the Word of God as the Spirit gave him understanding,* and was *directly responsible to God* for his life and behavior. A priest ministers to *God* and to *others* in God's name. The priesthood of the believer means that every believer is a *minister.* Everyone who is called to Christ is called to the *ministry.*[11]

Though leaders are given care of the flock, every single member of the flock is called to maturity and to helping others grow up in their faith. Each member of the church is given gifts for the sake of the body and each member is encouraged to *practice* the *use* of their gifts until they become able to distinguish good from evil. God's desire is that *each and every* believer becomes experienced in the gifts of the Spirit.

The form of the New Testament church then was more loosely structured around the gifts of the Holy Spirit which were given by God to each member, rather than placing a great emphasis between certain individuals as leaders, and the "rest of the group." Within the framework of the early churches, the group of elders assigned to each church were to lead the flock, but *all* people within each body participated in its maturing, *by operating in the gifts they had been given by the Holy Spirit.* In the second of these next two scriptures, the words "you" in the Greek are all *plural*, and therefore apply to every member of the body to whom the letter was written: that's you, and that's me!

> And in the church God has appointed first of all *apostles,* second *prophets,* third *teachers,* then *workers of miracles,* also those having *gifts of healing,* those able to *help others,* those with gifts of *administration,* and those speaking in different kinds of *tongues.* (I Corinthians 12:28)

> For though **by this time you ought to be teachers**, you need
> someone to teach you again the basic elements of the oracles
> of God. You need milk, not solid food; for everyone who
> lives on milk, being *still an infant*, is **unskilled in the word
> of righteousness**. But solid food is for the *mature*, for those
> whose faculties have been **trained by practice to distinguish
> good from evil**. Therefore let us go on toward perfection. . .
> (Hebrews 5:12-6:1, *NRSV*)

The Hebrews writer is lovingly rebuking his readers for
remaining immature. He tells us we should have already been
teaching the Word, but because we have not *practiced* and *used*
our faculties—our ability to discern—we are still "infants" in
our thinking. We are to exercise and use our faculties in order to
become skilled in the "word of righteousness." His call is to
go on to perfection, meaning the completion of our faith into
maturity.

Effects on the Church

As the first Anabaptist fellowship began in the town of
Zollikon near Zurich, this small band of believers recovered some
of the spontaneity which had been part of the house churches in
Acts. Once again believers met in homes where the Lord's
Supper was celebrated, new believers were baptized, and where
the "priesthood of all believers" was practiced.[12]

But, today the practice of the priesthood of all believers
is not the norm for our Anabaptist fellowships, or for much of
the worldwide body of Christ. There are two spiritual roots which
over the centuries have fostered an unhealthy pattern of keeping
the flock dependent on particular leaders. It is out of these two
roots that one of two things have occurred: either leaders have
inadvertently fed their fellowships a diet of spiritual milk, or the
members have never been able to see their personal call to
spiritual maturity. These two spiritual roots are *fear* and
unbelief, and we will address these two roots throughout the rest
of this chapter.[13]

Success and Failure

Success and failure are *both* a part of practicing anything. For example, a child who is learning to walk will fall down quite a few times before she is actually able to stand up and walk. When she finally does walk, at first she will only take a few steps. Gradually she will be able to walk more consistently and finally after several years, she will run fast and freely without falling down.

It is no different in our spiritual lives. The process of growing up from spiritual infants into spiritual adulthood requires the practice and use of our sense of discernment in distinguishing right from wrong and good from evil (Hebrews 5:14). A brotherhood then, will always be "in the process" of growth, since within each church there are always young believers who are maturing. These young believers will make a lot of mistakes as they learn to figure out the difference between the voice of the Holy Spirit, the voice of their own flesh, and the voice of the evil one. Allowing freedom where the gifts are practiced requires seeing *failure as part of the process* of helping younger believers to grow into the use and exercise of their gifts. Instead of tightening the controls of what happens in a church in order to prevent failure or error, failure needs to be seen as a normal part of eventually succeeding.

I have personally made many mistakes in my own practice of the gifts of the Holy Spirit. I have given prophetic words to people, which in time I understood were spoken out of my own personal hurts rather than coming from the Holy Spirit. When I understood my error, I contacted those people and asked forgiveness wherever possible and also repented before the Lord. God never condemned me for my error and thankfully, neither did my church. Neither discounted me as a "heretic," but gave me room to fail and to grow. As I have been growing in the spiritual gifts, I still make mistakes, but the mistakes are becoming farther apart and the accuracy of my ability to hear and discern is gradually increasing.

We will also have to learn how to address failure with mercy rather than fear, as we give room for practicing discernment. Unfortunately at present, spiritual error is not often addressed in a healthy and open manner. But if it is handled wisely, everyone can be edified in the process. On one occasion, that was exactly what happened. Someone gave a word which was discerned as being inaccurate. Since the word had been given publicly, a brother felt the freedom to address the correction publicly, and spoke up with gentleness, humility, and love, to the one who had given the word. As he did, he shared with honor, speaking "in *Spirit* and in truth." The result was that the church was edified even through the error, as they learned a lesson in discernment. The young believer also grew in the process as she was given grace in her failure, and afterwards affirmed as a person by individuals within the body.

Weaknesses Turned to Strengths

The pattern in both the Scriptures and in the present day is that when God comes into the lives of people, He changes their weaknesses into strengths. Their places of need become the avenues of their eventual ministry to others. God uses those whom the world and the religious church institutions think are useless, hopeless, cast off, and unsalvageable, to demonstrate His glory. These are the ones God delights in rescuing, and these are the ones He loves (Mark 2:17). The Scriptures declare this very truth:

> But God chose the *foolish things* of the world to shame the wise; God chose the *weak things* of the world to shame the strong. He chose the *lowly things* of this world and the *despised things*—. . . so that no-one may boast before him. . . . Therefore, as it is written: 'Let him who boasts boast in the Lord.' (I Corinthians 1:27-31)

In my own life, I have watched God take the areas of my greatest struggles and my greatest fears, and slowly change me so that His glory is beginning to be released in those places. Where fear had ruled, He is bringing boldness; where shame had been, He is establishing confidence; where unbelief existed, He is building trust.

The Scriptures reveal this pattern. Rahab was a prostitute, but became righteous and is mentioned in David's family line. Mary Magdalene was demonized, but as a follower of Jesus, was one of the first to whom He appeared after His resurrection. Gideon and his army defeated the Midianites, but he was the least in his family and came from the weakest clan. David was the youngest of eight sons, dismissed by his father as a candidate for kingship, but God chose him above the others. Paul the apostle "persecuted Jesus," yet through his writings God used him to minister to believers throughout all time. Mark (also called John) deserted Paul's ministry, yet later Paul instructs Timothy to bring Mark along to meet him, because of his helpfulness in ministry. The list of transformed people in the Bible is nothing short of miraculous!

It is important for us to understand this aspect of God's ways in light of our discussions on congregational life. God uses the weak ones. That means He will take those who make the most mistakes, who are the most helpless, and He will build them up. We are to honor and esteem the weak, not only because God loves the poor and needy, but because He intends to show His glory through their lives and make them noble vessels. The most damaging and harmful thing that can happen with the weak ones is that leadership or congregations, in order to control the atmosphere of a church or meeting, discount them as "dishonorable" or unusable vessels (II Timothy 2:20-21).

They may fall and fail often, yet we are to give Holy Spirit-led guidance and help them to mature. If we fear the effects of their failure in our fellowship and prevent them from practicing their gifts, they may never be able to rise up and take their place in the Kingdom of God. God already sees the *end* of their lives. If we are also able by His Spirit to perceive who they are to *become*, we will be able to love them through anything and will have hopeful expectation of their success and patient, loving endurance of their failure.

Release or Control

Many leaders have carried such a heavy weight of responsibility for making certain their flock is "safe" from heresies, that they have erred on the side of *control*. Maintaining a safe atmosphere through an overbearing control of what happens in our fellowships is one way to try and prevent spiritual error, but it will hinder the Holy Spirit from operating in our midst. Both congregations and leaders are often torn between wanting to grow and being afraid of the "messiness" that comes as a part of believers exercising and practicing their gifts. Out of the fear of error and fear of man, we can all hinder the Spirit by wielding a subtle or not-so-subtle control over the atmosphere of a church.

Leaders in particular can also be hesitant to risk the necessary "practicing" of gifts because they fear God's judgment. This fear is based on the following Scripture, yet the very next verse indicates the mercy of God:

> Let not many of you become teachers, my brethren, for you know that we who teach shall be judged with greater strictness. *For we all make many mistakes*, and if any one makes no mistakes in what he says he is a perfect man, able to bridle the whole body also . . . (James 3:1-2, *RSV*)

The actual Greek translation of verse one is *not* that the teachers will receive a "greater condemnation" as the King James Version translates it, but rather that the decision or determination about their faithfulness or unfaithfulness will entail a greater scrutiny. The "judgment" is not necessarily indicated as a condemning judgment, but a judgment which can be either positive *or* negative. And in the very next verse, God says we *all* make many mistakes, and that includes leaders. In these verses, God *is* calling leaders to accountability, telling us we are not to be careless. But at the same time, we are not to be afraid or to fear Him as if He were waiting to heap condemnation upon us. He knows the leaders of the flock will not be perfect.

We will see the whole body of Christ rise up in a confident use of their gifts, as we learn to *trust* rather than fear, and to *release* rather than subdue. Jim Goll puts it this way:

> Left unchecked, *a control spirit can cripple* and even destroy a church. So how do we deal with it? How can we keep it from taking over? It is primarily a heart issue. *The key is learning how to release rather than hold on;* how to give back to God what He has given to us. It's an issue of *faith and trust and of having a revelation of grace and mercy.* These little keys will unlock the prison door that has held and continues to hold hundreds of thousands of God's people at arm's distance from the presence and power of His Spirit.[14]

Releasing people to grow in their gifts is the key to a mature and healthy church. Then the whole church will walk into its intended calling, as the "joints and ligaments" of the body each do their part (Ephesians 4:16).

Both shepherds and the sheep can learn to trust God during the maturing process, and it is especially to the advantage of congregation members to have confidence in their leaders and yield to their leadership because in time, the leaders will give a report to God as those who "keep watch" over the flock:

> *Obey* (have confidence in) your leaders and *submit to them* (yield), for they are keeping watch over your souls and will *give an account.* Let them do this with *joy* and not with *sighing*—for that would be *harmful to you.* (Hebrews 13:17 *NRSV,* parenthesis mine)

In a healthy church, the leaders will be anointed and faithful in watching over the sheep, *and* in fostering an atmosphere where members of the flock can grow in their gifts. The flock, knowing they are free and safe, will be able to bless their leadership even when they make mistakes.

Fear of the World

There is also a very real fear today within our churches of losing our young people to the world. Those of us who are in American or European societies have seen much worldly influence through television, movies, computers, and so on. But, worldliness was no different in the times of the New Testament churches. The ingredients were different then, but in some ways the Roman empire's pagan idol worship, sexual perversions, and errant philosophies were worse than today's influences.

That is another reason we're instructed to be filled with the Holy Spirit, and to *practice distinguishing* between good and evil (Ephesians 5:18; Hebrews 5:14). If we understand by the Holy Spirit's prompting what is good and what is evil, we will be kept safe. We are "in the world, though not of it". We love those in the world as Jesus loved them, but we walk by the Spirit in increasingly confident discernment. We listen to Him and act according to His direction and we are kept safe.

There are many Christian ministries today which reach out to drug addicts, prostitutes, the demonized, and many other needy people. These ministries go into worldly environments and demonstrate God's love, just as Jesus did when He related to tax collectors and sinners in their own homes.

The answer to keeping our young people is not to control them by keeping them from all contact with the world, because that is virtually impossible. The best way to prepare our young people is to *equip* them to walk worthy of God (I Thessalonians 2:12), helping them to grow in discernment. Throughout the larger body of Christ, young people are being spiritually prepared. Even children are being taught to hear the voice of God, and miracles are happening through the prayers of these children.

Young people want excitement. They are full of energy and have incredible potential. God delights in "godly offspring," in youth who are full of His Spirit and walking by faith (Malachi

2:15). As we invest ourselves in bringing them to maturity, they will go from spiritual strength to spiritual strength. Daniel, speaking of the end times says, "the people that do know their God shall be strong, and do exploits." These youth are part of the Kingdom saints whom God will use to do those exploits (Daniel 11:32, *KJV*).

Preparing for God's Presence

If we are going to experience God's presence in today's church, it will be as we *release* each other, trusting God to bring each one to completeness in Him:

> One of the major hindrances to revival is that we have regulated, restricted, controlled, and limited *who* can do *what* in the Church rather than *releasing people* to function in the gifts, ministries, and service that Christ has called them to. Out of fear and unbelief and the desire to keep things *"under control,"* we have forgotten the spirit . . . of Jesus' commands: *Go* . . . into all the world and preach the gospel. . . . And *these signs will accompany* those who have believed . . .[15]

Many believers *with many gifts* are needed as the gospel is preached to all the nations (Matthew 24:14). Many within the church will become apostles, prophets, evangelists, pastors, teachers, apply gifts of healing, helps, giving, and more, so that new believers coming into the body can be fed, encouraged, taught and matured. As Goll sums it up,

> ...*all* the saints (need to) be equipped and functioning in ministry, not just the elite "chosen few".[16]

We are all to "become mature, attaining to the whole measure of the fullness of Christ," through the practice and use of our gifts, by the free and gracious presence of the Holy Spirit (Ephesians 4:13).

Lord, You are worthy of all control over Your church. Thank You that its rule and government is on Your mighty shoulders.[1] Let Your Kingdom come and let Your will to be done on earth, as it is in heaven.[2]

Confessing the sins of our fathers:

I confess the sins of our fathers, who have often grieved You by resisting Your control. We have hurt You deeply. You saw every time we made rules which brought bondage instead of freedom. You stood aside when we went our own way, rather than hearing Your desires for our congregations. You watched every time we quenched Your Spirit, so that things would stay orderly and safe in our fellowships. Forgive us. Forgive our stubbornness and our arrogance. Forgive us for taking control rather than giving You control.

Personal cleansing:

In my own life, I choose to forgive every person who has tried to control me or my family out of their fear or unbelief. I forgive each one whose name You choose to bring to mind (allow God to speak to You): I forgive _____ for their control. Where I have judged them, I repent. Cleanse me by Your blood.

Show me by Your Spirit how to trust You when people around me walk in a spirit of control. Help me to love them and to find Your guidance in each situation.

And Father, I know there have been times when I have controlled people or situations because of my own fear or unbelief. I know I have rejected Your headship and demanded my own way. I confess my sins. Forgive me and change me. I choose Your control and Your headship.

Help me yield more and more to You, Holy Spirit.

Silencing the strongholds:

In Your Name, Jesus, I now break off every generational spirit of control which has come down through my family lines. Take all ungodly control in my life and in my family to the cross, and cleanse us. I bring down every stronghold of control in my mind and in my family. I bind every demonic attachment to those strongholds, in Jesus' Name.

Prayers for restoration:

Father, I want to be able to walk in complete submission to You. Conform me to Christ's image.[3] Wash all my fears and heal every place of unbelief. Heal my family as well, and bring Your presence to the Anabaptists. We need You. Teach us how to release others instead of fearing, and show us how to allow failure and weakness as we walk together in trust and faith. We need You to guide us, because we can't see how to make these changes by ourselves, and we don't want to walk in our own strength.

Thank You for Your Scriptures. Thank You that You promise to guide me as I read them. Give me confidence in You, that when I err in my interpretation, You will set me back on the path of truth. Thank You for my church leaders who have taught me truths. Bless each one. Help them as they shepherd Your people. Give them more faith and more of Your presence. Refresh them. I choose to yield to their leadership and trust You to work in their lives as they guide our church.

Protect my family and me and my church fellowship from the evil one. Keep us hidden from his sight and bring his plans no avail.[4] Cause him to fall into every trap he has set for us.[5]

Thank You, Faithful One. Glorify Your Name in my life.

In Jesus' wonderful Name, Amen.

[1] Isaiah 9:6; [2] Matthew 6:10; [3] Romans 8:29; [4] Isaiah 54:17; [5] Psalm 35:7-8.

Promises for you from Philippians 1:5-6:

Because you believe, God has begun a wonderful work in your life. He is committed to finishing every aspect of His work in you. He will carry it and keep it in His possession. His work will be completed, right up to the very day when you see Jesus in heaven. *He* will do it!

24

COVENANT INCLUSION

OR

COVENANT EXCLUSION

Years ago, our Mennonite fellowship embraced a newly converted community person who had not grown up in Anabaptist heritage. He and his entire family became Christians and began attending church every Sunday. They sat in the front pew and were very excited about their newfound faith and their new spiritual family. God had met them in a wonderful true conversion of heart, and spiritually they were "growing like weeds." The problem was that this man was a local bartender.

No one was quite sure what to do with his "profession." Financially, he had obligations and expenses like everyone else. As the situation was considered by our Mennonite church, it was decided that time should be given for John to grow, and to hear God in providing another occupation as the Holy Spirit directed him elsewhere.

For several months, John and his family attended church on Sunday, while he tended bar during the week. The amazing thing is that John had the gift of evangelism and as he interacted with his patrons, he shared his love for Christ and his testimony. People in the bar were getting saved and he was bringing them along with him to church.

In less than a year after they became Christians, John and his wife Sandy, decided to close the bar and turn it into a restaurant. Years later, they would become the pastors of a church fellowship in their hometown.

I remember being amazed at the way our church handled John's work situation. The leadership had the wherewithal to recognize his need to make a living, and the faith to seek God's leading. Rather than forcing him to change careers and work at "any old job" that would have seemed more "Christian," they followed the Holy Spirit's solution. A legalistic response would have been to insist that John had to quit tending bar before he could really be considered part of the fellowship, or before there was a viable solution for his financial needs.

John had been transformed *internally*. His heart had been purified, his motives changed. Now, instead of serving himself, he desired to serve God. Recognizing that his heart was *pure* enabled his fellowship to "walk in the light" with him, and to trust in God's answer for John's needs.

An Historically Pure Church

Purity in Anabaptist churches has been interpreted in many different ways throughout the centuries. It all started in the State Churches of the 1500s, where, Sunday after Sunday, the wicked unbeliever and the righteous man stood side by side in services.[1] The godly and the ungodly both took communion. The evil and unrepentant were confirmed into the church, right along with those who truly believed. There was no practice of the biblical mandate to "expel the wicked man" from among the brotherhood, since the "brotherhood" was of all of society (I Corinthians 5:12-13).

As truth became apparent, this deplorable compromise of evil within the church brought grief of soul and spirit to new believers. Apostolic leaders Luther and Zwingli both purposed to be instruments of change. Though they differed in opinion on how reform was to occur, they both agreed that it should be applied *within* the status quo of the State Church system. Luther wanted to patiently instruct the masses in order to "bring over (to Christ) the whole people of the parishes,"[2] and Zwingli wanted to make the existing State Church into a "new" State Church system.[3]

As we know, the Anabaptists said Luther and Zwingli had missed the mark. They said of Luther that he:

'Tore down the old house, but built no new one in its place,'[4]

and of Zwingli that he:

'threw down all infirmities as with thunder strokes, but erected nothing better in place.'[5]

Our forefathers believed the church needed to become the *pure* bride of Christ once again.[6] The church was to be undefiled: a community of Christians who lived together with other *believing* Christians.[7] The early Anabaptists may have disagreed on various issues, but this one thing was certain: separation from the world was essential. Jacob Hutter wrote that we have "gone out of" the world and "sundered ourselves" from worldly society.[8]

You can understand then how *the ban* came into being. It was absolutely essential in the creation of this new church model that some guidelines be established for protecting the purity of the church, so that it would in no way resemble the worldly pattern of the State Church. Thus, in the earliest confession of Anabaptist faith, the Schleitheim Confession (1527), an article is included to instruct on the Matthew 18 procedure of discipline for those in the congregation who fall into sin.

"The ban" actually evolved from a phrase first used by Conrad Grebel and his friends to describe the Matthew 18:15-20 passage. Grebel said that in establishing this New Testament church, it was to be done:

. . . with the help of *Christ and his rule* as we find it initiated . . . in Matthew 18 . . . in the context of a covenanted, speaking, dialoguing community.[9]

This "rule of Christ" quickly became an integral part of the brotherhood as Anabaptism spread. It was to be used only in cases of open sin and where the name of Christ was put to shame.[10]

It was Balthasar Hubmaier who later tied the Matthew 18 "rule of Christ" with communion and baptism. He taught that the Lord's Supper was the "key of exclusion and binding."[11] Forbidden to those who were being disciplined, it eventually became a way of determining who among the Anabaptist communities was being shunned, or separated from the rest of the group.

Baptism was the "key of admittance (into the church) and loosing." It "served the practical function of determining who was 'in' and who was 'out.'"[12] Baptism brought believers into the church and at the same time, automatically put them in danger and cut them loose from the State Church and from the world. Because it was such a clear demarcation of commitment, it eventually became synonymous with church membership. Today in many Anabaptist churches, baptism and church membership are still joined together, hand in hand.

A Focus on Exclusion of the World

Historically, our church membership through baptism helped to restore a *purity* to the body of Christ that was greatly lacking. But in time, the church's purity became our primary focus. When it did, we began equating separation from the world, with the *exclusion* of others. Rather than preaching to the lost and bringing them *into* our fellowships, we concentrated more on keeping *out* of the church anyone or anything which could possibly cause contamination. Protecting our churches from impurities became a matter of priority, even more important than an evangelical witness.

The New Testament church endeavored to walk in purity, but they continued to reach out to people of different cultures in expanding their churches, recognizing that the gospel was for all men, both Jew and Gentile alike:

> He is the atoning sacrifice for our sins, and *not only for ours* but also *for the sins of the whole world.* (I John 2:2)

> For this is what the Lord has commanded us: 'I have made you a light for the Gentiles, *that you may bring salvation to the ends of the earth.'* (Acts 13:47)

We need to return to a balanced understanding of the purity of the bride of Christ. Her purity is *of the heart,* not the Pharisaical purity of religious avoidance. No matter where she goes in reaching out to the lost, her purity can never be taken away, since it is the purity of *heart motives.* Her purity is by the blood of Jesus, which has "purified us from all sin":

> But if we walk in the light, *as he is in the light, we have fellowship with one another,* and the *blood of Jesus,* his Son, *purifies us from all sin.* (I John 1:7)

As new converts experience both the inner baptism of God's Spirit and the outer baptism of water (see chapter 7), their *hearts* will be *transformed by God,* who is their internal Light. There is always a discipling of new believers by members of their church fellowship, just as my church discipled John and his family in their newfound faith. But the foundation of all external guidance, is the inner guidance which each Christian carries in their hearts, where God has written His laws (Hebrews 8:10).

A Focus on Exclusion of Other Churches

Our emphasis on the *exclusion* of all that is worldly has created problems in another arena. Originally, the Anabaptist definition of "the world" included everyone within the State Churches. Today, either in actual practice or in heart attitude, there are times when we have called other church denominations "worldly," because we disagree with some of their doctrines. Since they don't "line up" with our doctrines, we consider them impure and avoid fellowship with them. Yet Paul rebuked the apostle Peter, a Jew, for separating himself from Gentile believers for the sake of his Jewish traditions (Galatians 2).

Any attempts to keep our churches pure by our doctrine will not be effective. As Paul writes to the Colossians, we will only find ourselves walking in condemnation as we fail time after time in restraining our own flesh:

> Since you died with Christ to the basic principles of this world, why, as though you still belonged to it, do you *submit to its rules*: "Do not handle! Do not taste! Do not touch!?" *All these regulations* refer to things that perish with use; they are simply *human commands and teachings*. These have indeed an appearance of wisdom in promoting *self-imposed piety, humility, and severe treatment of the body*, but they are of *no value in checking self-indulgence*. (Colossians 2:16-23, *NIV/NRSV*)

Keeping a pure church will never be accomplished by creating doctrines to shield it from the world, just as following church doctrines will never keep its people from being worldly. It is always the *presence of God* who provides our purity. His Spirit in individuals and His Spirit in our congregations will bring a purity of attitude and gifts of repentance where we need to be corrected (Romans 2:4). He is our safety from the world because when we are transformed by God living *inside* of us, we will not *want* to walk impurely. When the Spirit of God is operating in our fellowships, directing, teaching, filling, speaking to leaders and lay persons, and guiding the interpretation of the written Word, there is no fear of contamination. There is only a desire to *press into Christ* and a holy understanding that we are to encourage one another daily, in order to keep from becoming hardened by sin's deceitfulness (Hebrews 3:13).

Our Heritage

Our ancestors did much to re-establish the church as a pure vessel, set apart from the world and the state political systems. Yet, because of our overemphasis on the church as our "safe place," apart from other influences, we have become rigid in our thinking about church doctrine and church history. As our churches were being established and Anabaptism continued to grow, we drew up doctrinal statements. We call them *confessions of faith*, but essentially they are the tenets by which we govern our churches. Early on, these confessions were valuable in helping us move forward in establishing the framework of this new church. They are still helpful today in providing viable guidelines for our church denominations.

However, for many of us, the doctrines and confessions of our faith have become a snare to our hearts. In our desire to keep a pure church and to protect ourselves from the influences and the harm of the world, we have made our confessions of faith, our heritage, and our beloved historical leaders, an object of pride, idolization, and separation. Our *tradition* has become more important than walking in unity with the rest of the body of Christ. But even Menno Simons warned against giving precedence to the doctrines, customs, or interpretations of man's making:

> Christ commands all true messengers and preachers to preach the gospel. *He does not say,* 'Preach the **doctrines** and **commands of men**, preach **councils and customs**, preach **interpretations and scholarly opinions**.' He says, 'Preach the Gospel!' [13]

Even the fact that our ancestors were martyred for their faith has been a source of idolization for some. But the Scriptures declare that though a person may surrender their body to the flames, *without love*, he gains nothing (I Corinthians 13:3). Our ancestors may have died bravely, but as their descendants, if we do not have the love of God in our hearts, we gain nothing.

True Purity

As we ask God to return us to a true purity which is created *by His Spirit*, we will become a people who once again, like our early forefathers, have a heart focus on the *inclusion* of others into the body of Christ. Our motives for purity will become motives of love rather than motives of fearful exclusion.

God is a God of redemption! When we give Him everything, He redeems it and makes it truly pure. We have been a people who have yearned for purity. God desires to fulfill our longings to be pure, but by His Spirit, rather than by our own efforts. He is able, and He will do it as we yield to Him and allow Him to purify with His refining fire, all that is ours, both past and present!

> For he will be like a refiner's fire or a launderer's soap. He will sit as a refiner and *purifier* of silver; he will **purify the Levites** (priests of God) and **refine them like gold and silver**. Then the Lord will have **men who will bring offerings in righteousness,** and the offerings of Judah and Jerusalem *will be acceptable* to the Lord, as in days gone by, as in former years. (Malachi 3:2-4)

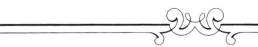

Father, thank You that my early ancestors cared about Your bride, and wanted the church to be pure. Thank You that they desired to walk in holiness before You and before men. I also want to walk in purity before You, so I now confess to You our sins.

Prayers for corporate cleansing:

I know our desires to be pure have been sincere. We have wanted to keep all worldly influences out of our churches. But Father, we have erred by our religious piety. We forgot that You are the One who makes us pure in our hearts, and we avoided reaching out to others with Your salvation. We stopped sharing about You because we didn't know what to do with worldly people's sins. Forgive us for making our purity more important than people's souls.

And forgive us for making purity from worldly influences more important than walking in unity with other believing churches. Forgive us for denying fellowship with others who love You, because they didn't abide by our own church traditions. Jesus, You died for them and You died for us, and we are all purified by Your blood.[1] Forgive us for denying our brotherhood. I repent on behalf of my fathers. I repent on behalf of my family and I repent for my own sins. Forgive us and cleanse us from all our unrighteousness.[2]

Laying down our idols:
Thank You for the faith and the example of our church fathers. But Lord, we want You to be our all in all, and everyone else to be in their proper place in our hearts. Wherever we have idolized any church father—Jakob Ammann or Menno Simons, Conrad Grebel, Felix Manz, or any other leader throughout history—forgive us. (If there are other names that come to mind, take time to confess them as well). We repent and turn from our idolization.[3]

And wherever we have honored our confessions of faith more than we have honored You, forgive us. For every time we have placed our heritage—even the martyrdom of our heritage— above Your glory, forgive us.

You, Lord, are worthy of all adoration.[4] I'm thankful for my heritage, but I give it to You and ask You, sanctify it in my heart by taking it to the cross and bringing it to death, resurrecting it by Your Spirit, to be pure. Bring down any idols in my heart that I have set above You. I want You to be Lord of all my life. I invite You—have Your way.

We are pure because have been washed, we have been sanctified and justified by Your Son, and by nothing else.[5] Give us once again a pure church by Your Spirit among us.

Thank You Father, for hearing me. Thank You for Your

great love. Thank You that You have set Your attention and
affection on me. I love You, my Redeemer and my Refuge.
In the Name of Jesus, Amen.

---

[1] I John 1:7; [2] I John 1:9; [3] Jonah 2:8; [4] Revelation 4:11; [5] I Corinthians 6:9-11.

Promises for you from Psalm 128:

Because you revere God and obey Him, He will bless you
for your entire life, even until you're old! Your family will be
blessed, like a grape stalk that is just *filled* with large bunches of
sweet grapes. He'll make your work prosperous and pleasant,
and you'll get to enjoy the results of your efforts. Because you
revere Him, God will bless you every single day!

25

THE POWER OF WORDS

From the very start, Anabaptists have been cursed by men's tongues. We have been branded as "heretics," "blasphemers," "enemies of God and humankind," "wicked," "thieves," "murderers," "hypocrites," "possessed and blinded by the devil," and given many other condemning names and descriptions.[1] Jesus warned us in the Scriptures that we would be cursed just as He was cursed, yet He tells us not to be afraid but to continue to speak out on His behalf (Matthew 10:23-28). We are also promised that a curse without cause will not find a resting place in us (Proverbs 26:2). In other words, a curse will not harm us if it is spoken without reason.

Many of our early ancestors were able to forgive the slanderous tongues of their enemies and in mercy, extinguish their verbal darts. Loving prayers were offered for those who were spewing vile condemnation, their curses unable to find a resting place in the souls of the martyrs.

But in time, when we withdrew quietly into the sadness of worldly sorrow, embitterment, and rejection, their curses took effect in crushing our spirits. As we judged those who cursed us, we received the judgments back into our own souls and the curses were able to find a resting place in our hearts through our wounding.

The Spiritual Power of Words

The Scriptures declare that words have the power to bring to *life,* or power to bring to *death.* Words have power to *pierce a heart* and *crush a spirit*. They also have power to bring *healing*:

> If anyone is *never at fault* in **what he says**, *he is a perfect man*, able to keep his whole body in check. . . The tongue also is a fire. . . . It corrupts the whole person, **sets the whole course of his life on fire**, and **is itself set on fire by hell** . . . no man can tame the tongue. It is a restless evil, full of deadly poison. (James 3:2-7)

> **Death** and **life** are in the **power** of the tongue, And those who love it will eat its fruit. (Proverbs 18:21. *NKJV*)

> Reckless words **pierce like a sword**, but the tongue of the wise **brings healing**. (Proverbs 12:18)

> The tongue that **brings healing** is a tree of life, but a *deceitful tongue* **crushes the spirit**. (Proverbs 15:4)

I once cut off my fingertip with a knife, and it hurt! I can only imagine the pain of being pierced by a sword. Of course, unlike a sword or knife, words don't cut into the physical body, but into the soul or the spirit, where another verse tells us they have enough power to *crush*. No wonder James writes that the tongue can corrupt or defile the whole person and affect the whole course of his life!

If we realized that our words actually do have *power* in the spiritual realm, we would be much more careful to speak *life* rather than death, and healing rather than cursing. Derek Prince, in *Blessing Or Curse—You Can Choose*, writes about the *spiritual* nature of our words:

> Both **blessings** and **curses** belong to the **invisible, spiritual realm**. They are vehicles of **supernatural, spiritual power** . . . Both are major themes of Scripture . . . mentioned in the Bible more than 640 times. . . . The **main vehicle** of both **blessings** and **curses** is **words**. Such words may be **spoken or written** or **merely uttered inwardly**.[2]

Why do our words have such power? It is because we have been made in the image of our Creator, God Almighty. His words have power to create and like Him, our words also have a creative power.

The Tongue's Creative Power

When God created the earth, he *said*, "Let there be light." or, "Let there be a firmament." or "Let the earth bring forth grass," and so on. Everything was created by God *speaking* it into existence. Hebrews explains it this way:

> By faith we understand that the worlds were framed by **the word of God**, so that the things which are seen were not made of things which are visible. (Hebrews 11:3, *NKJV*)

God spoke, and matter was formed. God spoke and the waters were given boundaries. God spoke and the stars came into being. God spoke. There is creative *power* in God's words, which are *alive* (Hebrews 4:12).

Our words have life and power as well, as we have seen in the previous Scriptures. But because there are two spiritual kingdoms in this world where we live, our words can also bring the power of *death*. We can create either good for the Kingdom of God, or cursing in the realm of the world and of the evil one. If we slander our brother, for example, James says we are allowing our tongue to be "set on fire by hell." He continues with these admonishments to believers:

> With the tongue we *praise our Lord and Father*, and with it we **curse men**, who have been **made in God's likeness** . . . **Out of the same mouth come praise and cursing**. My brothers, this should not be. Can both fresh water and salt water flow from the same spring? (James 3:9-12)

> Brothers, **do not slander one another**. Anyone who **speaks against** his brother or judges him *speaks against the law* and judges it . . . But you—who are you to judge your neighbor? (James 4:11-12)

When we curse another human being, God says we are condemning one He has made in *His likeness*. When we speak against a
brother, we are speaking against God's own law.

But, when we speak blessing, we bring *life*. Words can be
like "apples of gold in fittings of silver" if they are fitly spoken
(Proverbs 25:11). Words can actually bring healing, and a tongue
that speaks healing is called a "tree of life" (Proverbs 15:4). It is
not only for the sake of others that we are not to speak words of
cursing, but also *for our own health and wellbeing*. We are to
bless, being kind and:

> . . . not returning evil for evil *or reviling for reviling,* but *on
> the contrary **blessing**,* knowing that you were called to this,
> ***that you may inherit a blessing***. For *"He who would love
> life And see good days, Let him **refrain his tongue from evil**,
> And his lips from **speaking deceit**.* (I Peter 3:9-10, *NKJV*)

We are to speak blessing even when we are reviled—or
insulted—*so that* we may inherit a blessing. God declares His
favor, praise, and blessing over our lives when we declare
blessings over other human beings, even over those who have
spoken reproachfully against us. One of the reasons some of us
have not experienced victory in our lives is that our tongues
have caused us to forgo the blessing of God. Through the
negative words we have spoken about others and even about
ourselves, we have forfeited inheriting favor.

Think about your own life: what kind of words were
uttered in your home as you were growing up? Were words
spoken which blessed and praised and favored one other? Were
there negative and harmful words? Are there any phrases which
haunt your memory as a "curse" against you? All of these words
can have effect, if they are given a "place to rest" in our wounded
hearts.

Recently, at a small meeting of Anabaptists who had
gathered for prayer, we discussed the words of our own
childhood experiences. A few had heard occasional words of
blessing, but most remembered negative words. One commented

that his parents did not want to speak words of blessing, for fear that their children would become proud! And another shared that her parents didn't speak negative words, but neither were there many words of praise or encouragement. At the close of the prayer meeting we took time to bless each other in obedience to God's Word, which tells us to encourage one another daily (Hebrews 3:13).

The Words of our Ancestry

The words spoken by our ancestors against each other were at times words of blessing and at times curses. As divisions began to occur between our different Anabaptist groups, we tended to be less than gracious as we began "delivering each other unto satan" and calling each other "servants of the devil" (see chapter 22). In our own heritage, we have dangerously called each other these names, without realizing the seriousness of our words. We have also called the Reformers "antichrists" and worse (chapter 17). Yet Jesus rebuked the Pharisees when they called Him Beelzebub (a name for satan) and warned them they were *blaspheming against the Holy Spirit* who lived inside of Him (Matthew 12:24-32, Matthew 10:25).

We can, by God's grace, begin walking in a lifestyle of blessing those whom God has created in His image, both the righteous and the unrighteous. In the prayer at the end of this chapter, we will take time to pray a prayer of cleansing from generational curses spoken against us *and* which we or our fathers may have spoken, that we may grow in using our tongues righteously as children of our heavenly Father (II Corinthians 6:7; Matthew 5:44-45).

The Power of Oaths

Our forefathers understood very well the power of words as they were used against them in the swearing of oaths. In today's society and in particular in our judicial systems, an oath is used as a promise to *tell the truth*. For example, the oath taken by a witness in trials of law is something like this: "I swear to tell the truth, the whole truth, and nothing but the truth. . . . " But for the political leaders and the State Church leaders of the Middle Ages, the oath was used to demonstrate *loyalty* to leaders, to churches, or even to a religious deity. This type of oath is known as an *oath of fealty*.[3]

Its use dates back to ancient Rome, and forward to as late as the nineteenth century in some parts of the world.[4] In ancient Rome, the oath of fealty was used to swear loyalty to the emperor and even to the emperor's gods. It was used in Constantine's era, and it was also used in the Middle Ages during the Inquisitions of the State Catholic Church.

During the time of our ancestors, the oath was used to swear loyalty to the government and to both State Church systems. By requiring everyone to swear by an oath, they were able to identify and condemn dissenters.[5] New oaths were created specifically to "catch" Anabaptists. Under threat of serious punishment for violation, entire populations in political domains were made to swear oaths as loyal subjects, promising to turn in Anabaptists to the authorities.[6] It is no wonder that our ancestors disliked the oath so intensely, since it was used as a weapon against them, and anyone else who thought differently than those who were in power.

Our forefathers, by their understanding of the Scriptures, could not swear by an oath of fealty, or by any other oath. Instead, they believed, as Jesus taught, that our "yea" or "nay" was to be enough and that anything beyond that came from the evil one (Matthew 5:33-37). But if they agreed with the matter at hand, they were free to *confirm* and to give their word by a promise of their lips, understanding that:

> . . . we must always, in all matters, and with everyone, adhere to, keep, follow, and fulfill the same, as though we had confirmed it with a solemn oath.[7]

The Anabaptists were faithful men and women of their word. If they affirmed or confirmed, it was as good as an oath because they understood they had given their promise to fulfill what they had spoken. For example, when the Mennonites who had recently arrived in the new world (America) signed a commitment *giving their word* to remain loyal to the throne of England, they were grieved afterwards that they had not really understood the foreign English language of the paper they had signed. They felt bound by their signatures to be loyal to the throne, though they did not necessarily agree with its government, because they had "confirmed" their word.[8]

The Power Of Vows

In the New Testament, the meaning of the word *oath* has to do with a *binding restraint*, as if by giving our oath we have erected a fence around something in order to hem it in.[9] When James warns believers not to swear by heaven or earth or with any other oath, he is doing so in order to protect us from the power of words which hem us in like a fence and lead us to condemnation through their binding power (James 5).

Vows also have the power to hem us in and bind our lives. The biblical meaning of a vow has to do with the *promises we make to God*. Vows and oaths have similar strength, but a vow is usually heaven-directed and an oath is usually man-directed.

As Anabaptists, we have been well-schooled in the strength of words when they are used in making an oath. However, we have not been nearly so aware of the power that a vow can wield over our lives. For this reason, in the rest of this chapter we will focus on the vows we make to God, in order to understand how some of our words—whether actually spoken by our lips or merely uttered strongly by our heart—really can determine the entire course of our lives, just as James has written.

Making a vow to God is a serious thing. We are told in Ecclesiastes that it is better not to make a vow at all, than to make a vow to God, and not be able to fulfill it:

> Do not be **quick with your mouth**, do not be **hasty in your heart to utter** anything **before God**. God is in heaven and you are on earth, so let your words be few. . . . When you make a **vow to God,** do not delay in fulfilling it. He has **no pleasure in fools; fulfill your vow**. It is **better not to vow** than to make a vow and not fulfill it. Do not let your mouth lead you into sin. And do not protest . . . "My vow was a mistake." (Ecclesiastes 5:2-6)

We are not to be hasty or quick when we commit do something before God, because whether the vow is only uttered in the heart *or* spoken with our mouths, God *expects* us to fulfill it! He holds us responsible for our commitments to Him, and "has no pleasure in fools" who will not keep their word.

The book of Numbers also instructs us not to break our word, and to do *everything* we have said we would do:

> When a man makes a **vow** to the Lord or takes an **oath** to bind himself by a pledge, **he must not break his word** but must do **everything** he said. (Numbers 30:2)

Proverbs warns us it is harmful to make a vow carelessly:

> *It is a trap* for a man to dedicate something rashly *and only later to consider his vows.* (Proverbs 20:25)

Paul fulfilled a *vow* in Acts, because of the threat of violence against him by the Jews:

> . . . so do what we tell you. There are four men with us who have **made a vow**. Take these men, join in their purification rites . . . so that they can have their heads shaved. Then everybody will know there is no truth in these reports about you. . . . (Acts 21:23-24)

The meaning of this word *vow,* is a prayer to God that is *held fast* by its promise.[10] Just like our marriage vows are binding before God and hold us fast to a promise that we are not to break, other vows we make are also spiritually binding, and "hold us fast" before God.

It is possible to make vows, especially unspoken vows uttered in the heart, which actually bind us to acting and responding in certain ways. We may not even be aware of some of the vows that we have made earlier in our life, but they are nevertheless binding, since they have been made "before God" in the realm of the spirit.[11] In my own journey of spiritual growth, God has revealed numerous vows uttered in my heart, most of them unknowingly, until God made them apparent by His Spirit. One vow made at an early age, was that *I would never trust those in authority over me.* As a result of that vow, I spent much of my adult life withholding my heart from family members, school teachers, pastors, youth group leaders and other sincere leaders whom God had placed in my life in order to train me and bring me to maturity. When God brought this vow to my awareness, I was able to be set free from its binding power. Since that time, I have been increasingly free to receive teaching and blessing from those who are the authorities in my life.

Vows of Baptism

Just as we make a marriage vow publicly before both God and man, there is another public vow made in many of our more conservative Anabaptist churches. It is the vow of baptism. This vow is made solemnly and includes both a *confession of faith* and a *commitment to joining the church*, as well as a promise to *obey the church and all its doctrines and regulations.* One written copy of these vows asks four questions to which the baptismal candidate is to respond:

1.) Can you confess with the eunuch, "I believe that Jesus Christ is the Son of God?"

2.) Do you also confess this to be a ***Christian doctrine, church, and brotherhood to which you are about to submit?***

3.) Do you now denounce the world, the devil and all his doings, as well as your own flesh and blood, and desire to serve only Jesus Christ, who died on the cross for you?

4.) Do you also promise, in the presence of God and His church, with the Lord's help to support these *doctrines and regulations*, to earnestly *fill your place in the church*, to help counsel and labor, and *not to depart from the same, come what may, life or death?*[12]

These vows, as with every vow we make, are to be taken seriously. If you have personally taken this vow or spoken similar words in the presence of your own church, you probably remember the day well since it was an important occasion in your life.

Yet, I find a hesitancy in my spirit as I consider the binding of these vows of baptism. Since we are not to make a vow rashly or carelessly, I need to ask several hard questions about their veracity. As we are binding ourselves *not to depart,* even in *life* or *death*, to whom or to what have we pledged our undying allegiance? Is it to the *body of Christ*, that is, the greater eternal church, from which we are committing not to depart? Are we subjecting ourselves to supporting the *doctrines* and *regulations* of the Scriptures? If so, then we are honoring God, who has bought us with the precious blood of Christ. We do well to commit ourselves to Him and to His holy Word.

But if, by speaking these vows we are binding ourselves to obey all the doctrines and regulations of our *local church* or our *denomination*, *come what may in life or in death*, then please allow me to pose some difficult "what if" questions. What if we are called to another church through entering into missions or through moving away to another geographical region? How are these vows then fulfilled? What if in fulfilling our destiny in the Kingdom of God, we are called to join our hearts to a different local church body because of our similar strengths and spiritual gifting? What if in my search of the Scriptures, I discover the doctrines of my local church contain some teachings which are unbalanced or inaccurate? Haven't I bound myself to obey *all* the doctrines, accurate or inaccurate? What if as I grow in my faith, I realize some of the doctrines and regulations of my local church are really "the traditions of men" rather than ordained by God's Spirit (Mark 7:8)? Am I not still bound to their obedience by my vow?

Perhaps we need to reconsider what we are requiring for baptism and church membership. Perhaps our "vows" should not be vows at all but rather, an affirmation or a commitment to covenant. Otherwise, we may be forcing a binding which we should not be forcing. And perhaps our "Yea" or "Nay" should be enough, without promising obedience to our death (Matthew 5:37).

We have been so careful about not swearing oaths to men, but have given less attention to our vows before God which are as binding, if not more so, than our oaths. If we are "condemned" by swearing oaths, how much more will we be bound if we make a vow to God and are unable to fulfill it with all of our heart (James 5:12)? Our forefathers wrote that we were not to swear oaths because we are imperfect and cannot "perform our oath" as God could, when He swore an oath to Abraham. Therefore, they continued, "we should not swear."[13] If we cannot keep our oaths, the probability of being imperfect in "performing our vows" is even greater, and when we do not keep them we are "trapped" (Proverbs 20:25).

In questioning the kinds of vows we have made, I am not advocating that we break away from our local churches or refuse to be in covenant with other believers. Being a part of a church body is a command of God, and essential for every believer (Hebrews 10:25). We simply need to understand that we *will tie ourselves* to whatever it is we have vowed to obey. Menno Simons wrote that we are *not to be bound* by the commands of men—not the "councils of fathers," not "customs of long standing," not decrees. We are only to be *bound* by Christ and His teachings:

> We *look not* to **councils of the fathers** nor to **customs of long standing**. For no . . . council or **decree** can stand against the *Word of God*. **We dare not be bound by men.** *We are bound by the commands of Christ,* by the pure teachings and practice of the apostles. . . .[14]

Menno said it so well, when he said we are to be *bound by the commands of Christ.* This particular issue, perhaps more than any other subject in this entire book, is the most delicate one I have addressed so far. I am fully aware that encouraging us to "repent" from a vow to obey the doctrines and regulations of a church leaves us in a quandary. Repenting from a vow to not depart from our local church, in life or in death, seems unfaithful. We want to be faithful, and it is a fearful thing to take steps which are in direct opposition to a vow we may have already made. The very act of turning from the vow is disobedience to our vow! But, if we are to walk *by the Spirit*, we cannot walk by the doctrines of men. Until vows are broken which tie us to obeying regulations and doctrines (other than those found in Scripture), we will stumble in following Christ wholeheartedly, because we will be serving another "master":

> Don't you know that *when you offer yourselves to someone to obey him as slaves,* you are slaves to the one whom you obey . . . (Romans 6:16)

> But now, *by dying* to what *once bound us,* we have been *released from the law* so that we *serve in the new way of the Spirit,* and not in the *old way of the written code*. (Romans 7:6)

We no longer serve a *written code.* Therefore, the first prayer at the end of this chapter is a prayer to break *only* the part of these baptismal vows which bind us to men's doctrines, or to *never* departing from our local church or denomination. It is *not* a prayer to deny honor or voluntary submission to brotherhood, but only a prayer to free our hearts to *obey by the direction of the Holy Spirit and according to God's Word*, rather than being bound by our vows.

I encourage you not to pray this prayer until you are ready. Seek God personally about what I have written and be at rest in His answer, so that you can pray this prayer in faith. And preferably, because of the binding power of vows, it would be better to pray with someone else who walks in faith. The agreement of two is more effective than one standing alone (Ecclesiastes 4:12). However, if there is no one with whom you can pray, the Father and the Son will stand with you as your witnesses (John 8:18).

The second prayer is for the breaking off of curses which may have found a resting place in your life. Remember to pray both prayers aloud.

Prayer to break vows to doctrine and regulations, and allegiance until death to a local church or denomination:

*In the mighty Name of Jesus, I renounce the vow "not to depart from my church and my denomination **come what may, in life or in death.**" I renounce the vow to "support the doctrines and regulations of my church and my denomination **come what may, in life or in death.**" By Jesus' power and His name, I break these vows over my mind, my will and my emotions. I break their power over my spirit and my body and untie them from my being. I declare that I am now **free to obey** my church and my denomination **by direction of the Holy Spirit and according to God's Word.***

In the name of Jesus Christ, my Master and Lord, Amen.

Prayer to break curses from your life:

The following information is from Derek Prince's book, *Blessing or Curse: You can Choose!*[15] (see Recommended Reading section) It is so helpful, I felt it would be best to reprint it in a slightly expanded form (to include additional prayer for cleansing of our heritage) as a prayer for your use. The prayer includes seven aspects which are first broken down and listed individually so that you may understand the scriptural basis for what you will be praying. It would be good to look up the scriptures and consider them before you actually pray.

Aspects of prayer to break curses from my life:
1. *Confess* your faith in Christ and in His sacrifice on your behalf. (Romans 10:9-10)
2. *Repent* of all your rebellion and your sins. Submit yourself to God (James 4:7)
3. *Claim* forgiveness of all sins. (I John 1:9)
4. *Forgive* all other people who have ever harmed you or wronged you. (Mark 11:25)
5. *Renounce* all contact with anything occult or satanic. (if unsure about something, ask God to clarify) (II Corinthians 6:14-17)
6. You are now ready to pray the prayer for release from any curse. (Based only on *Jesus' sacrifice* on the cross: You do not have to *earn* it.) Be real with God as you pray this—in His presence. (Galatians 3:13)

Lord Jesus Christ, I believe that You are the Son of God and the only way to God; and that You died on the cross for my sins and rose again from the dead.

I give up all my rebellion and all my sin, and I submit myself to You as my Lord. I confess all my sins before You and ask for Your forgiveness-especially for any sins that exposed me to a curse.

Release me also from the consequences of my ancestors' sins. I forgive those who have cursed us, and release all unforgiveness to You now. Wash us and cleanse us by Your blood. Heal our souls from the effects of being cursed. I also repent on behalf of my fathers for the curses we have spoken against our brothers and against our enemies. Please forgive us for cursing

those whom You have said to bless. I now break every genera-
tional curse in my family lines by the power of Your Name, Jesus.

    By a decision of my will, I forgive all who have harmed
me or wronged me—just as I want God to forgive me. In particu-
lar, I forgive _____ (any persons who come to mind).

    I renounce all contact with anything occult or satanic—if
I have any "contact objects" (objects that are idols or have
demonic influence), I commit to destroy them (see chapter14).
I cancel all satan's claims against me.

    Lord Jesus, I believe that on the cross you took on Your-
self every curse that could ever come upon me. So I ask You now
to release me from every curse over my life—in Your name, Lord
Jesus Christ! By faith I now receive my release and I thank You
for it.

Derek's final prayer point is this:

    7. Now *believe* that you have received, and go on in
God's blessing!

    He continues by encouraging us to find scriptures of
blessing and to begin to pray them aloud over our lives. The
blessings in Deuteronomy chapter twenty-eight are an example.
Not only are we to be free from curses, but we are to speak
blessing and life with our tongues! This point is essential to build
our faith.

    If there are specific words or phrases spoken over you
that have settled into your heart as a negative message, you may
want to renounce those curses individually. For example, a curse
can be a hurtful phrase which your heart received as true, like
You'll never amount to anything, or *You're stupid.* Once you've
renounced specific curses, search the scriptures for blessings
or promises that counteract their negative words. For the above

curses, two examples would be Ephesians 2:10 and I Corinthians 2:16. Declare the scriptures you have found over your life. I also highly recommend reading Derek's book as a resource tool for further freedom and helpful information.

A few of the promises from Deuteronomy 28, which for you, are "yes" and "amen" in Christ (II Corinthians 1:20):

You are blessed wherever you live, if it's in the country or the city. Your work is blessed, your children are blessed. Your bread basket is blessed. When you leave your house you are blessed, and when you come back home, you are blessed.

Your enemies are defeated. They'll run away from you in seven different directions! Everything you touch will be blessed! YOU are blessed!

~ My Prayer For You ~

I would like to offer a prayer for you. I have written this prayer, because it is the only way I can communicate it to you, the reader. But God is not bound by time or space, so He will receive it. God *bless* you abundantly, as you walk forward with our heavenly Father!

My Father, thank you so much for my spiritual sibling, who is reading this page. Thank You that they have done the hard work of reading all about their heritage, in order to extract its treasure. Thank You for their desire to find precious spiritual gold. Reward them, Father, reward them with your heavenly riches. Reward their thirst with a spiritual *river* of water! Reward them with the fullness of Your Spirit. Reward them with Your deep love. Reward them with heaven's bounty. Father, pour out Your gifts into their lives, both for themselves, and for the body of Christ. Bless them in every way and give them great, abundant joy!

Thank You for hearing me.
I ask boldly, in the name of Jesus, Amen.

~ Epilogue ~

In recent years there have been repeated times of reconciling with descendants of some of our former persecutors. Leaders of the Swiss Reformed State Church have reached out in recognizing their need to repent in order to repair a breach in the wall of the Kingdom of God. That breach occurred many years ago, but as we have seen throughout this book, the repair of its effects has been ongoing.

Swiss believers who have expressed regret for the State Reformed Church's persecutions have also committed to a long term process of healing and restoration. They understand that true reconciliation means not only forgiveness, but also a return to unity and fellowship.

For this reason, I felt it was important to chronicle several of the gatherings which have already occurred. As I write, plans are under way for a reconciliation conference in Lancaster County, Pennsylvania, USA, in April 2005. Other recent works have included a conference in May 2003 in Winterthur, Switzerland; a small conference in Montana, USA, in January 2004; and a conference in June 2004 in Zurich where leaders of the Reformed State Church commemorated a memorial to Felix Manz, one of our early Swiss forefathers martyred for his faith. Following are articles detailing these gatherings. Thanks to J. Lemar and Lois Ann Mast of Masthof Press for the use of their article.

ANABAPTIST RECONCILIATION
WITH THE REFORMED STATE CHURCH
OF SWITZERLAND

© 2003, Janet Keller Richards

Most of us can understand, at least to a degree, the heart of a father who is estranged from his son. We know he carries a certain inward pain until the day his son returns home and they are reconciled and restored. Today, such a "father" in the faith exists who has carried the ache and burden of estrangement for years. His name is Geri Keller, the founder of *Stiftung Schleife*, a parachurch ministry in Winterthur, Switzerland.

The "son" is the Mennonites and Amish and all those who are of Anabaptist heritage. Geri, as a member of the Reformed State Church of Switzerland and a retired Reformed pastor, longed to bring healing between the Reformed church of Switzerland and the Anabaptists whom they persecuted, executed, and banished from their land for several hundred years.

Encouraged by God that the time was right for such a reconciliation, Geri and Stiftung Schleife convened a conference called, *Heal Our Land*, from May 1-4, 2003, in Winterthur. The call to attend was for all "fathers" and "sons" who were willing and ready to recreate a spiritual home for each other through repentance and forgiveness.

In addition to Anabaptists who attended from Switzerland, Germany, France, Austria, and other parts of Europe, there were two main groups of Anabaptists who attended from the United States. One was a group of Amish families from two communities in Idaho and Montana. The other was a conglomerate of eighteen Mennonites from Lancaster Mennonite Conference, Franconia Mennonite Conference, and the Hopewell Network.

As representatives from the Lancaster area, we understood that we were not attending a formal church event, but rather an event of intercession, where we were "standing in the gap" for our respective people groups, much like Daniel stood in the gap as he prayed for Israel in Daniel, chapter 9.

As the conference began, those from each people group agreed with calls from the pulpit for forgiveness and repentance toward each other. But repentance moved from mental assent to personal experience when a Reformed State pastor began to express the burden of guilt he personally carried because of the devastation his ancestors had perpetrated against us. That was the moment when healing started to well up in our Anabaptist hearts. Tears flowed freely. We also recognized anger in our hearts which needed to be confessed and released.

We Lancaster Anabaptists shared the next day about our own sinful attitudes towards our former persecutors and our need for cleansing and healing. We spoke of our need to grieve the losses which occurred as a result of having our spirits broken by oppression and persecution, much like the plight of the Israelites in their Egyptian slavery or the Native Americans who were dispossessed by the European white man. We asked for help to heal and to find revival again. We asked the "fathers" for forgiveness for the bitterness and resentment we carried.

We listened to Reformed pastors openly share their struggles regarding infant baptism, which is still required as a sacrament in the State Church. These men and women who love God are being faced with the reality of a possible loss of job and income through their obedience to Scriptures. We felt a kindred spirit as we heard their fears and weaknesses confessed in brokenness.

Through many symbols of repentance, our hearts were gradually restored to our spiritual fathers and their hearts to us: Reformed pastors in their clerical robes washed the feet of the Amish delegation and then stood and removed their clerical collars to give them to Ben Girod, an Amish bishop, as a sign of their desire to be reconciled; thirty Reformed State Church Pastors knelt down on stage before the Lancaster Mennonite and Amish leaders and tearfully asked for and received a verbal affirmation of forgiveness from every Anabaptist leader and his wife; Reformed State Church pastors lined up across the front of the auditorium, receiving prayers of blessing from individual

Anabaptist representatives; water spilled out on hands all over the auditorium, as Reformers and Anabaptists asked each other to wash their hands in a symbolic cleansing of guilt and repentance; and for the first time in history, an Amish Bishop preached from the pulpit of the Grossmünster church in Zurich, where many "guilty" verdicts had been brought against the first Anabaptists who were executed.

Later in the week, the reconciliation continued as Reformers reached out in acts of sacrifice and humility. At Trachselwald castle, where many Anabaptist ancestors had been incarcerated and tortured before being taken to execution, a leading government official of the region and a brother in Christ, Markus Grossenbacher, publicly asked forgiveness on behalf of the government of the Trachselwald region for the sins done there against the Anabaptists. In Schaffhausen, Sabine Aschmann, a Reformed State Church pastor sensed God asking her to return a part of what had been stolen from the Anabaptists. In response, she gave as a gift of restitution to the Lancaster Mennonites, her family's rare copy of a Froschauer Bible. The Bible, printed by Anabaptists in the 1500s, had been confiscated during the persecution years. It remains as one of a few copies of these Anabaptist Bibles which exist today.

In regards to the Scriptural doctrine of baptizing adult believers, which originally gave our ancestors the name, "Anabaptists", meaning, "re-baptizers", Geri Keller stood on the last day of the conference, boldly and humbly proclaiming to all Anabaptists on behalf of the Reformed State Church , "We were wrong and you were right. You were right."

When true reconciliation occurs, joy and hugs abound. Tears course down faces. Dancing, singing, shouting, waving of banners, and celebration erupt. We found all of these amidst the waves of repentance, forgiveness and cleansing which washed over our group. At last, our hearts felt at home with our Reformed brothers and sisters. We truly felt restored to our spiritual father. May God take the seeds of what began at *Heal Our Land* and sow them over the Anabaptist communities throughout the world! As unity is restored in the body, may the oil of the Spirit again flow down on the priesthood of believers, as it flowed down on Aaron's beard in Psalm 133. May God heal each Anabaptist from the effects of the persecution years, that we may all grieve, forgive, and find the restoration to the fathers that we need.

A SMALL GATHERING IN MONTANA
JANUARY 2004

In addition to the larger conferences in Winterthur and Zurich, a group of believers from Anabaptist and Swiss Reformed backgrounds met at the Amish community in Libby, Montana, and shared together for three days in song, teaching, and fellowship. Believers from other "nations" also joined us, including some First Nations Native believers, as well as Canadian Mennonites from Saskatchewan, Canada.

It was a rich time of learning to appreciate each other's differences even while we enjoyed the unity of God's Spirit. In the midst of the cold Montana Winter, our hearts were warmed as we laughed, cried, prayed, worshiped, and broke the bread of fellowship together over the delicious meals prepared by our Amish hosts. God met us wonderfully, as we celebrated being family through His unifying and sweet presence among us.

WHAT DOES OUR ANABAPTIST HERITAGE
MEAN TO US TODAY?[1]

by J. Lemar and Lois Ann Mast

When we received an invitation to participate in "The Reformation and the Anabaptists," a historical conference in Zurich, Switzerland, our first response was to ask, "Why does the Reformed Church of Zurich want to ask for forgiveness from descendants of Anabaptists for the persecution that the Reformed ancestors did almost 500 years ago?"

But after attending this June 26-27, 2004, conference, we now understand the importance of joining over 100 other Mennonites to extend the forgiveness that was requested. What an experience to be asked for forgiveness and then grant it after 500 years!

In 1524, it was important to some Reformed (soon to be Anabaptist) families in Switzerland to stop baptizing their infants and adopt "believer's baptism." Also, they believed that they should follow the New Testament teaching of separation of church and state. This was the beginning of the first Anabaptist congregation.

Ulrich Zwingli and other Reformation leaders definitely did not understand these Anabaptists. Interestingly, the Reformed Church leaders today cannot understand why these early church leaders who also had been persecuted by the Catholic Church, in turn persecuted the Anabaptists. "Why?" they asked.

Emotions welled up in most persons' eyes as the leaders of the State Reformed Church offered a public confession stating, "The persecuted do not forget their history, but the persecutors by contrast would prefer to do so. . . . We honor the radical approach of the Anabaptist movement to be the salt of the earth and the light of the world as a free community of committed

---

[1] From *Mennonite Family History*, edited by J. Lemar and Lois Ann Mast, Volume XXIII, Number 4, 2004, p. 136.

believers putting into practice the message of the Sermon on the Mount . . . we belong to Jesus Christ who tore down the wall of enmity and united people near and far in one body."

Forgiveness also was important to a young Swiss theology student who sat beside Lois Ann during the Saturday afternoon session. After the session, she hugged and wept in her broken English, "I'm sorry, I'm sorry!" She had recently completed several university classes on Reformation history and thanked us for standing up for what we believe just as our ancestors did 500 years ago. She said that she now understands why the first Anabaptists chose to follow Jesus instead of the state church leaders. What an experience!

Our Anabaptist forefathers asked radical questions about what they were taught—questions that were hard to ask since they went against what their church leaders were teaching-and they did it with courage and steadfastness that even resulted in death. The questions for us today are, "Can we learn from our past so that Christians never again persecute each other?" "How do we share our faith to ensure that our church history never repeats itself?" "What radical questions should we be asking each other as followers of Christ in this century?"

Copies of the confession made by the Reformed Church of Zurich leaders, as well as the response given by the Swiss Mennonite Conference leaders, may be found in volume XXIII, Number 4, of the quarterly publication, *Mennonite Family History*, 219 Mill Road, Morgantown, PA 19543.

~ Recommended Reading ~

God's Love and Relationship:
The Divine Romance by Gene Edwards, Alba House Publishers.
The God of all Comfort by Hannah Whitall Smith, Moody Press.
Father—A Look Into The Heart Of God by Geri Keller, MorningStar Publications.

Basic Christian Growth:
There Were Two Trees In The Garden by Rick Joyner, MorningStar Publications.
Destined for the Throne by Paul E. Billheimer, Christian Literature Crusade
The Hidden Power of the Blood of Jesus by Mahesh Chavda, Destiny Image Publications.
Blessing or Curse—You Can Choose by Derek Prince, Chosen Books (a division of Baker Book House). Chapter seventeen is excellent for understanding all our salvation has provided for us.

Present Day Visions, Encouragements, and Strengthening Books:
The Final Quest by Rick Joyner, MorningStar Publications.
The Call by Rick Joyner, MorningStar Publications.
The Fear of the Lord by John Bevere, Charisma House Publishing.
Breaking Intimidation by John Bevere, Charisma House Publishing.
The Devil's Door by John Bevere, Charisma House Publishing.
Wild at Heart by John Eldredge, Thomas Nelson Publishers (a book to men about their quests for *life*).
Possessing Your Inheritance by Chuck D. Pierce and Rebecca Wagner, Systema Regal Books, Gospel Light, Ventura, Calif.
John G. Lake, His Life, His Sermons, His Boldness of Faith by Kenneth Copeland, Copeland Publications, Fort Worth, Texas
Overcoming fear by Rick Joyner, MorningStar Publications

Healing for Our Lives:
The Transformation of the Inner Man by John and Paula Sanford, Victory House, Inc., Tulsa, Okla.
Healing of the Wounded Spirit by John and Paula Sanford, Victory House, Inc., Tulsa Okla.
Deliverance and Inner Healing by John and Mark Sanford, Chosen Books.
God's Remedy for Rejection by Derek Prince, Impact Christian Books.
"Elijah House" is an excellent resource ministry for learning about the healing of the soul. They may be reached at www.elijahhouse.org or at Elijah House, 17397 W. Laura Lane, Post Falls, ID 83854-4611.

Spiritual Warfare:
Possessing the Gates of the Enemy by Cindy Jacobs, Chosen Books or Zondervan Publishing.
Warfare Prayer by C. Peter Wagner, Regal Books.

Blessing or Curse—You Can Choose, Derek Prince, Chosen Books (a division of Baker Book House).

Church History and Its Effects on Our Day:
Floods Upon the Dry Ground by Charles P. Schmitt, Destiny Image Publishers (Giving foundation and understanding to the progressive move of the Holy Spirit in the earth).
The Eternal Church by Dr. Bill Hamon, Christian International Publishers, Santa Rosa Beach, Fla. (an overall spiritual history of the greater body of Christ, from its inception to present day).
Rekindling the Anabaptist Flame by Ben Girod, Carlisle Printing, Sugarcreek, Ohio.
The Story of Liberty by Charles Carleton Coffin, Maranatha Publications, Gainesville, Fla. (History of the Church and ruling powers of Europe during the Middle Ages).
The Secret of the Strength by Peter Hoover, Benchmark Press, Shippensburg, Pa. (Anabaptist history with some spiritual applications).
The Reformers and Their Stepchildren by Leonard Verduin, The Christian Hymnary Publishers, P.O. Box 7159 Sarasota, FL 34278. (941) 373-9351 (Anabaptist history).
There is a Way Back by Vaughn and Ilona Martin, (another look at the Anabaptist heritage in light of spiritual understanding).

Others:
Daring to Live on the Edge by Loren Cunningham, (trusting God with finances) YWAM Publishing.
The Hidden Power of Prayer and Fasting by Mahesh Chavda, Destiny Image Publishers.
The Elijah Task by John and Paula Sanford, (a call to today's prophets and intercessors). Elijah House Ministries.
Intercession, Thrilling and Fulfilling by Joy Dawson, YWAM Publishing.
Women of Destiny by Cindy Jacobs, Regal Books.
Discover Your Spiritual Gifts by C. Peter Wagner, Regal Books.
The Power of a Praying Wife by Stormie Omartian, Harvest House Publishers, Eugene, Ore. (encouragement for women and prayers for husbands).

~ Bibliographic Footnotes ~

Chapter One, A God-Given Heritage:
[1] The fourth article of the Schleitheim Confession requires separation from all popish and repopish works and idolatry, gatherings, church attendance . . . meaning the State Churches, which were an "abomination . . . to Christ Jesus, who has freed us from the servitude of the flesh. . . ."

Chapter Two, Grace in the Fire:
[1] The accounts in this chapter of the testimonies of the martyrs are taken from *Martyrs Mirror* compiled by Thieleman J. van Braght, translated from the original Dutch or Holland language from the 1660 edition by Joseph F. Sohm (Scottdale, Pa.: Herald Press).

[2] Ibid., p. 571.
[3] Ibid., p. 570.
[4] Ibid., p. 1093.
[5] Ibid., p. 430.
[6] Ibid., p. 1068.
[7] Ibid., p. 431.
[8] Ibid., p. 432.
[9] Ibid., p. 426.
[10] Ibid., p. 1057.
[11] Ibid., p. 437.
[12] Ibid., p. 437.
[13] Ibid., p. 843.
[14] Ibid., p. 982.
[15] Ibid., p. 1069.
[16] Ibid., p. 1115.

Chapter Three, Freedom From Religion:
[1] Coffin, Charles C. *The Story of Liberty* (Gainesville, Fla.: Maranatha Publications, 1987), p. 37.

[2] Ibid., p. 24.
[3] Ibid., pp. 165-166.
[4] Ibid., pp. 162-169.
[5] Ibid., pp. 162-169.
[6] Ibid., pp. 36, 189.
[7] Ibid., p. 192.
[8] Ibid., chapters XII, XIII.
[9] Horsch, John. *Mennonites In Europe, Volume 1* (Scottdale, Pa.: Mennonite Publishing House, 1942), pp. 24-26, 37.
[10] Littell, Franklin Hamlin. *The Anabaptist View of the Church* (Beacon Hill, Boston: Starr King Press, 1957), p. 18.

[11] Ibid., p. 13, and Verduin, Leonard, *The Reformers and Their Stepchildren* (Sarasota, Fla.: The Christian Hymnary Publishers, 1964), pp. 107, 116, quote and footnote.

[12] Littell, Franklin Hamlin, *The Anabaptist View of the Church*, p. 79.

[13] More than once, Reformers alluded to this matter of chaos and confusion resulting from refusing to give allegiance to the government or the church. One example is in Leonard Verduin's *The Reformers and Their Stepchildren*, p. 251.

[14] Blanke, Fritz. *Brothers In Christ* (Eugene, Ore.: Wipf and Stock Publishers, 1961), p. 23.

[15] Littell, Franklin Hamlin. *The Anabaptist View of the Church* (Beacon Hill, Boston: Starr King Press, 1957), p. 137.

Chapter Four, Salvation By Grace Through Faith:

[1] Dyck, Cornelius J. *An Introduction to Mennonite History* (Scottdale, Pa.: Herald Press, 1993), pp. 19-20.

[2] *Confession Of Faith And Minister's Manual* (Crockett, Ken.: Rod and Staff Publishers, Inc.), p. 14. Article VI.

Chapter Five, Evangelistic Zeal:

[1] van Braght, Thieleman, *Martyrs Mirror* (Scottdale, Pa.: Herald Press, trans. from the 1660 original Dutch or Holland language by Joseph F. Sohm).

[2] Ibid., p. 1059.

[3] Ibid., p. 1059.

[4] Ibid., p. 1089.

[5] Ibid., p. 1127.

[6] Shenk, Wilbert R., ed. *Anabaptism and Mission* (Scottdale, Pa.: Herald Press, 1984) p. 100.

[7] Littell, Franklin Hamlin. *The Anabaptist View of the Church* (Beacon Hill, Boston, Starr King Press, 1957), p. 109.

[8] Ibid., pp. 121-122.

[9] Ibid., p. 121.

[10] Ibid., p. 121.

[11] Gingerich, Ray C., *The Mission Impulse of Early Swiss and South German-Austrian Anabaptism* (Nashville, Tenn., May 1980). A doctrinal dissertation submitted to the Faculty of the Graduate School of Vanderbilt University in partial fulfillment of the requirements for the degree of Doctor of Philosophy In Religion.

[12] Shenk, Wilbert R., ed. *Anabaptism and Mission* (Scottdale, Pa.: Herald Press, 1984, pp. 89-90.

[13] Zeman, Jarold Knox. *The Anabaptists and the Czech Brethren in Moravia, 1526-1628: A Study of Origins and Contacts* (The Netherlands: The Hague, 1969, p. 179.

[14] Hoover, Peter. *The Secret of the Strength* (Shippensburg, Pa.: Benchmark Press, 1999), p. 4.

[15] Shenk, Wilbert R., ed. *Anabaptism and Mission* (Scottdale, Pa.: Herald Press, 1984), p. 90.

[16] Littell, Franklin Hamlin, *The Anabaptist View of the Church* (Beacon Hill, Boston: Starr King Press, 1957), pp. 132-133.

[17] Shenk, Wilbert R., *Anabaptism and Mission*, p. 128.

[18] Littell, Franklin Hamlin, *The Anabaptist View of the Church*, p. 112.

Chapter Six, A Change of Mind:
[1] *Strong's Concordance, #3794.*

Chapter Seven, Two Baptisms:
[1] Anabaptist Encyclopedia at http://www.anabaptists.org/history and Littell, Franklin Hamlin. *The Anabaptist View of the Church*, p. xv.

[2] *Ausbund*, pp. 823-830, as quoted by Mary M. Miller, *Our Heritage, Hope, and Faith,* (Sugarcreek, Ohio: Carlisle Printing, 2000, Author, p. 413.

[3] *Martyrs Mirror*, p. 1039.

[4] Ibid., p. 434.

[5] Ibid., p. 429.

[6] Littell, Franklin Hamlin. *The Anabaptist View of the Church,* pp. 117, 120.

[7] Gingerich, Ray C. *The Mission Impulse of Early Swiss And South German-Austrian Anabaptism*, pp. 28-32.

[8] Muralt, Leonhard Von, ad. Schmid, Walter (eds.) *Zurich*, p. 20, and Williams George, and Mergal, Angel (eds.), *Spiritual and Anabaptist Writers* as quoted in Gingerich's . . . *Mission Impulse* . . . p. 31.

[9] Muller, Lydia (ed.), *Glaubenszeugnisse Oberdeutscher Taufgesinnter,* Vol. I, (a quote from Hans Hut) as quoted in Gingerich's . . . *Mission Impulse* . . . p. 101.

[10] Ibid., p. 102.

[11] Ibid., pp.103-104.

[12] Rideman, Peter, *Account of Our Religion, Doctrine, and Faith,* (London: Hodder & Stoughton/Plough Publishing House, 1950), pp. 38-39, as quoted by Littell in *The Anabaptist View of the Church*, p. 110.

[13] Marpeck, Pilgram, *Confession of Faith Composed at Strasburg* . . . ,ed. by John C. Wenger, *Mennonite Quarterly Review* (1938) 3:167-202, 171,197. as quoted in Littell, *Anabaptist View,* p. 66.

[14] Hoover, Peter, *The Secret of the Strength*, p. iii.

[15] Ibid., p. iii.

[16] Hoover, Peter. *The Secret of the Strength*, p. 72.

[17] Ibid., p. 73.

[18] Ibid., p. 58.

[19] Ibid., p. 59.

[20] Wenger, John Christian, *The Complete Writings of Menno Simons,* (Scottdale, Pa.: Mennonite Publishing House, 1956), p. 326.

[21] Ibid., p. 326-327.

[22] Ibid., p. 341.

[23] Dyck, Cornelius J. *An Introduction To Mennonite History,* p. 101; and Littell, Franklin Hamlin. *The Anabaptist View of the Church,* p. 148.

[24] Miller, Mary M., *Our Heritage, Hope, and Faith.*

[25] Ibid., p. 87, as quoted from *Lust Gärtlein,* p. 201.

[26] Ibid., p. 149, as quoted from *Christenpflich,* p. 138.

[27] Littell, Franklin Hamlin. *The Anabaptist View of the Church,* chapter 3.

[28] Peachy, Paul, *Anabaptism and Church Organization,* XXX *Mennonite Quarterly Review* (1956) 3:213-28, 217, as quoted in Franklin Hamlin's *The Anabaptist View of the Church,* pp. 94-95.

[29] Introductory cover letter of the Schleitheim Confession.

Chapter Eight, Brotherly Love and Community:

[1] Detweiler, Lowell *The Hammer Rings Hope—Photos and Stories from Fifty Years of Mennonite Disaster Service* (Scottdale, Pa.: Herald Press, 2000), p. 59.

[2] Ibid., p. 34.

[3] MDS Website: www.mds.mennonite.net

[4] *Mennonite Central Committee 2003/2004 Workbook* presented in two annual sessions at Akron, Pa., June 2003 and 2004.

[5] MCC website: www.mcc.org for more information.

[6] *Mennonite Central Committee 2003/2004 Workbook,* p. 181.

[7] Verduin, Leonard, *The Reformers and Their Stepchildren* (Sarasota, Fla.: Christian Hymnary Pub., 1964), p. 228.

[8] Shenk, Wilbert R. ed., *Anabaptism and Mission* (Scottdale, Pa.: Herald Press, 1984), p. 98.

[9] Verduin, Leonard. *The Reformers and Their Stepchildren,* p. 234.

[10] Ibid., p. 231.

[11] Horsch, John. *Mennonites In Europe, Volume I* (Scottdale, Pa.: Mennonite Publishing House, 1942), p. 296.

[12] Emil Egli, *Aktensammlung* No. 623, as quoted in Verduin's *The Reformers and Their Stepchildren,* p. 233.

[13] Zieglschmid, A. J. F., ed. *Die älteste Chronik der Hutterischen Brüder* (Ithaca, N.Y., 1943), p. 436, as quoted by Wilbert Shenk in *Anabaptism And Mission,* p. 99.

[14] Detweiler, Lowell, *The Hammer Rings Hope—Photos and Stories From Fifty Years of Mennonite Disaster Services,* pp. 64-65.

Chapter Nine, We Have a Talent:

[1] Ruth, John Landis, *The Earth Is The Lord's: A Narrative History of the Lancaster Mennonite Church* (Scottdale, Pa.: Herald Press, 2001), pp. 74-81.

[2] Blough, Neal, *The Anabaptist Vision and Its Impact Among French Mennonites*. From the website of Goshen College. "Google®" search, type Neal Blough and title of article.

[3] Dyck, Cornelius J., *An Introduction to Mennonite History)*, pp. 208-209.

[4] Ibid., p. 77.

[5] Moore, John Allen, *Anabaptist Portraits* (Scottdale, Pa.: Herald Press, 1984), pp. 18, 101, 120, 127, 136, 150, 166-167.

[6] Thanks to Elijah House Ministries, Inc., and their founders, John and Paula Sanford, for this valuable insight.

[7] Website: www.tenthousandvillages.com

[8] *Mennonite Central Committee 2003/2004 Workbook,* p. 133.

[9] Website: www.mcc.org for more information.

[10] *Mennonite Central Committee 2003/2004 Workbook.* p. 20.

[11] Ibid., p. 61.

[12] Ibid., p. 92.

Chapter Eleven, Extracting the Treasure:

[1] *Strong's Concordance*, #18.

[2] *Strong's Concordance,* #505.

[3] *Strong's Exhaustive Concordance*, #266.

[4] Dyck, Cornelius J., *An Introduction To Mennonite History,* p. 31.

[5] Ibid., p. 110.

[6] Littell, Franklin Hamlin. *The Anabaptist View of the Church*, pp. 20-21, and Dyck, Cornelius J., *An Introduction to Mennonite History*, p. 106.

[7] Elijah House Ministries in Idaho teaches these concepts in several excellent teachings: "Bitter Roots" and "Generational Sins." See Recommended Reading for more information.

[8] Paul's letters to the Corinthian and Galatian churches contain examples of a call to corporate repentance, as do the letters in Revelations chapters two and three and the Old Testament prayers of Daniel, Ezra, and Nehemiah, confessing the sins of their entire nation of Israel before God.

[9] *Strong's Concordance, #3077.*

Chapter Twelve, False Peace—Inability to Witness:

[1] Taken from a related essay by Neal Blough, on website: *(www.goshen. edu/mhl/Refocusing/)* Roth, John D., ed., *Refocusing A Vision: Shaping Anabaptist Character in the 21ˢᵗ Century* (Mennonite Historical Society), 1995.

[2] Shenk, Wilbert R., ed., *Anabaptism and Mission* (Scottdale, Pa.: Herald Press, 1984), p. 126.

[3] Ruth, John Landis, *The Earth Is The Lord's*, p.107.

[4] Littell, Franklin Hamlin, *The Anabaptist View of the Church*, pp. 114-116.

[5] Ibid., p. 113.

[6] Horsch, Johm, *Mennonites In Europe* (Scottdale, Pa.: Mennonite Publishing House), p. 315, as quoted in Little's *The Anabaptist View of the Church,* p. 112.

[7] Dyck, Cornelius J., *An Introduction to Mennonite History*, p. 151.

[8] Ibid., p. 164.

[9] Gerhard Lohrenz in Dyck, C.J., ed., *A Legacy of Faith* (Newton, Kans.: Faith and Life Press, 1962), p.173, as quoted in Dyck, *An Introduction to Mennonite History,* p. 178.

[10] Shenk, Wilbert R., ed. *Anabaptism and Mission*, chap. 8; van der Zijpp, N., *From Anabaptist Missionary Congregation to Mennonite Seclusion,* pp. 121-122.

[11] Dyck, Cornelius J., *An Introduction to Mennonite History*, p. 191.

[12] Ibid., p. 169.

[13] Ibid., pp. 202, 169.

Chapter Fourteen, False Peace—Giving Up the Spiritual Fight:

[1] Wenger, John Christian, ed., *The Complete Writings of Menno Simons*, p. 326.

[2] Ibid., p. 326.

[3] Online Bible Version 2.5.2, software by Ken Hamel, Box 168 Oakhurst, NJ 07755. (Online Bible Software, 1995), *Strong's Concordance, #3003.*

[4] *Strong's Concordance, #1228.*

[5] *Strong's Concordance, #4074.*

[6] *Strong's Concordance, #4073.*

[7] This is another valuable insight learned from John and Paula Sanford of Elijah House Ministries.

Chapter Fifteen, Worldly Sorrow and Unbelief:

[1] A clarification made by John Ruth, author and historian.

[2] *Martyrs Mirror* includes many accounts of parents' letters to their young children

[3] Gingerich, Ray C. *The Mission Impulse of Early Swiss and South German-Austrian Anabaptism*, pp. 105-108.

[4] Dyck, p. 158.

[5] Ruth, p. 136.

[6] Dyck, p. 162.

[7] Dyck, p. 125.

[8] Hoover, p. 264.

Chapter Sixteen, Embitterment and Comfort:

[1] *Strong's Concordance, #3874, 3870.*

[2] McReynolds, Paul R., ed. *Word Study Greek-English New Testament* (Wheaton, Ill.: Tyndale House Publishers, 1998), p. 790.

[3] *Strong's Concordance, #3894.*

[4] *Strong's Concordance, #3870.*

[5] Keller, Geri. *Father—A Look Into The Heart of God* (Wilkesboro, N.C.: Morning Star Pub, 2004), p. 142.

Chapter Seventeen, Bitterness Towards Authority:
[1] Blanke, Fritz, *Brothers in Christ* (Eugene, Ore.: Wipf and Stock Publishers, 1961), p. 8.
[2] Ibid., pp. 7-8.
[3] Wenger, J.C., *The Christian Faith* (Scottdale, Pa.: Herald Press, 1971, pp. 68-69.
[4] Moore, John Allen, *Anabaptist Portraits* (Scottdale, Pa.: Herald Press, 1984), pp. 22, 25.
[5] Ibid., pp. 48-49.
[6] Blanke, Fritz, Leonhard von Muralt, and Walter Schmid, eds., *Quellen zur Geschichte der Täufer in der Schweiz* (Vol. I, Zurich, 1952), as quoted in Blanke's *Brothers in Christ*, p. 17.
[7] Blanke, Fritz, *Brothers in Christ*, p. 19.
[8] Wenger, J.C., *The Christian Faith*, p. 70.
[9] Blanke, Fritz, *Brothers in Christ*, p. 10.
[10] Ibid., p. 11.
[11] Ibid., p. 10.
[12] Ibid., p. 9.
[13] Ibid., p. 16, parentheses are mine.
[14] Littell, Franklin Hamlin, *The Anabaptist View of the Church*, pp. 13-14.
[15] Egli, Emil, ed., *Actensammlung zur Geschichte der Zuricher Reformation in den Jahren 1519-1533*, as quoted in Littell, *The Anabaptist View of the Church*, p. 14.
[16] Loserth, Johann, and Josef R. Beck, "Georg Blaurock und die Anfange des Anabaptismus in Graubundten und Tirol," VII *Vortrage und Aufsatze aus der Comenius-Gesellschaft, 1889,* as quoted in Littell, *The Anabaptist View of the Church*, p. 14.
[17] Littell, Franklin Hamlin. *The Anabaptist View of the Church*, p. 146.
[18] Horsch, John. *Mennonites in Europe, Volume 1* (Scottdale, Pa.: Mennonite Publishing House, 1942), pp. 122-123.
[19] For attitudes of ancient Reformers and Catholics, see Littell's *Anabaptist View*, pp. 143-148, as one of many historical examples.
[20] Verduin, Leonard, *The Reformers and Their Stepchildren*, p. 50.
[21] Littell, Franklin Hamlin, *The Anabaptist View of the Church*, p. 11.
[22] Calvin calls Anabaptists enemies of God who speak blasphemies, the devil speaking through them . . . Verduin, *The Reformers and their Stepchildren*, pp. 80-81.
[23] *Strong's Concordance, #4088,4089.*
[24] *Strong's Concordance, #4805.* Also its root, *#4784.*
[25] Dyck, p. 104.

Chapter Eighteen, Fear of God and Fear of Death:
[1] Dyck, *Introduction To Mennonite History*, p. 46; Littell, *Anabaptist View*, pp. 28-29.

[2] Stein, Jess Stein, ed. in chief, *The Random House College Dictionary* (New York, N.Y., Random House, Inc, 1975).

[3] For a few examples of the use of the ban and of divisions, see John Ruth, *The Earth Is The Lord's*, pp. 520, 132, 134, 319: other divisions, see chapter 20, etc. Also, Dyck, *An Introduction To Mennonite History*, pp. 153, 162, 214, 238.

[4] McReynolds, Paul R., ed., *Word Study Greek-English New Testament*. (Wheaton, Ill.: Tyndale House Publishers, 1998), p. 817; *Strong's Concordance, #47, 1459, 998.*

[5] Horsch, John, *Mennonites in Europe*. (Rod and Staff Publishers, 1942, 1995), pp. 70-78; website: anabaptists.org/history/sattler.html

[6] *Strong's Concordance, # 673.*

Chapter Nineteen, Reverence for God or Reverence for Man:

[1] Read *Martyrs Mirror* where there are numerous court records of Anabaptists' bold testimonies

[2] Littell, *Anabaptist View of the Church*, p. 42.

[3] *Strong's Concordance, #5288.*

[4] *Strong's Concordance, #5218, 5219, 3958.*

Chapter Twenty, Division or Unity:

[1] Dyck, Cornelius J., *An Introduction To Mennonite History.* pp. 54-55.

[2] Ibid., p. 54-55.

[3] Ibid., p. 55.

[4] From Anabaptistnetwork.com. *The Schleitheim Confession*, cover letter.

[5] Bishop Lloyd Hoover, sources: Kraybill, Donald B., and Nelson C. Hostetter, *Anabaptist World USA* (Scottdale, Pa.; Herald Press, 2001), #2; and Ruth, John Landis, *The Earth Is The Lord's* (Scottdale, Pa.: Herald Press, 2001)

[6] Ruth, John Landis. *The Earth Is The Lord's*, p. 132.

[7] Littell, Franklin Hamlin. *The Anabaptist View of the Church*, p. 32, parenthesis and emphasis mine.

[8] Oyer, John S. and Robert S. Kreider, *Mirror of the Martyrs (*Intercourse, Pa.: Good Books, 1990), p. 58.

[9] Shenk, Wilbert R., ed., *Anabaptism and Mission*, chapter 8, especially pp. 123-125.

Chapter Twenty-one, A Religious Approach to God:

[1] *Strong's Concordance, #3954.*

[2] *Strong's Concordance, #3954.*

[3] *Strong's Concordance, #5273.*

[4] *Strong's Concordance, #6041.*

[5] *Strong's Concordance, #5223.*

Chapter Twenty-two, Religious Legalism or Walking in Relationship:
[1] Jim is now ministering in Kentucky and can be located at "Rivers Of Living Water Ministry," P.O. Box 22155, Louisville, KY 40241.
[2] Littell, Franklin Hamlin. *The Anabaptist View of the Church*, pp. 4-5.
[3] Ibid., pp. 7-8.
[4] Ibid., pp. 8-9.
[5] Wenger, J.C., *The Christian Faith* (Scottdale, Pa.: Herald Press, 1971), p. 74.
[6] Dyck, Cornelius J., *An Introduction to Mennonite History,* (Scottdale, Pa.: Herald Press, 1993), p. 97.
[7] Ibid., p. 99.
[8] Wenger, J.C. *The Christian Faith*, p. 75.
[9] Dyck, Cornelius J., *An Introduction to Mennonite History,* p. 107.
[10] Bach, Jeff, *Voices of the Turtledoves—The Sacred World of Ephrata,* (University Park, Pa.: The Pennsylvania State University Press, 2003, pp. 28-29.
[11] Ibid., p. 30.
[12] Ibid., pp. 38-39.
[13] See chapter 15 of this book and Ruth, John Landis, *The Earth is the Lord's,* p. 136; Cornelius J. Dyck, *An Introduction to Mennonite History*, pp. 122-123, 162.
[14] Ruth, John Landis, *The Earth is the Lord's,* p. 133; Dyck, Cornelius J. *An Introduction to Mennonite History,* p. 237.
[15] Ruth, John Landis, *The Earth is the Lord's,* pp. 133, 136.
[16] Ibid., p. 133.
[17] Hoover, Peter, *The Secret of the Strength* (Shippensburg, Pa.: Benchmark Press, 1999), p. 26.
[18] Dyck, Cornelius J., *An Introduction to Mennonite History,* p. 123.
[19] Littell, Franklin Hamlin. *The Anabaptist View of the Church*, p. 13.
[20] Excerpted from "Living with the King" by Rick Joyner, *Word for the Week*, April 5, 2004. www.morningstarministries.org <http://www.morning starministries.org> Used by permission.
[21] Examples are too numerous to mention specifically. A few of the many men and women who are operating regularly in these gifts are Mahesh Chavda, Randy Clark, Todd Bentley, Reinhard Bonnke, Titus Mbai, and Heidi Baker.

Chapter Twenty-three, Religious Control or Spiritual Release:
[1] Acosta, Noé S., *Comparative Study of the Official Doctrine of the Roman Catholic Church and the Holy Bible,* a doctrinal dissertation submitted to the Faith Theological Seminary Graduate Board: May 1999, p. 24.
[2] Ibid., p. 25.
[3] Hoover, Peter, *The Secret of the Strength* (Shippensburg, Pa.: Benchmark Press, 1999), p. 262.
[4] Ibid., p. 262.
[5] *Van die gheestelicke verrysenisse . . . ca1558,* as quoted in Hoover, *The Secret of the Strength*, p. 260, emphasis is mine.

[6] For a deeper study of this topic, read *Floods Upon the Dry Ground* by Charles P. Schmitt, chapter three in particular. Also, chapter five in *Father Forgive Us!* by Jim Goll.

[7] Schmitt, Charles P., *Floods Upon the Dry Ground* (Shippensburg, Pa.: Destiny Image Publishers, 1998), pp. 16-17, parentheses are mine.

[8] Ibid., pp.16-17, parentheses are mine.

[9] Ibid., p.16, parentheses and emphasis are mine.

[10] Qualben, *A History of the Christian Church*, pp. 94-95, as quoted in Schmitt, *Floods Upon the Dry Ground*, p. 27; parentheses and emphasis are mine.

[11] Goll, Jim W., *Father Forgive Us!* (Shippensburg, Pa.: Destiny Image Publishers, Inc., 1999), p. 80; boldface and italics are mine.

[12] Blanke, Fritz, *Brothers in Christ* (Eugene, Ore.: Wipf and Stock Publishers, 1961), p. 53.

[13] Goll, Jim W., *Father Forgive Us!* p. 77.

[14] Ibid., p. 84, emphasis is mine.

[15] Ibid., p. 88.

[16] Ibid., p. 88, parentheses are mine.

Chapter Twenty-four, Covenant Inclusion or Covenant Exclusion:

[1] According to historian John Ruth, there were no pews in churches for people to sit down: they stood for services!

[2] Littell, Franklin Hamlin, *The Anabaptist View of the Church*, p. 6.

[3] Moore, John Allen, *Anabaptist Portraits* (Scottdale, Pa.: Herald Press, 1984), p. 69; Horsch, John, *Mennonites in Europe, Volume 1* (Scottdale, Pa.: Mennonite Publishing House, 1942), p. 45.

[4] *American Journal of Theology*, "The Zurich Anabaptists and Thomas Muntzer," IX, as quoted in Littell, *The Anabaptist View of the Church*, p. 2.

[5] Beck, Josef, ed., *Die Geschichts-Bucher der Wiedertaufer in Oesterrich-Ungarn,* as quoted in Littell, *The Anabaptist View of the Church*, p. 2.

[6] Shenk, Wilbert R., ed., *Anabaptism and Mission* (Scottdale, Pa.: Herald Press, 1984), p. 98.

[7] Ibid., p 114.

[8] *WTQ* 1938, p. 170, as quoted in Littell, Franklin Hamlin. *The Anabaptist View of the Church*, p. 90.

[9] Von Muralt, Leonhard, and Schmid, Walter, eds., *Zurich*, p. 20; and George Williams and Angel Mergal, eds., *Spiritual and Anabaptist Writers*, p. 85, as quoted in Gingerich, *The Mission Impulse of Early Swiss and South German-Austrian Anabaptism.*

[10] Gingerich, Ray C., *The Mission Impulse of Early Swiss and South German-Austrian Anabaptism,* dissertation submitted to the faculty of the Graduate School of Vanderbilt University in partial fulfillment of the requirements for the degree of Doctor of Philosophy in Religion, May 1980 (Nashville, Tenn.), pp. 61, 71; and Franklin Hamlin Littell, *The Anabaptist View of the Church* (Beacon Hill, Boston: Starr King Press, 1957, p. 85.

[11] Gingerich, Ray C., *The Mission Impulse of Early Swiss and South German-Austrian Anabaptism,* dissertation submitted to the faculty of the Graduate School of Vanderbilt University in partial fulfillment of the requirements for the degree of Doctor of Philosophy in Religion, May 1980 (Nashville, Tenn.), p. 71.

[12] Ibid., p. 72.

[13] *Dat Fundament des Christelycken leers* . . . 1539, as quoted in Peter Hoover, *The Secret of the Strength,* p. 261.

Chapter Twenty-five, The Power of Words:

[1] Verduin, Leonard, *The Reformers and Their Stepchildren* (Sarasota, Fla.: The Christian Hymnary Publishers, 1964), pp. 55, 80, 81, 110, 184, 262.

[2] Prince, Derek, *Blessing Or Curse—You Can Choose* (Grand Rapids, Mich.: Chosen Books, 1990, 2000) by Derek Prince Ministries-International, pp. 32-33.

[3] Verduin, Leonard, *The Reformers and Their Stepchildren,* p. 244.

[4] Ibid., pp. 245,252.

[5] Ibid., p. 247.

[6] Ibid., p. 250.

[7] *Confession of Faith and Minister's Manual* (Crockett, Ken.: Rod and Staff Publishers, Inc.), Article XV, pp. 26-27.

[8] Ruth, John Landis, *The Earth is the Lord's,* p. 222.

[9] *Strong's Concordance, # 3727.*

[10] *Strong's Concordance, #2192* and *#2171.*

[11] Elijah House Ministries has an excellent teaching on *Spiritual Vows* which may be obtained by contacting their ministry. See Recommended Reading on pages 337-338.

[12] Miller, Mary M., *Our Heritage, Hope, and Faith* (Sugarcreek, Ohio: Carlisle Printing, 2000), p. 156.

[13] Article #7 of the Schleitheim Confession.

[14] *Dat Fundament des Christelycken leers . . . 1539,* as quoted in Peter Hoover, *The Secret of the Strength,* p. 261.

[15] Prince, Derek, *Blessing Or Curse—You Can Choose,* chapter 18. Reprinted with permission.